SCIENCE FICTION

Science Fiction explores the genre from 1895 to the present day, drawing on examples from over forty countries. It raises questions about the relationship between science fiction, science and technology, and examines the interrelationships between spectacle, narrative and self-reflexivity, paying particular attention to the role of special effects in creating meaning and affect. It explores science fiction's evocations of the sublime, the grotesque, and the camp, and charts the ways in which the genre reproduces and articulates discourses of colonialism, imperialism and neo-liberal globalization. At the same time, *Science Fiction* provides a thorough analysis of the genre's representation of race, class, gender and sexuality, making this text an essential guide for students, academics and film fans alike.

Key films discussed include:

- *Le voyage dans la lune* (1902)
- *20,000 Leagues Under the Sea* (1916)
- *L'Atlantide* (1921)
- *King Kong* (1933, 2005)
- *Gojira* (1954)
- *La Jetée* (1962)
- *The Abominable Dr Phibes* (1971)
- *Tetsuo* (1989)
- *Sleep Dealer* (2008))
- *Avatar* (2009)

Mark Bould is Reader in Film and Literature at the University of the West of England and co-editor of *Science Fiction Film and Television*. He is co-author of *The Routledge Concise History of Science Fiction*, author of *The Cinema of John Sayles* and *Film Noir*, and co-editor of *The Routledge Companion to Science Fiction*, *Fifty Key Figures in Science Fiction*, *Red Planets*, *Neo-noir* and *Parietal Games*.

Routledge Film Guidebooks

The Routledge Film Guidebooks offer a clear introduction to and overview of the work of key filmmakers, movements or genres. Each guidebook contains an introduction, including a brief history; defining characteristics and major films; a chronology; key debates surrounding the filmmaker, movement or genre; and pivotal scenes, focusing on narrative structure, camera work and production quality.

Bollywood: a guidebook to
popular Hindi cinema
Tejaswini Ganti

James Cameron
Alexandra Keller

Jane Campion
Deb Verhoeven

Horror
Brigid Cherry

Film Noir
Justus Nieland and Jennifer Fay

Documentary
Dave Saunders

Romantic Comedy
Claire Mortimer

Westerns
John White

Crime
Sarah Casey Benyahia

Science Fiction
Mark Bould

SCIENCE FICTION

MARK BOULD

Routledge
Taylor & Francis Group

LONDON AND NEW YORK

First published 2012
by Routledge
2 Park Square, Milton Park, Abingdon, Oxon OX14 4RN

Simultaneously published in the USA and Canada
by Routledge
711 Third Avenue, New York, NY 10017

Routledge is an imprint of the Taylor & Francis Group, an informa business

British Library Cataloguing in Publication Data
A catalogue record for this book is available from the British Library

Library of Congress Cataloging in Publication Data
Bould, Mark.
Science fiction / by Mark Bould.
p. cm. – (Routledge film guidebooks)
Includes bibliographical references and index.
1. Science fiction films – History and criticism. I. Title.
PN1995.9.S26B58 2012
791.43'615 – dc23
2011047958

ISBN: 978-0-415-45810-8 (hbk)
ISBN: 978-0-415-45811-5 (pbk)
ISBN: 978-0-203-14332-2 (ebk)

Typeset in Joanna
by Taylor & Francis Books

Printed and bound by CPI Group (UK) Ltd, Croydon, CR0 4YY

CONTENTS

INTRODUCTION

In *The Practice of Everyday Life*, Michel de Certeau compares the urban planner's rational model of the city with the sprawling, chaotic reality of urban life. The former is an idealised virtual construct, free from the stubborn materiality of history, people and places, viewed from above as if by a transcendent, disembodied deity. The latter consists of unstable, constantly becoming entanglements of pathways 'below the thresholds [of] visibility', like 'intertwining, unrecognized poems' (93). Many discussions of genre and of specific genres display the planner-deity's desire for a neatly ordered totality, clamouring for – and often producing – definitions and origin points, inclusions and exclusions, borders and limits. Such discussions, and the discrepancies, anomalies and exceptions they inevitably throw up, reveal several contradictions. Genres are heterogeneous, but grouping diverse films under a single rubric tends to homogenise them, to emphasise similarities to such an extent that differences are not only marginalised but often made invisible. Genres are discursive phenomena, constantly defined and redefined by a host of different voices, with different degrees of influence, for many different reasons, but genres are frequently regarded as clearly defined objects, as boxes into which individual texts can be smoothly slotted. Genres are produced by the complexly determined, socially situated positions from which they are viewed, but are often treated as if they are pre-existing phenomena with fixed, essential forms.[1]

Consequently, this book does not define or delineate science fiction (sf). Indeed, it rejects the 'god-trick' involved in claiming an objective position from which to impose order, offering instead a 'situated knowledge' that is conscious of at least some of its partialities and limitations (see Haraway 1991b). While engaging with the Film Studies sf canon, it embraces more than a century's worth of sf production worldwide. It refers to films from more than 40 countries, from 1895–2011, including shorts, animations, blockbusters and B-movies, and independent, art-house, avant-garde, cult, trash, sexploitation and pornographic sf films. The danger in such an encyclopaedic approach is losing sight of specificities and reducing films to examples of a homogenous genre. To avoid this, in addition to trying to remain sensitive to cultural contexts, this book eschews definitions and generalisations. Whenever it refers to 'sf', it envisions the genre not as a sleek Monolith, pristine, transcendent and unassailable, but as a shape-shifting Thing, constantly becoming and without fixed form. Furthermore, the clusters of titles interspersed throughout the chapters are concerned with variety, not repetition – they are invitations to dive deeper into the genre's heterogeneous possibilities.

This book is divided into three chapters, each one a street-level tour through the sf city, viewing the familiar sights and pausing at the tourist traps but also taking roads less well travelled and nipping up obscure alleyways. Chapter 1 addresses the often misunderstood relationship between sf and science. Instead of fruitlessly berating the genre for its scientific errors, it begins by examining the ways in which scientific-sounding language and technological artefacts are deployed in sf films, and the ways in which 'bad' science nonetheless creates meanings and affects. Drawing on material from science studies, it then considers the representation of the scientist in relation to public and professional discourses about the proper (and the actual) functioning of science. It explores the dilemmas posed for scientific practitioners by economic, industrial, political, cultural and social contexts, and finds in the mad scientist a figure representative of modern subjectivity. In closing, it turns to the position of women in sf's labs, who are far less likely to be scientists than experimental subjects.

Chapter 2 begins with the tension between sf's spectacular and conceptual elements. It considers the relationship between sf and the cinema of attractions that emerged as part of capitalist modernity, dominated by the shock of the new and a proliferation of spectacular commodity forms. Building on theoretical material from 'the affective turn' in cultural studies, it rethinks cinematic spectacle as more than just a mind-numbing, overwhelming force, focusing in particular on the complexity of special effects sequences. It then considers three varieties of sf spectacle: the sublime, the grotesque and the camp. In conclusion, it examines sf's self-reflexive use of special effects and depictions of technologies of vision and representation.

Chapter 3 is more overtly concerned with the politics of sf. It begins with the colonialist and imperialist discourses prevalent in the late nineteenth and early twentieth centuries when both cinema and sf emerged. It outlines sf films' reproduction of and complicity in colonialist and imperialist ideology, paying particular attention to the late silent and early sound period, but also finding numerous recent examples. It explores the post-imperial melancholy typical of British sf after anti-colonial revolutions tore European empires apart, and considers Vietnam-era US sf as a tentative, contradictory articulation of countercultural anti-imperialist sentiments, particularly as the genre attempts to address US racial politics. The chapter – and the book – concludes with a discussion of the ways in which Western hegemony has been maintained through globalisation, focusing on contemporary sf's figuration of neo-liberal capitalism and its transformations of the experience of time and space.

These three chapters, if not exactly the kinds of poems de Certeau describes, offer three journeys through global sf. They do not aspire to the omniscience of a planner deity, and are far from exhaustive. Hopefully, they provide some new ways to think about sf and suggest new possibilities to explore.

Writing a book is gnarly, recursive, surprising and, although it seems to happen in solitude, profoundly social. The University of the West of

England funded some teaching remission in 2010–11, which freed up some time to write this book, but it was only ever feasible because of the generosity of friends and colleagues there, and the patience, sympathy and support of Aileen Storry and Eileen Srebernik at Routledge. I owe more than I can adequately express to the following for help, advice, guidance, tolerance, reading lists, obscure DVDs, meals and drinks, for answering idiotic questions (as well as hard ones), for sitting through films that they sometimes (and sometimes very clearly) found less interesting than I did, and for supporting my students during the 2010 occupation: Susan Alexander, Mark Barton, Pete Broks, Andrew M. Butler, Andy Channelle, Istvan Csicsery-Ronay, Mike Davis, Neil Easterbrook, Pawel Frelik (Soviet bloc and queer sf pimp *extraordinaire*), Carl Freedman, Ximena Gallardo C., Kathrina Glitre, Mike Hodges, Rehan Hyder, Gwyneth Jones, Jessica Langer, Rob Latham, Roger Luckhurst, China Miéville (*architeuthis* cadre), Aris Mousoutzanis, Kim Newman, Humberto Perez-Blanco, Kim Stanley Robinson, Steve Rosevear, Lee Salter, Steven Shaviro, C. Jason Smith, Vivian Sobchack, Jesse Soodalter, Greg Tuck, Sherryl Vint (science studies *sensei*), Peter Wright and my local UCU branch. But I'm sorry, Billy, this one's for the hardCore24, especially Steve Presence, Anthony Killick, Paddy Besiris and Matt Hollinshead. Throughout a very difficult year, they inspired even more than they distracted. This book, this year, would not have been possible without them. Love and respect.

1

THE SCIENCE IN SCIENCE FICTION

In February 2010, newspapers carried a pronouncement by Professor Sidney Perkowitz – a member of the US National Academy of Science's programme to provide 'entertainment industry professionals with access to top scientists and engineers to create a synergy between accurate science and engaging storylines'[1] – that sf films 'should be allowed only one major transgression of the laws of physics' (Sample online). Six weeks later, another physics professor, David Goldberg, posted an open letter to the writers and director of Hot Tub Time Machine (2010), complaining that the film was full of scientific errors and unresolved paradoxes. BootHillBossanova immediately responded: 'No shit. That's why physicists don't write movies. I bet you were a joy to sit next to in the theater'. Unfortunately, he had not actually read Goldberg's spoof letter, which praises the film for understanding 'that time travel may only be undertaken while in the nude', as in The Terminator (1984), but criticises the sequence in which Jacob (Clark Duke), cast back in time to the night of his conception, 'interrupts his parents mid-coitus' and thus 'temporarily disappears from existence'. As Goldberg explains, 'Mathematical models demonstrate ... conclusively that he would fade from existence a bit at a time, starting with images in photographs', as in Back to the Future (1985).

Such incidents, organisations and outbursts reveal the extent to which different people and communities have different investments in sf, many of which are articulated around the genre's relationship to science. For some, science is more or less irrelevant, but for others this relationship is profoundly debased, in need of discipline and repair (see Landon: 3–58). However, because there is no necessary, fixed or consensus relationship between sf and science, and because the science in sf can only ever be 'figurative', 'an image of science' (Csicsery-Ronay, Jr 2008: 111),[2] attempts to police the genre in terms of scientific accuracy rather miss the point. This chapter will consider the representation and uses of science and scientists in sf. Drawing on material from science studies, it will argue that filmic scientists, caught between multiple and often irreconcilable ideological and material interpellations, exemplify the condition of the modern subject under capital. It will conclude by examining sf's tendency to depict women in the lab not as scientists but as experimental subjects.

THE SOUND (AND LOOK) OF SCIENCE

Mark C. Glassy contends that criticism of sf films must consider two factors specific to the genre: 'the verisimilitude or accuracy of the science (otherwise they would not be "science" fiction) and the success of the special effects', with 'the former generally tak[ing] a back seat to the latter' (2). This problematic position – why privilege the accuracy rather than the fictionality of the science in science fiction? What does it mean for special effects to be successful? Are special effects really that central to the genre? – has many precursors. For example, H.G. Wells's review of Metropolis (1927) berates the film for ignoring 'the question of [the] development of industrial control [and] the relation of [the] industrial to [the] political' in favour of 'furlong after furlong' of spectacular but 'ignorant old-fashioned balderdash' (2004: 12). Forty years later Susan Sontag likewise observed that sf 'movies are ... weak ... where science fiction novels ... are strong – on science', providing 'sensuous elaboration' rather than 'an intellectual workout' (1994a: 212). Carl Freedman offers the most rigorous statement of this opposition between the conceptual and the spectacular. He understands sf cinema in terms of the dominance of special effects and sf literature in terms of 'cognitive estrangement' – that is, the depiction of rational, material but counterfactual worlds that prompt readers to see their own world anew and re-engage with it critically and politically (see Suvin).

Freedman describes special effects as 'filmic moments of a radically filmic character' that marshal the full resources of cinema and 'self-consciously foreground their own radicality' (1998: 305, 307). In sf, 'special effects are deliberate triumphs of cinematic technology' that 'enact, on one level, the technological marvels that the typical science-fiction film thematizes on a different level' (307). However, because the cinematic experience reduces the viewer 'to a passive, atomized spectator in a darkened room', 'forced to consume the proffered aesthetic experience strictly according to the temporality determined by the filmmaker', the 'tendency' of special effects 'to overwhelm the viewer' intensifies 'the authoritarian aspect of film' (306) by minimising the 'breathing room in which anything like a cognitive response might be formulated' (311). The sole exception Freedman recognises is 2001: A Space Odyssey (1968), which finds a specific solution to 'the all but hopeless contradiction between' critical cognition and authoritarian spectacle (315). Faced with films that are 'less radically cinematic (as with Ridley Scott) or less authentically science-fictional (as with Spielberg or Lucas)', he concludes that sf film 'may well be intrinsically impossible' (315).

There are numerous problems with Freedman's argument. It not only ignores sf's long history across media forms so as to privilege literature but also relies on Darko Suvin's definition of the genre, which is so prescriptive as to exclude most of what is actually published as sf.[3] It also conflates such abstract notions as 'the purely cinematic' with a single mode of film production (big-budget Hollywood spectacle) and 'the authentically science-fictional' with a narrow range of exemplary (rather than typical) novels. The Marxist and film theory traditions upon which Freedman draws are profoundly anxious about affect and embodiment, and tend to focus on the apparatuses of (economic, political, social or cinematic) power at the expense of individual and collective subjects positioned by and responding to them; but even with *Avatar* (2009), a film in which spectacle massively outweighs any cognitive–conceptual elements, viewers might as easily be moved, inspired or bored, have their thoughts provoked or their sensibilities offended, as be overwhelmed.

Freedman elsewhere points to the ways in which science tends to operate in sf, arguing that what is 'at stake' is not cognition itself but 'the *cognition effect*' (2000: 18), produced by the rhetorical move that 'tricks' one 'into an unwary concession to some plausible assumption' so as to '*domesticate* the impossible hypothesis' (Wells 1980: 241). This effect is not generated by scientific accuracy so much as by the 'appearance of command over the *language* of science' (Jones: 16). For example, in *The Thing from Another World* (1951), Captain Hendry (Kenneth Tobey) is sent to investigate a mysterious crash landing 48 miles east of an arctic research station. Briefing him, Dr Carrington (Robert Cornthwaite) instructs Nikki (Margaret Sheridan) to read out his notes detailing how the object's impact was picked up by sound and seismographic readings. When Hendry asks how they 'determine[d] the point of impact' in relation to the base, Carrington replies, 'By computation', and turns away to talk with someone else over the intercom. This diffident response, typical of Carrington's self-absorption, is so perfunctory as to highlight both the generic expectation and frequent redundancy of expository dialogue. Indeed, when the friendlier Dr Stern (Eduard Franz) tries to give a fuller explanation, he quickly switches from explication to assertion: 'It's quite simple, captain. We have the time of arrival of the sound waves on the detectors and also the arrival time of the impact waves on the seismograph. By computing the difference it becomes quite obvious that they were caused by a travelling object, and the distance from here is approximately forty-eight miles'. Offering no real new information, Stern's words – like the surrounding laboratory equipment – nonetheless lend the scene generic verisimilitude, just as the way in which they are partially overlapped by Carrington's background conversation offer the generic setting a more general verisimilitude. Stern's dialogue also indicates the extent to which sf's evocations of science express and address different kinds of interest and degrees of knowledge on the behalf of filmmakers and audiences. It partially explains the possibility of measuring the distance to the crashed saucer from the different speeds at which the shockwave travelled through air and ground but, having implied the scientifically derived certainty of this information, abandons exposition in order to reiterate Hendry's next goal.

There is a similar moment in *The Thing* (1982) when Childs (Keith David) asks whether Dr Blair (Wilford Brimley) believes that the Antarctic base is being attacked by a shapeshifting alien. The film cuts to Blair running a computer simulation that models an 'intruder' cell approaching and assimilating a dog cell, and the resulting 'imitation' cell assimilating another dog cell just as quickly, implying a geometric progression. The computer simulation, by making visible the invisible, pseudo-authenticates the biological process by which the alien takes over life-forms, while the ticking of Blair's pocket watch, audible beneath the haunting score, emphasises the relentlessness of these simulated events. The simulation is replaced on the computer screen with the following text: 'PROBABILITY THAT ONE OR MORE TEAM MEMBERS MAY BE INFECTED BY INTRUDER ORGANISM: 75%' and 'PROJECTION: IF INTRUDER ORGANISM REACHES CIVILIZED AREAS ... ENTIRE WORLD POPULATION INFECTED 27,000 HOURS FROM FIRST CONTACT'. By demonstrating a more-than-human mathematical ability – made to seem all the more rational and precise by measuring time in hours rather than more immediately comprehensible units – the computer pseudo-authenticates the pace of global infection.

Sf films often use scientific-sounding language to communicate things other than, or more than, scientific information. For example, in *Flash Gordon* (1936), Dr Zarkov (Frank Shannon), forced to serve Emperor Ming (Charles Middleton), informs his new sovereign, 'I've discovered a new ray which will be of great help in furthering your plans. ... The ray is a variation of the one you've been using but being of a higher frequency is much more flexible. It is built up from the negative side rather than the positive'. Ming replies, 'Hmmm, I see'. This exchange reflects on knowledge differentials between individuals, and suggests that the cognition effect does not necessarily depend upon scientific accuracy but on various forms of persuasion. Even if the viewer recognised the meaninglessness of Zarkov's words, the fact that they are spoken by Zarkov in a laboratory and that they conform to the norms of the broader franchise – in comic strips, radio shows, books and toys – could have increased their implicit authority and persuasiveness. Moreover, both Zarkov and Ming utilise the authority effect of scientific-sounding language to persuade, even as their conversation reveals the extent to which multiple criteria might be relevant in assessing the science in sf. Shannon's rather awkward delivery suggests that Zarkov might be deliberately spouting gibberish to test the limits of Ming's scientific knowledge; and Ming's response could convey that he is out of his depth or, more cunningly, that he is tricking Zarkov into thinking so.

Sf does not just rely on dialogue to create cognition effects, but also on visual and aural design that, according to Piers D. Britton, are governed not by the physical laws of science but by persuasive varieties of 'extended common sense', which resonate with audiences through their experience, real or mediated, of similar phenomena. For example, while sound cannot travel in a vacuum and the fieriness of explosions in space are restricted by the availability of combustible gas, the attack on the Death Star in *Star Wars* (1977) derives authority from a persuasive regime of verisimilitude involving the cultural memory of aerial dogfights and bombing missions in war movies such as *The Dam Busters* (1955) and *633 Squadron* (1964). Similarly, during the climactic Mutara Nebula cat-and-mouse battle, *Star Trek II: The Wrath of Khan* (1982) draws on submarine war movies, such as *Run Silent, Run Deep* (1958); and *Starship Troopers* (1997) draws upon imagery of the island-hopping Pacific War and, more self-reflexively, US wartime propaganda films. *2001: A Space Odyssey* evokes/produces a rather different regime of verisimilitude through its insistence on the silence of space and its resolutely undramatic attention to the routine procedures of spaceflight. A similar regime of verisimilitude is evoked by the quarantine procedures and the 'grindingly thorough' examination of a crystalline alien virus in *The Andromeda Strain* (1971), the lengthy surgery in *The Terminal Man* (1974), the shuttlecraft's descent in *Alien* (1979) and the mundane repetitions of daily life in *Moon* (2009). The latter two also derive verisimilitude from the sense that – as in *Eolomea* (1972), *Solyaris/Solaris* (1972), *Dark Star* (1974), *Acción mutante* (1992) and *Cargo* (2009) – equipment and people are worn out, exhausted and on the verge of breaking down.

Cargo also features a common solution to the dilemma that the silence of space poses for spectacular images of spacecraft. As the giant space freighter *Kassandra* passes through the shot, it is accompanied by a deep, almost subsonic rumbling, which lends materiality to the digitally created craft while mediating between extended common sense (surely a vehicle of that size must make some noise), knowledge that an audience may or may not possess (that sound cannot travel in a vacuum) and generic expectations (in some SF films, spaceships do make noise and, in some of them, they make this kind of noise). This particular aural solution garners further verisimilitude by its unglamorous signification of industrial noise – like the sound of an engine vibrating through the hull and interior walls – which matches the look of the ship's interior of dark, rusting passageways, metal bulkheads and cargo hold full of shipping containers. A slightly different solution is found in *Test Pilota Pirxa/Pilot Pirx's Inquest* (1979), which in place of *Cargo's* 'perceptual realism' (see Prince) develops an ambiguity that simultaneously implies and denies the audibility of the spaceship *Goliath*. External shots are accompanied by an extra-diegetic thrumming – sometimes ascending, sometimes descending – and other electronic noises, one of which, a hissing, might be diegetic. The first time it is audible, it appears to be diegetically motivated by the engine's plasma flare. It can, however, also be heard in later external shots in which the flare cannot be seen, making this sourcing rather more tenuous. Furthermore, in the sequence in which a sabotaged probe fails to launch and *Goliath* plunges towards Saturn's rings, the extra-diegetic electronic sounds, including the hissing, continue to be audible despite intercutting between the ship's exterior and interior. These ambiguities about the nature and source of the hissing provide an opportunity to interpret the sound, and thus the film, as being, in this regard at least, either scientifically accurate or inaccurate.

Galaxy Quest (1999) indicates the extent to which SF's depictions of science and technology depend upon an 'extended common sense' built upon earlier representations rather than upon scientific accuracy. The beleaguered Thermians, mistaking the long-cancelled television series *Galaxy Quest* for factual historical documents recording the heroic missions of the NSEA *Protector*, recruit the washed-up cast into their struggle against tyranny. The spaceship and costumes seen in glimpses of the old television episodes derive one kind of authenticity by resembling those of *Star Trek* (1966–69). The replica *Protector* created by the Thermians derives another kind of authenticity by its difference from the television series' set and models (and by variations in the quality of the image that emphasise the difference between video and film stock), but also by updating them so as to more closely resemble the sets, models and CGI of the *Star Trek* films and sequel series. The importance of signification – of signs over referents – is underscored when the Thermians reveal that they have no understanding of the science or technology upon which their *Protector* depends, having constructed it by working from the series' signifiers of advanced technology and the actors' gestures while operating the fictional equipment. In a further twist, saving the 'actual' *Protector* from destruction depends upon fan knowledge of the 'fictional' ship. When Jason Nesmith (Tim Allen) and Gwen DeMarco (Sigourney Weaver) – who played the television series' Captain Peter Quincy Taggart and Lieutenant Tawny Maddison – race to disarm the self-destruct device, they are guided by Brandon (Justin Long), a fan on Earth who has a walkthrough of the 'fictional' *Protector*'s technical specifications on his computer. Turning a corner, Jason and Gwen come upon a 'bunch of chompy crushy things in the middle of the hallway'. Gwen protests that this meaningless hazard 'serves no useful purpose … makes no logical sense' even if it did appear in the series. Fortunately, Brandon's friend Hollister (Jonathan Feyer) has been rewatching the relevant episode so as to time the sequence in which the low-fi 'fictional' chompers open and close in order to navigate Jason and Gwen through the 'real' chompers.

THE CRITICAL POTENTIAL, PLEASURES AND POLITICS OF 'BAD' SCIENCE

Freedman insists that, despite the 'formal distinction' between them, cognition remains 'the readiest means of producing a cognition effect' (2000: 18–19). However, this presupposes an ideal reader who embodies critical rationality and is immune to other forms of persuasion. Furthermore, as with invocations of scientific accuracy as the sole measure of quality, it privileges and normalises certain kinds of cultural capital, rather than recognising that in practice the cognition effect arises from complex negotiations between a text and its audience.

While inadequate or unpersuasive evocations of science might interrupt or detract from some films, 'bad' science can serve a variety of purposes and produce different pleasures, as *Gojira/Godzilla* (1954) and *Plan 9 from Outer Space* (1958) demonstrate. Before *Gojira*'s Emiko Yamane (Momoko Kochi) can tell her fiancé, the scientist Daisuke Serizawa (Akihiko Hirata), that she wishes to break their engagement because she is in love with Marine Safety Bureau officer Hideto Ogata (Akira Takarada), Serizawa insists on demonstrating the results of his secret research. The film cuts to her point of view, panning across his basement laboratory from a large fishtank and an array of familiar chemistry equipment on her right, past a strange-looking generator in front of her and to another fishtank and more chemistry equipment on her left. A reverse shot shows her dwarfed in this environment. Gazing at the equipment with incomprehension, she moves into the foreground to examine the aquarium. The faint churning hum of an electric pump is the only sound. As Emiko bends down to look at the fish, the camera tracks to the right so that the murky aquarium briefly fills the entire screen before revealing the laboratory's other half. Serizawa, wearing dark rubber gloves, carries a dish into the foreground. After a close-up of the fish,

Emiko joins Serizawa as he lifts a pellet from the dish; another close-up of the fish shows the pellet sinking to the bottom of the aquarium. There is a cut on the 180° line to show Serizawa in long medium-shot, throwing a lever on the generator, which comes to life with a loud chirring. In a closer medium shot, Emiko lurches forward to look into the aquarium. Serizawa tells her to stand back, and an awkward cut overlaps the action as he seizes her shoulders and pulls her away. The water fizzes and glows. In two shot, Serizawa dominates the top left of the screen while Emiko cowers fearfully in the lower right, peering into the out-of-shot aquarium. She screams, covers her eyes and turns away, taking refuge against Serizawa's shoulder. A crashing piano chord drowns out the machine noise, which then ceases, replaced by the chord's long reverberation and the sound of bubbling. Serizawa continues to stare at the aquarium. There is, however, no reverse shot to reveal what has happened to the fish. Instead, the reverberation bridges into a shot, set some time later, of Emiko, again dwarfed by her surroundings, staggering traumatised from the laboratory.

Intriguingly, this scene withholds the moment of revelation to which it seems to build. Another half hour of screentime passes before Emiko, devastated by the sheer number of Gojira's casualties, tells Ogata what she saw. Her flashback begins with the shot of the pellet sinking into the aquarium, and cuts to what appears to be the full version of one of the two shots clumsily edited together in the original sequence, before cutting to the two-shot. At last, there is a reverse shot as the metal pellet releases gas into the water, gurgling loudly, accompanied by mechanically scratching violins. Another shot shows the fish swimming around the rising streams of bubble, and after a cut, semi-concealed by a fade, fish skeletons, stripped of their flesh. As the piano chord crashes again, there is a cut to the shot of Emiko screaming and turning away, into which a further shot of the sinking fish skeletons is interpolated. There is another reverse shot of the aquarium in which the water con-tinues to bubble. Ominously throbbing piano and cello take over the soundtrack as Serizawa walks Emiko to a seat in front of another aquarium. The repetition of shots from the earlier sequence, made to stutter by the newly introduced reverse shots, betoken Serizawa's urge to speak and then, as if to make amends for the film's earlier reticence, there is a sudden torrent of words:

> It's an Oxygen Destroyer. It destroys oxygen in the water and liquidates aquatic life. It can't live without oxygen. I wanted to learn about oxygen in every respect. I discovered the lethal energy hidden in it. A deadly power. When I found it, I was terrified. I felt sick. Even a small ball of this could reduce Tokyo Bay to an aquatic graveyard in an instant. ... I didn't set out to discover such a thing. If used as a weapon it could destroy civilization just as H-bombs could. That's why I can't let people know until I find a peaceful use for the power. That's why I kept quiet. If they know about it and make use of it as a weapon, I'll destroy all the data I've compiled and kill myself.

Withholding this information generates suspense and sidelines the romance narrative so as to concentrate on Gojira's destructive rampage. Simultaneously, it betrays an anxiety that the Oxygen Destroyer is so ludicrous – does it destroy the oxygen atoms in the water molecules? If so, what happens to the energy released by this destruction? Or does it just destroy the free oxygen suspended in the water? How does it do either of these things? And why does it strip the fish down to their skeletons? – that an earlier revelation would detract from the film's mournful tone.

However, the 'bad' science – the absurdity of the Oxygen Destroyer – is essential to the film's engagement with the nuclear bombings of Hiroshima and Nagasaki and with the *Daigo Fukuryū Maru/Lucky Dragon* incident.[4] Jacques Derrida argues that 'the terrifying reality of nuclear conflict can only be the signified referent, never the real referent ... of a discourse or a text', and that nuclear war takes on 'a fabulous textuality' because it exists only 'through what is said of it' (23). According to Peter Schwenger, circular time-sequences, twists, turns and deferrals are common features of nuclear texts – as are hesitations, suppressed memories and attempts 'to locate the experience of nuclear disaster by surrounding the inexpressible with verbal strategies' (Dowling 11). In the first of these two scenes, the Oxygen Destroyer represents the inexpressibility of nuclear destruction. The sequence is fragmented by the impossibility of showing it, and this absent core is surrounded by tangential textual fragments that fail to 'assimilate the … wholly other' (Derrida 28). Traumatised, Emiko becomes – like Serizawa – an agent of suppression and forgetting. Her flashback elaborates upon what we saw, restoring the missing reverse shots and dialogue. However, the mismatches between the two versions of the sequences suggest a struggle to narrativise, rather than merely to recollect, trauma – just as Serizawa, who barely speaks in the first version, becomes in the second almost hysterical in his attempt to 'surround the inexpressible' if not with 'verbal strategies' then at least with words. Prefiguring *Dr Strangelove or: How I Learned to Stop Worrying and Love the Bomb* (1964), the Oxygen Destroyer gives some sense of the absurdity of nuclear 'reality' by reducing nuclear war to the dissolution of some fish, which is in no way proportionate to the horror and hysteria Emiko and Serizawa express. What the Oxygen Destroyer is and does makes no sense whatsoever, but the 'bad' science justification only adds to its symbolic power.

In *Plan 9 from Outer Space*, the alien Eros (Dudley Manlove) contends that humankind's development of ever greater bombs, such as the new solarbenite bomb, could result in 'the total destruction of the entire universe served by our sun'. While atom bombs 'split the atom' and hydrogen bombs 'actually explode the air itself', a solarbenite explosion will destroy the invisible particles of the sun's rays. He explains this nonsensical science with the aid of a desperately inadequate analogy:

> Take a can of your gasoline. Say this can of gasoline is the Sun. Now, you spread a thin line of it to a ball, representing the Earth. Now the gasoline represents the sunlight, the sun particles. Here we saturate the ball with the gasoline – the sunlight – then we put a flame to the ball. The flame will speedily travel around the Earth, back along the line of gasoline to the can – or the Sun itself. It will explode this source and spread to every place that gasoline – our sunlight – touches. Explode the sunlight here, gentlemen, you explode the universe. Explode the

sunlight here and a chain reaction will occur direct to the Sun itself
and to all the planets that sunlight touches, to every planet in the
universe.

Rather than merely dismissing Eros's explanation as 'bad' science, it might
prove more productive to consider it in relation to the social-situatedness of
the film and its audiences and to different repertoires of cultural capital. *Plan
9* roots itself in the 1950s flying saucer craze being played out in newspapers, comics, films, rock'n'roll novelty singles and so on. The aliens'
leggings and silky tabards look like the costumes from pulp illustrations,
comics and such television space operas as *Space Patrol* (1950–55) and *Rocky
Jones, Space Ranger* (1954), while the tone Eros adopts to explain solarbenite evoke such science education television as *Watch Mr Wizard* (1951–65).
Perhaps most importantly, the meagreness of Eros's metaphoric resources is
matched by the barrenness of the flying saucer's interior and the lack of
props with which to illustrate his analogy, just as the shakiness of his science
is matched by the instability of the soon-to-be-overturned wooden table
beside him. In this context, the very weakness of *Plan 9*'s science, along
with the poverty of its spectacle, can be a source of pleasure.

Eros's insistent repetition of the correspondences between the paired
terms of his analogy (ball/Earth, can/Sun, gasoline/sunlight) reminds
us that *all* scientific explanations are metaphorical, that even in science
there is no direct relationship between sign and referent. Indeed, the
gulf between sign and referent often reveals the discursive and material
factors involved in scientific practice. For example, *I Am Legend* (2007)
opens with Dr Alice Krippin (Emma Thompson) being interviewed on
television, directly after a heartily masculine sports segment speculating
on the baseball world series. While headlines about sport, finance,
international politics and a missing boy crawl across the bottom of the
television screen, African American Karen (April Grace) questions
Krippin about her 'miracle' cure for cancer. Krippin explains:

The premise is quite simple. Take something designed by nature and
reprogram it to make it work for the body rather than against it. … in

> this case the measles virus, which has been engineered at a genetic level to be helpful rather than harmful. … the best way to describe it is if you can … imagine your body as a highway and you picture the virus as a very fast car … being driven by a very bad man. Imagine the damage that that car could cause. But then if you replace that man with a cop, the picture changes. And that's essentially what we've done.

This sequence suggests a gendering of science and its representation. Despite the significance of Krippin's breakthrough, the interview's position in the broadcast and the accompanying screencrawl bracket it off from such masculinised, and thus more 'important', subjects as economics, politics and sport. Karen is introduced by a male colleague as being at 'the Health Desk' rather than, say, 'the Science Desk', where two women discuss biology rather than, say, physics. Dominant ideology doubly associates women of colour with the body rather than the mind, thus doubly excluding them from science. Furthermore, Karen is positioned as an audience surrogate (both diegetically and extradiegetically) in need of a childishly oversimplified explanation.

Krippin's analogy evokes a simple world of moral binaries and, by collapsing the distinction between humans as biological entities and humans as the subjects of political structures of domination, indicates the frequent complicity between scientific practice and social control. Appeals to science as neutral and objective, and as the arbiter of sf quality, often betray a similar politics, as when Gary Westfahl takes the 'charming idiocies that permeate' This Island Earth (1955) as his starting point in issuing advice to young sf scholars. Emphasising the film's 'quintessential stupidity' about scientific matters, he suggests that 'if the phrase "conversion of lead to uranium" doesn't immediately make you giggle, you should either brush up on your science or find another area of literature to study' (Westfahl 1999: 53).[5] Westfahl does not 'claim any expertise in scientific matters' beyond knowing 'what anyone who studies science fiction should know', since sf 'is a genre founded upon, and sometimes claiming authority from, a commitment to scientific accuracy' (53). This argument unquestioningly privileges a tradition of sf literature originating in the *Amazing Stories* pulp (see Westfahl 1998, 2007), which from its 1926 launch editorialised about the centrality of science to sf. Westfahl dismisses film analysis in relation to sociohistorical contexts because it reduces filmmakers to 'recorders of current events' (Westfahl 1999: 53).[6] He even describes a specific instance of such an approach to *This Island Earth* as yet another case of 'tenure-seeking academics' sending sf through 'their grinders to make some tired point about man's inhumanity to woman, the insidious persistence of postcolonial thought, or the impossibility of crafting coherent narratives in our postmodern world' (54). He suggests it would be much better, if probably career damaging, to 'dedicate yourself to the unending challenge of thoughtfully analyzing science fiction, employ[ing] only those tools that are appropriate for the task at hand, and [thus to] wrestle with the bewildering variety of issues raised by its numerous texts, including the foundational questions raised by humanity's existence in an immense and incomprehensible cosmos that will always remain important, no matter how naïvely they are expressed or how clumsily they are confronted' (54). Westfahl's escalation of a methodological disagreement treats science as if it is a neutral, objective practice, and then claims its authority effect for his own critical approach. This manoeuvre conflates the white male critic with rationality, while denying reason and rationality to women, peoples of colour and others who are marginalised by contemporary power relations. It also poses the white, middle-class, male critic as a self-denying, self-sacrificing, guileless, unappreciated and victimised hero.[7] In doing so, it exemplifies 'the god-trick of seeing everything from nowhere' (Haraway 1991b: 189), a notion central to the science studies critique of science.

UNPICKING SCIENCE'S SELF-IMAGE

An influential strand of Western philosophy proposes a distinction between consciousness and the world. René Descartes argues that the only thing of whose existence a consciousness can be certain is itself as it questions its own existence. While Descartes ultimately accepts that there are relationships between thoughts and material reality, Immanuel Kant insists on separating the noumenal (which cannot be known through the senses) from the phenomenal (which can be perceived by the senses). Such dualisms, which encourage the subject to perceive itself in isolation from the world (including separating its consciousness from its own body), also underpin the development of positivist, empirical science, which depends on two related notions: that the scientist can disengage from the world in order to observe and measure it impartially; and that behind the perceptible surface of things lies the possibility of understanding, connecting and explaining material phenomena through theorising the laws that govern them. This sense of rational detachment fosters the belief that science itself is grounded in the reality of the material universe but purified of social, political, economic, ideological and psychological influences. However, science studies increasingly challenges science's self-image of objectivity, neutrality and universality. As Thomas Gieryn argues, '"science" is not a single thing' and its 'boundaries ... are ambiguous, flexible, historically changing, contextually variable, internally inconsistent, and sometimes disputed' (1983: 781, 792).[8]

Noting the tendency to detach science from the social world and the impossibility of ever doing so, Bruno Latour traces 'imbroglios of science, politics, economy, law, religion, technology, fiction' whose 'fragile thread[s] will be broken into as many segments as there are pure disciplines' (2, 3). For example, a newspaper story about the expanding hole in the ozone layer includes: corporate CEOs who are 'modifying their assembly lines in order to replace ... chlorofluorocarbons, accused of crimes against the ecosphere'; 'heads of state of major industrialized countries who are getting involved with chemistry, refrigerators, aerosols and inert gases'; meteorologists who 'don't agree with the chemists' and are 'talking about cyclical fluctuations unrelated to human activity'; and 'Third World countries and ecologists' who are concerned with 'international treaties, moratoriums, the rights of future generations, and the right to development' (1). This single story 'mixes together ... the most esoteric sciences and the most sordid politics, the most distant sky and some factory in the Lyon suburbs, dangers on a global scale and the impending local elections or the next board meeting' (1). The same newspaper carries similarly exfoliating stories about AIDS, computer chips, frozen embryos, forest fires, whale migration, contraception, high-definition television and 'a slag heap in northern France', once 'a symbol of the exploitation of workers' but now classified as an ecological preserve because of the rare flora it has been fostering' (2). However, 'the analysts, thinkers, journalists and decision-makers will slice the delicate network' of the total, inextricably interconnected story 'into tidy compartments where you will find only science, only economy, only social phenomena, only local news, only sentiment, only sex' (2). They refuse to 'mix up knowledge, interest, justice and power' or 'heaven and earth, the global stage and the local scene, the human and the nonhuman' or the 'knowledge of things' and 'power and human politics', treating such categories as not merely separable but in reality separate (3). This compartmentalisation, which involves 'rigidly maintained distinctions between the scientific and the social, between real science and its technologies and applications, between basic and mission-directed research, and between contexts of discovery and contexts of justification' arguably 'protects individuals from having to understand' or even 'question ... the actual social consequences of their research' (Harding 2008: 55).

The relative collapse of state funding of science and technology research in the US and Europe after the Cold War led to a massive outflow of scientists from universities and into industry. Consequently, Helga Nowotny, Peter Scott and Michael Gibbons argue, barriers between pure research and its application, between science and society, are dissolving, making 'demands' and 'expectations that research' will 'yield socioeconomic benefits' more 'pervasive' (96)[9] and recontextualising research in terms of people

> as users, as target groups in markets or addressees of policies, even as 'causes' for further problems to be tackled, – or as 'real' people in innumerable interactions and communicative processes, ranging from

new modes of investment and financing for research, to legal regulations and constraints that shape the research process, to markets and media, households and Internet users, other scientists and millions of sophisticated and highly educated lay people.

(246)

However, the enrolment of these larger, more varied networks of social actors in a potential democratisation of research goals, agendas and practices simultaneously decouples 'science's useful outcomes ... from its cognitive authority' (184), with enormous consequences for what constitutes 'good' science. Moreover, since this vision of socially accountable science refuses to engage with real issues of power, politics and neo-liberal economics, it might merely be 'improv[ing] the public image of sciences which are increasingly under corporate and state military control' (Harding 2008: 93).

Many science studies' concerns were already evident in the 1920s and 1930s, when the still-influential cinematic images of mad science first coalesced. For example, even J.B.S. Haldane's pro-science pamphlet *Daedalus, or Science and the Future* (1924) begins by hypothesising that the appearance of a new star might actually be 'the last judgment of some inhabited world, perhaps a too successful experiment in induced radio-activity on the part of some of the dwellers there' (3), and concludes with the observation that scientific and technological progress has outstripped human moral development, with potentially apocalyptic consequences. Bertrand Russell's response, *Icarus, or the Future of Science* (1924), notes that 'long experience' has 'compelled' him 'to fear that science will be used to promote the power of dominant groups, rather than to make people happy', before outlining 'some of the dangers inherent in the progress of science while we retain our present political and economic institutions' (5, 6).

In 1942, Robert K. Merton outlined the shared values and normative structures of science as a self-regulating system in terms of four 'sets of institutional imperatives' (1973c: 270). First, universalism dictates that 'truth-claims, whatever their source, are to be subjected to *preestablished impersonal criteria*: consonant with observation and with previously confirmed knowledge' and that the 'acceptance or rejection' of such claims does not 'depend on the personal or social attributes of their' proponent (270). Everyone, regardless of 'race, nationality, religion, class, and personal qualities' (270), should have 'free access to scientific pursuits' (270, 272). Second, the 'findings of science' are the 'product of social collaborations' and subject to 'common ownership': the 'scientist's claim to "his" intellectual "property" is limited to that of recognition and esteem' (273). Third, scientists are disinterested and, fourth, they operate according to an 'organized skepticism' – the 'temporary suspension of judgment and the detached scrutiny of beliefs in terms of empirical and logical criteria' (277).

However, Merton constantly betrays anxieties about real-world conditions contradicting these imperatives. Universalism is undermined by personal and institutional prejudice against those considered 'of inferior status, irrespective of capacity or achievement' (272);[10] by the demands of the state, which favours 'ethnocentric particularism' in 'times of international conflict' (271); and by the extent to which 'laissez-faire democracy permits the accumulation of differential advantages for certain segments of the population', and thus requires political intervention 'to put democratic values into practice and to maintain universalistic standards' (273). Common ownership, already threatened by conflicts over priority and esteem, is incompatible with 'the definition of technology as "private property" in a capitalistic economy' (275) and with the secrecy that state and industry often demand. Disinterestedness is compromised by self-aggrandising individuals and groups, and scepticism is often seen to threaten 'the current distribution of power', frequently placing science in opposition to social institutions – 'organized religion', 'economic and political groups' – that demand 'uncritical respect' (278).

In earlier essays, Merton admits that 'scientific research is not conducted in a social vacuum' (1973d: 263) and that research agendas 'are determined by social forces as well as by the immanent development of science' (1973b: 204), even conceding that in some cases 'extra-scientific elements' may have 'wholly determined' rather than merely 'significantly influenced ... the foci of scientific interest' (1973a: 203). He also notes that although they are often thought of as 'dispassionate, impersonal', scientists are professional workers with 'a large emotional investment in [their] way of life' (1973d: 259). Just as scientists' motives 'may range from a passionate desire' to further human knowledge to 'a profound interest in achieving personal fame', so science's functions may range from 'enlarging our control of nature' to 'providing prestige-laden rationalizations of the existing order' (1973d: 263).[11]

These concerns are discernible in films of the period, too. In *Verdens undergang/The End of the World* (1916), news of potential collision with a comet causes a stockmarket collapse. Millionaire Frank Stoll (Olaf Fønss) buys up stocks at rock-bottom prices and forces a newspaper to falsely report that scientists believe that the comet will pass by harmlessly, restoring public confidence, prompting stock prices to rise and enabling him to sell at a massive profit before the truth comes out. In *F.P.1* (1933),[12] Captain Droste (Leslie Fenton) – visionary architect, builder and commander of the eponymous Floating Platform 1, designed for aeroplanes to land and refuel mid-Atlantic – bemoans the espionage and sabotage undertaken by 'vested interests, international concerns, perhaps some great trust or combine, something impersonal, without a soul'. He imagines progress as an irresistible metaphysical force, but recognises that its enemies in this instance are those who typically might finance innovation acting to maintain 'the old order of things' from which they derive their wealth and power. In *Frau im Mond/Woman in the Moon* (1929), Professor Georg Manfeldt (Klaus Pohl) dismisses his illustrious colleagues as calcified, unimaginative intellects when they mock his vision of mining the lunar mountains for gold. Discredited and ostracised as much for breaching social convention as for his unconventional science, he spends the ensuing 30 years living 'like a dog for the sake of [his] ideas'. He violently refuses an offer to buy his notebooks 'as a curiosity', prompting the pseudonymous Walter Turner (Fritz Rasp) – an agent of 'five brains and chequebooks', a group of financiers anxious about losing control of the world's gold reserves – to steal the notebooks, rocket designs and mission plans from Wolf Helius

(Willy Fritsch), the idealistic engineer-industrialist who intends to build and fly the professor's moon rocket. Turner gives Helius the option of making the trip on behalf of the five brains 'or not at all', preferring to 'annihilate all of [his] plans' rather 'than let [him] shut [them] out of the picture'. When Helius proves recalcitrant, Turner destroys one of his hangars and threatens to target his workers and the rocket itself with further bombs.

By 1939, J.D. Bernal saw science as inherently less stable than any shared scientific ethos might suggest: 'We can no longer be blind to the fact that science is both affecting and being affected by the social changes of our time' (3) and 'violent events from the outside world' (392). The Depression, fascism and widespread preparations for war must surely cause scientists 'to consider more seriously than ever before [their] position and function in society' (392). Such concerns were already familiar from sf. For example, in *A Connecticut Yankee* (1931), Hank Martin (Will Rogers) dreams that he is cast back in time to the days of King Arthur where, knighted 'Sir Boss', he wisecracks about the Depression and the rise of Mussolini, and introduces Fordist industrial practices under his monopolistic control. The film also anticipates elements of President Roosevelt's New Deal and, in a darker vein, the imminent return of mechanised warfare, including artillery and aerial bombardments of civilians. The opening section of *Things to Come* (1936) – made while Italy invaded and annexed Ethiopia, and released just months before the fascist coup in Spain, the declaration of war between Japan and China and the German invasions of Austria and the Sudetenland – depicts the growing fear of and preparations for imminent war, culminating in scenes of mass conscription and of air raids and gas attacks against civilian populations. Images of scientific/technological warfare – battleships, fighter planes and futuristic tanks clash and waves of bombers fill the sky over peaceful country towns – give way, after decades of conflict, to trench warfare, ragtag armies and devastating plague, culminating in a precarious existence among the ruins of a once great city under the brutal, feudal Mussolini-esque Boss (Ralph Richardson).

For Bernal, though, science's equivocal position had much deeper historical roots. The very notion of science as a 'purely intellectual occupation' or quest for truth, he argues, is 'essentially self-contradictory' (5): 'the most elementary reading of the history of science shows that both the drive which led to scientific discoveries and the means by which those discoveries were made were material needs and material instruments' (6). The growing centrality of organised science to the modern industrial state, largely unrecognised until the First World War, made the scientist 'as much a salaried official as the average civil servant and business executive' (10). As such, the scientist, like any worker, must choose between job security, personal fulfilment and more lucrative, but riskier, opportunities: 'no longer, if ever he was, a free agent', the scientist's 'real liberty ... is effectively limited, by his needs of livelihood, to actions which are tolerated by his paymasters' (388), often resulting in servile conformism. Under monopoly capitalism, which is unconcerned with the 'progress of science or the possibilities of its gifts to humanity' (121), scientific research is 'effectively controlled, if not in the detail, then in the general direction ... by the interests that control the productive processes as a whole' (10) and, for them, science is just another means of maximising the extraction of surplus value (profit). While monopolies are capable 'of expending large sums on research' (138), there is little 'incentive' for them to do so (139). The 'existence of competition and the necessary secrecy which it entails' (316), along with monopoly control and exploitation of patents, further restrict the circulation and development of scientific knowledge, often with massive human and social consequences. Together, the demands of the state and of industry produce 'unbalanced' research (40). Particularly in the US, this is exacerbated by 'the importance of publicity' in 'the struggle for success' (206), which 'enables a good deal of purely scientific work, whose direct utility value would be small, to be done' but 'places an undoubted emphasis on branches of science which have high publicity value ... to the detriment of other and equally important branches of science' (207).

While there are a number of biopics in this period celebrating the lives of real scientists, such as *The Story of Louis Pasteur* (1936), *The Story of*

Alexander Graham Bell (1939), *Dr. Ehrlich's Magic Bullet* (1940), *Edison, the Man* (1940) and *Madame Curie* (1943), the issue Bernal raises is better addressed by *The Man Who Changed His Mind* (1936).The recruitment of Dr Laurience (Boris Karloff) to the Haslewood Institute of Modern Science is accompanied by all the ballyhoo – headlines, articles, features, bunting, public lectures – that the newspapers owned by Lord Haslewood (Frank Cellier), an industrialist and press baron, can generate, but when Laurience presents his research on mind transference to a highly publicised gathering of scientists, he is met with ridicule. Haslewood, furious at this public relations disaster and absolutely uninterested in the truth of Laurience's claims, fires him on the spot. According to Reynold Humphries, the 1930s mad scientist – who treats animals, people and even the dead as nothing more than raw materials – is 'a stand-in for the capitalist, acting as the return of the repressed of the latter's real historical function: assuming "rights" that are not his' (221). However, in this instance, as Haslewood's assertion of ownership over the product of Laurience's labour shows, the mad scientist is merely proletarian, 'an intellectual … but nevertheless a social subject forced to sell his knowledge to produce more knowledge that, transformed into a social commodity, will benefit' (224) Haslewood's business. Haslewood is only concerned with 'exploiting' Laurience 'for profit and power', whether transforming him into a celebrity to sell more newspapers or turning his research into commodities, while Laurience 'believes that he will have the right to use the results of his experiments for the common good', as if 'the fact of having produced this extra knowledge under precise working conditions had not inscribed him, along with the magnate, into an equally precise power relation based on production and exchange' (223–24).

Bernal concludes that 'the full development of science in the service of humanity is incompatible with the continuance of capitalism' (409), noting that the 'practical success at the very depth of the world slump' of the Soviet Union's first Five Year Plan (1928–32) prompted socially aware scientists to consider the advantages of centralised planning over capitalism's chaotic system of economic competition (392). *Gabriel over the White House* (1933) gets as close as a Hollywood film could to espousing this position. Newly elected President Judson Hammond (Walter Huston) has a near-fatal car crash and – brain damaged, or perhaps under angelic influence – abruptly ceases to toe the party line. He refuses to criminalise or violently disperse a million unemployed men who march on Washington, instead forming an 'army of construction', employing them to pursue their trades 'without one dollar of profit accruing to anyone' until the economy has sufficiently recovered to absorb them back into the workforce. He repeals prohibition, goes into competition with bootleggers and wages war on racketeers; and when debtor nations try to avoid repayments, he blackmails the world into universal disarmament and the abolition of war. However, he can only achieve all this by suspending Congress and becoming a dictator. *Just Imagine* (1930), despite the magnificent, well-ordered, harmonious metropolis it depicts, demonises planning because the future state extends its reach too far, dictating eugenically favourable marriages over the wishes of the romantic leads. In contrast, *Aelita* (1924) suggests that daydreams of exotic sexual and revolutionary adventures – like corruption, profiteering, petty officials, scheming women, jealous husbands and the blandishments of American commercial culture – have no place in the planned, collective endeavour of building the Soviet republics. *Kosmicheskiy reys: Fantasticheskaya novella/The Space Voyage* (1935), less obviously based in the realities of the fledgling Soviet Union, criticises bureaucratic managerialism for lacking vision and exuberantly celebrates the accomplishments of such ordinary Soviets as an ageing professor, a female technician and an inventive Komsomol lad.

THE SOCIAL SUBJECTIVITY OF (MAD) SCIENTISTS

Peter J. Kuznick writes that, 'with courageous exceptions', the 'twentieth century' saw scientists 'repeatedly disregard their own values and code of ethics' in the service of 'rulers exploiting science for ignoble purposes' (1). For example, in 1936–45, scientists everywhere capitulated 'to nationalist and ideological pressures':

The Soviet scientists' knuckling under to Lysenkoism, the ideological and technical support provided by German scientists to the Nazi regime, and … the role played by American scientists in developing and deciding to drop atomic bombs made abundantly clear the willingness with which scientists would serve existing powers and accept prevailing ideologies.

(1–2)

Bernal would attribute such complicities to the typical scientist's 'psychological abnormality':

He is driven to satisfy his curiosity for its own sake, and, in order to be free to do this, he is willing to fit into any kind of life which will offer the least mental and material disturbance to his main concern. Besides this science itself is an eminently satisfactory occupation; its pursuit withdraws interest from external things and offers as well a means of solace and escape from those who find the events of the outside world distressing. The great bulk of scientists are therefore, as long as their science is not threatened, likely to be the most docile and amenable of citizens.

(389)

Gojira's Serizawa exemplifies the scientist who struggles with the dilemma between science and its uses. By 'framing Serizawa's project as private', the film 'erases the deep connection between scientific development and state military mobilization' (Anderson 32), even though it also hints at his role in Japanese imperialist expansion into Asia and the Pacific. Serizawa's fear that politicians will weaponise the Oxygen Destroyer, along with his decisions to destroy his research and to commit suicide after using the Oxygen Destroyer to kill Gojira, positions him alongside scientists, such as Einstein, whose work was later used in the development of atomic weapons. However, his overly strenuous denial of having German friends suggests a more active wartime role. Moreover, while his wartime injuries – he lost an eye and his cheek is scarred, perhaps burned – seem to identify him as a victim of US bombing, they might as easily implicate him in the Japanese atom bomb project or other weapons research.

Kala Dhandha/Black Mail (1973) sketches the tension between 'pure' research and applied science in a corporate context when industrialist Kailash Gupta (Dharmendra) invites Professor Ramakant Khurana (Madan Puri) to dinner. Khurana insists that he is not paid 'to have food and relax but to do something worth mentioning', despite earlier insisting just as strenuously that he was hired to 'do some research' that 'may or may not come with a result'. Khurana recognises the contradictory impulses underpinning scientific labour: 'Actually doing research itself is sufficient, no matter whatever time has gone into it. It's a kind of addiction, a kind of love where the researcher gets lost. So you should keep reminding me that I should achieve something from my research so that it benefits you, me and the Nation'. While Merton argues that the scientific ethos, once internalised, fashions the scientist's 'scientific conscience' or 'super-ego' (1973c: 269), *Kala Dhandha* suggests that 'pure' research is driven as much by ego or id, with other imperatives – profitability, nation-building, modernisation – functioning as super-ego. Similarly, in *Yakeen* (1969), Dr Sharma (Bramha Bhardwa) prefers to be murdered rather than betray India by revealing a secret formula, proving 'that life does not take precedence over the nation'.

In 1945, Lionel Trilling observed that 'no one who has ever lived observantly among scientists will claim that they are without an unconscious' (170) – a point made abundantly clear in *Forbidden Planet* (1956) when alien technology manifests the incestuous desires of Dr Morbius (Walter Pidgeon) as an invisible monster when his daughter, Altaira (Anne Francis), becomes attracted to Commander Adams (Leslie Nielsen). Trilling suggests that scientists' 'devotion to science' and 'relative indifference' to 'manifestations of personality' are evidence of neurosis rather than 'sign[s] of normality' (170). Moreover, since scientists, like other professionals, are typically required to 'practice concealment and conformity', a psychoanalytical investigation would show 'that the strains and imbalances of their psyches are … of the same frequency as those of writers, and of a similar kind' (171). Indeed, cinematic mad scientists often display the tensions between physical embodiment and social entanglement *and* a drive to deny their bodies, sever social ties and contract into an isolated consciousness.

The impossibility of fulfilling this drive is reiterated throughout *Dr Jekyll and Mr Hyde* (1931), which starts with a slightly irised, three-and-a-quarter minute-long, subjective point-of-view sequence as Dr Henry Jekyll (Fredric March) rises from playing Bach, leaves his house and travels to St Simon's to lecture to medical students and fellow scientists. This extended use of a subjective camera provides a strong sense of an anchored perspective and identity. Although shots in which Jekyll talks to his servant, Poole (Edgar Norton), are mostly edited in a conventional shot/reverse-shot pattern, the irising, a pan and the slight motion of the camera help to create the impression of a continuous take; the chor-eographing of Jekyll's appearance in a mirror reinforces the relationship between Jekyll's eyes and the camera; the cut when Jekyll climbs into his carriage is more or less concealed; the cross-dissolve that elides most of the journey arguably makes the subjective camera even more subjective, representing not so much a temporal break as Jekyll's drifting attention. However, the visibility of these techniques simultaneously serves to destabilise the subject, as does the more general sense of dis-embodiment that accompanies a sustained subjective viewpoint: the camera does not replicate the human gaze, and its movement through space is too slow; Jekyll's body is fragmented as his arms appear in shot at not quite the right angle in relation to his 'eyes', while his voice and footsteps do not seem to come from quite the right place. The manner and tone in which Poole, the cab driver, students and the doorman interact with the subjective viewpoint generate a sense of Jekyll being interpellated as a subject, as if he is being constructed through these brief exchanges. At the same time, Jekyll seems to present himself to these interlocutors, performing a public role that is emphasised by his histrionic lecturing style. His lecture itself develops this idea of the subject as simultaneously, and contradictorily, unified and splintered when he declares: 'man is not truly one, but truly two. One of him strives for the nobilities of life. ... The other seeks an expression of impulses that bind him to some dim animal relation with the earth'.

The subjective viewpoint reappears when Jekyll, looking into a mirror, raises to his lips the chemical concoction that will change him into Hyde. The transformation is represented through three distinct shots, the second of which involves a whip pan that then becomes a whirling montage of voices from earlier in the film: his two objects of desire, Muriel (Rose Hobart) and the prostitute Ivy (Miriam Hopkins); disapproving older men; his own angry pronouncements. The combination of subjective viewpoint and (apparent) reflection in a mirror heightens the sense of contradiction between a unified and multiple subject, while the delirium montage simultaneously suggests the pressure placed on this uncertain subject by the multiple and contradictory interpellations involved in social interactions. Ironically, this becomes clearest just as Jekyll succeeds – as the subjective viewpoint implies – in withdrawing from the world and into isolated consciousness and pristine rationality.

Science's self-image demands the scientist's withdrawal from worldly entanglement, but this should also be understood as a particular example of a dilemma faced by all modern subjects required to reduce themselves to 'subjects-for-capital' – that is, the abstract proletarians who function as 'productive instrument[s]' for 'capital within the sphere of production' (Lebowitz 138), such as: the shuffling rows of workers in *Metropolis*, exhausted even at the start of a shift; the Martian workers in *Aelita* deemed superfluous to current requirements and refrigerated for later use; the narcotised commuters of *Equilibrium* (2002), barely aware of their surroundings; the cyborged *maquiladora* day labourers of *Sleep Dealer* (2008), who remotely operate robots on the other side of the closed Mexico–US border. These films also imagine 'subjects-for-themselves', the full human beings who exceed reduction to mere labour power: some rise as revolutionary mobs, others try to make lives for themselves outside the domination of the workplace and beyond the wage relationship that treats them as commodities to be bought and sold. As *The Man Who Changed His Mind* suggests, the scientist who withdraws from physical embodiment and social entanglement is not identical to the subject-for-capital, but to the extent that science is inextricably bound up in capitalism these positions overlap and converge.

Some of these tensions are played out in *Metropolis*. The opening sequence combines images of dynamic machines with abstract graphics, symbolising a social order in which industrial systems dominate people. While the functions of particular machines remain unclear, they are all apparatuses designed to discipline the workers, who must respond to their displays and readouts with exhausting physical exertions. The M-Machine even scalds enfeebled workers with jets of steam when they fail to function perfectly as components within its regulatory systems. From an immense office, the centre of a network of information and communications technologies, Joh Fredersen (Alfred Abel) calmly and dispassionately overlooks this domain, betraying none of his assistants' nervous energy. The 'brain of the city', he has effectively withdrawn from the social realm into almost total identification with the system over which he autocratically presides. When the M-Machine explodes, killing a number of workers, Joh's only concern is the potential effect on the smooth running of the city, but the disaster makes his son, Freder (Gustav Fröhlich), recognise that his privileged life of carefree leisure is built on the immiseration of the workers who maintain the city. He renounces Joh's distance from and disregard for the workers, and descends into the subterranean realm in which they live and work. His fresh engagement with the world is signalled by the febrile haste with which he races around the city and by the lingering, if chaste, caresses he shares with Maria (Brigitte Helm), the worker with whom he falls in love.

While Joh is happy to cast the workers out of the city, he is also anxious about what might occur out of sight of his cybernetic control systems. He aspires, in effect, to make the city transparent, knowable and thus governable; but his efforts at control are thwarted by the city's labyrinthine reality. An oneiric space, it is haunted by those things repressed by the dream of reason, such as the 'strange house' – which seems too large on the inside, with cellars extending down beneath the city – 'that the centuries had overlooked'. It belongs to Rotwang (Rudolf

Klein-Rogge), a scientific genius given to supernatural and alchemical paraphernalia. Whereas *Himmelskibet/A Trip to Mars* (1918) uses mise-en-scène to contrast scientific modernity with the unhealthy pursuit of ancient esoteric knowledge,[13] *Metropolis* insists on the inseparability of modernity from history. It locates Rotwang's ancient-yet-modern house in the 'middle' of the city, an uncanny remnant recalling those things otherwise excluded from Joh's purview.

The uncanny is often connected to a failure of vision, and thus to castration anxiety. Long ago, Joh stole Hel away from Rotwang, but she died giving birth to Freder, making him a constant reminder of desire, reproduction, death and sexual difference (the female's phallic lack also triggers castration anxiety). Rotwang has created a beautiful deco robot capable of labouring for 24 hours every day, rendering the proletariat superfluous. However, Joh instructs Rotwang to give the robot the appearance of Maria, effectively corrupting the 'pure' woman and turning the female body into a source of corruption: robot-Maria will rouse the workers into an uprising that will enable Joh to justify further repression, but she is also despatched to a nightclub, where her erotic dancing drives the ruling class to madness. The narrative heads towards a catastrophe that is only averted by a preposterous solution, which recuperates all this hysterical excess into an expanded system of cybernetic control, with Freder mediating between the workers and his father.

THE SCHIZOID SCIENTIST, SEXUAL TERROR AND POLITICAL COMPLICITY

In contrast to Rotwang, who seems to thrive on his ambiguous situation, mad scientists more commonly strive to leave behind desiring, embodied entanglements, to withdraw from direct engagement with the world. This tension between contrary impulses – reason/embodiment, subjects-for-capital/subjects-for-themselves – underpins the schizoid personality types demonstrated by so many mad scientists: Manfeldt, who prefers 30 years of social isolation; Serizawa, who expresses no feelings for

Emiko and chooses self-destruction; Carrington, who rather than speak to Hendry has his assistant read his notes aloud; and Krippin, who nervously mutters and stutters about her cure for cancer. In *Dr Cyclops* (1940), the 'strange' and 'abnormally secretive' biologist Dr Alexander Thorkel (Albert Dekker) exemplifies the 'anaesthetic schizoid', whose social disengagement and affective detachment indicates a 'yawning emotional emptiness', 'the cold breath of an arctic soullessness' (Kretschmer 126). Thorkel's appearance – bald-headed with thick glasses, his oddly bloated body and awkward movements confined by a battered linen suit that is both baggy and too tight – is larval, an infantilism emphasised by his impulsive outbursts and his inability to perceive other people (and animals) as beings independent of his will. After two years based in a remote, Amazon compound, he summons self-important Dr Rupert Bulfinch (Charles Halton) and microscopy expert Dr Mary Robinson (Janice Logan) ten thousand miles to assist him in his work – for just an afternoon, in order to confirm the result of an experiment. He is surprised when this high-handedness offends them, raving: 'You are merely my employees, whom I've discharged and instructed to leave'. Later, he uses them as experimental subjects, intending to kill them afterwards so that they cannot interrupt his work again.

Some films question the motivations of such extreme detachment, such as *The Damned* (1963), in which children of women irradiated in a nuclear accident are raised without direct human contact in a subterranean facility. Bernard (Alexander Knox) believes that only his cold-blooded, radioactive mutant charges are capable of surviving in a world devastated by an inevitable nuclear war, and would produce more such children if he could. He is avuncular when interacting with them via two-way television, but he dispassionately arranges the deaths of intruders and murders his lover when she sees too much. However, he considers himself merely a public servant in 'the age of senseless violence', duty bound by the state and a greater morality to disregard sentiment. In *Dead Ringers* (1988), identical twins and noted gynæcologists Elliot and Beverly Mantle (Jeremy Irons) are psychologically and socially co-dependent. The outgoing, superficially charming Elliot handles the public aspects of their work, while the shy Beverly undertakes research and deals with patients. Elliot urges Beverly to become involved with actress Claire Niveau (Genevieve Bujold), but the romance flounders when she discovers Beverly has a twin (Elliot slept with her first and, pretending to be Beverly, continues occasionally to do so). When the lovers are reunited, Beverly – now addicted to prescription medications – suspects her of infidelity. His growing derangement reveals the contempt for both women and embodiment that underpins the twins' behaviour. He uses a gold-plated Mantle retractor – an award for designing the actual device – to examine a patient, even though such instruments are only intended 'for surgical retraction', insisting that 'there's nothing the matter with the instrument, it's the body – the woman's body' that is 'all wrong'. Convinced that their 'patients are getting strange', he designs and tries to use 'gynæcological implements for working on mutant women'. Incapable of dealing with social, sexual and emotional entanglements beyond the Beverly/Elliot dyad, he retreats into a scientific (ir)rationality that disavows bodies and other people's subjectivity.

Zaveshchaniye professora Douelya/Professor's Dowell's Testament (1985) criticises fantasies of disembodied reason. Professor Dowell (Olgert Kroders), who compares his organ-transplant and life-extension experiments to God creating Eve from Adam's rib, arranges for his brain to be kept alive after his body dies so that he can continue his work. The pallid, post-humous-but-still-alive head, attached to a life-support trolley, emphasises his disdain for embodiment – as do the chimera he creates (dogs and chimpanzees with transplanted heads, a cat with duck's feet) and his failure to realise that his assistant, Dr Marie Laurent (Valentina Titova), sacrificed everything to work with him out of love rather than devotion to science. Dowell's estranged son, Arthur (Aleksei Bobrov), argues that while Einstein 'never thought his work would lead to an atomic bomb', 'noble ideas' will always be 'appropriated by people in uniform – then it's strontium in the bones, children born with two heads'. Representatives of the Mercury Chemicals Corporation boast that they are 'active in all five continents' – six, if you include the 'traces of [their] chemicals' discovered 'in Antarctic penguins'. Seeking to appropriate Dowell's work (to sell 'immortality' to the rich and to 'create humans ... who obey orders without asking questions'), they offer his successor, Dr Kern (Igor Vassiliev), unlimited resources while also threatening, if he does not cooperate, to buy up the Dowell Institute's debts and force him to work for them.

Kern grafts the head of one dead woman onto the body of another. This chimeric Eve (Natalya Saiko) does not remember either of her previous lives, but traces of the two personalities start to emerge. When Kern finds her preparing for a nocturnal rendezvous with Arthur, he loses his temper. Running his hand over her body, he tells her, 'I picked you up, piece by piece. I stitched you together like a doll. None of this is yours. I gave you a new body. You're nothing, you understand? You don't exist'. His sweat-beaded forehead and the hint of sexual violence suggest that his denial of her personhood is not that of a dispassionate scientist. Later, having bullied her into submission, he unveils her at a scientific congress as an 'experimental sample', a 'biological combination' of elements from 'two different biological units'. Meanwhile, Dowell realises the error of rejecting embodiment and social entanglements. He longs to feel the breeze on his skin, and for the first time ever he calls Laurent 'Marie'. The film ends with his public suicide after he tells the congress:

> I struggled my entire life in search of truth. When I believed I had learned it, I learned as well that the truth can be stolen. The ray of light is transformed into the deadly spark. The formula for life becomes a number in a bank account. The vultures snatch on the prey. ... you must be ready for the responsibility. You must take care for your fellow man. And all living things.

Typically, the mad scientist's withdrawal from the world reveals those things that science disavows about its own practices, particularly as the 'God trick' functions to deny the economic and social power relations (of class, race and gender) underpinning science's self-mythology and its real-world existence and operations. Ernst Kretschmer's description of schizoids as 'oversensitive and cold at the same time, and ... in quite different mixes' and as 'full of antitheses, always containing extremes' but lacking a stable, middle ground (152, 245) also fits Henry Frankenstein (Colin Clive), Doctor Gogol (Peter Lorre) and Jack Griffin (Claude Rains) in, respectively, *Frankenstein* (1931), *Mad Love* (1935) and *The Invisible Man* (1933). In order to pursue his experiments, Frankenstein retreats from the traditional institutions of knowledge represented by Goldstadt Medical College, where he was formerly a student, and from the bodily, familial, social and romantic/sexual aspects of life represented by 'a decent home, a bath, good food and drink and a darned pretty girl'. While the Baron (Frederick Kerr) suspects that the 'sordid experiments' delaying his son's wedding to Elizabeth (Mae Clarke) involve another woman, the film associates their 'unnaturalness' with homosexuality. Various conversations about Henry's secretive behaviour and sequestered existence suggest that he is engaged in what is understood as a final queer fling before settling down to the normative heterosexuality demanded of his feudal role. His reckless pursuit of the artificial creation of life also expresses fear of contagion by the female body and anxiety over his ability to reproduce the social order by producing a 'son for the House of Frankenstein'.

European feudalism is historically underpinned by the Decree of the Three Orders, 'sketched out by a powerful group of prelates in the eleventh century', which 'stated that God had assigned three separate tasks to mankind': 'in descending order, to pray for salvation for all (priests and bishops); to fight to protect all (the knights or nobles); and to labour in order to provide the resources necessary to support the first two groups (the peasants)' (Hobson 113). This 'new Christian moral code' (113) legitimised economic and political inequities, while enabling the church to construct the notion of Christendom, and thus of Europe, as a unified entity in opposition to Islam. Significantly, *Frankenstein* opens with exhausted Catholic funeral rites in a barren, disorderly cemetery being mocked by a grave-robbing Frankenstein, who mutters that the corpse is 'just resting, waiting for a new life to come'. But the film is unable to separate science from history or to imagine a purer, scientific modernity. Henry's laboratory is located inside a derelict, medieval watchtower. Suggesting a drive to establish and protect borders from external invasion, to purify and preserve a national identity, this crumbling edifice has obvious metaphorical appeal for Frankenstein, with his desire for bodily/social integrity in a world he fears has been superseded.[14]

This tension between declining feudalism and emergent capitalism, also evident in the *Frankenstein* sequels' confused historical settings, resonates with uncertainties about the desirability, efficacy, priorities and future of a capitalist economic and social order that had plunged Europe into four years of devastating war and produced the Great Depression. Consequently, *Frankenstein*'s evocation of class issues deeply rooted in the practice of science is unsurprising. The watchtower, for example, recalls debates over the proper spaces and places in which to conduct science. Steven Shapin's examination of the 'physical and the symbolic setting of experimental work' (479) in seventeenth-century England uncovers the class dimensions of this foundational period, when the Royal Society considered it acceptable to pursue scientific investigations in private but based the legitimacy of research on its findings being demonstrated in public. However, only certain classes were considered appropriate witnesses: mercantile interests undermined merchants' reliability, and the working class technicians who built, maintained and operated the experimental apparatus were also tainted by economic considerations, but a 'gentleman's word might be relied upon partly because what he said was without consideration of remuneration' (492). This logic underpins the moment when Frankenstein, having decided to demonstrate his work to the uninvited Elizabeth, Victor Moritz (John Boles) and Dr Waldman (Edward Van Sloan),[15] poses theatrically before the table upon which the creature (Boris Karloff) lies and says to the four people in front of him, one of whom is his hunchback assistant, Fritz (Dwight Frye), 'Good scene, isn't it? One man crazy, three very sane spectators'. By presenting his experiment and himself to spectators, Frankenstein reinforces his sense of separation from the social realm[16] while expunging from the scene the character upon whose labour his experiments depend.[17]

While the creature's costume associates him with the industrial proletariat (Wood 76), his monstrosity is also constructed around the sexually aggressive black buck stereotype. The film cuts away from the monster's apparent attack on Elizabeth, whose wedding dress accentuates her virginal whiteness, leaving it unclear whether he has raped her. A later cut associates Elizabeth's unconscious form with the dead body of the innocent little girl he accidentally drowned. In a film released in the year of the Scottsboro Boys case, the sight of an officially sanctioned, murderous torch-wielding crowd setting out to find the creature cannot help but evoke a racist lynch mob defending white womanhood. These associations undercut the superficially happy ending in which Henry and Elizabeth, finally married, are discreetly left to their wedding night. The baron, toasting a 'son to the House of Frankenstein', does not for a moment suspect that any promptly forthcoming grandchild might be the product of class pollution, racial miscegenation and necrophiliac rape.[18]

Psychoanalytic accounts tend to see the schizoid subject, stalled at an infantile stage of emotional and character development, as 'seek[ing] to dissolve the tension between the desire for union and the fact of separation, either by imagining an ecstatic and painless reunion with the mother or ... by imagining a state of complete self-sufficiency' (Lasch 1985: 177). While the latter alternative describes the arrested development of Dr Thorkel and Professor Dowell, the former is explored in the self-consciously Freudian *Mad Love*. Dr Gogol, who 'cures deformed children and mutilated soldiers', is obsessed with the actress Yvonne Orlac (Frances Drake). The film opens with a Grand Guignol stageplay, at the climax of which Yvonne's character, bound and stretched over a torture wheel by a husband who suspects her of infidelity, refuses to name her lover. As a red hot fork is applied to her flesh, implying genital mutilation, she screams, 'Yes! Yes! It was your brother!' Her ecstatic, sexualised performance is framed by two shots of Gogol, watching from between partially drawn curtains, his face half in shadow: 'The first shot tracks in on his ... face as the torture begins, his one clearly visible eye focused with startling intensity on the woman stretched on the torturer's frame. The second shot, at the performance's end, shows us that same eye closing in a kind of orgasmic satisfaction as her screams of pain reverberate around the theatre' (Tudor 189). In this primal scene fantasy, Gogol simultaneously 'identifies with the position of the victim as a mother figure' and 'with the sadistic husband deriving intense pleasure from having his unfaithful wife branded', but is also positioned so that he can 'occupy the absent place of the wife's lover' – the husband's presumably younger brother (Humphries 92).

Despite spurning Gogol's attentions, Yvonne asks him to save the hands of her concert pianist husband, Stephen (Colin Clive), damaged in a train crash. Gogol secretly replaces them with those of an executed circus knife thrower. Arrested in his Oedipal trajectory, Gogol frequently becomes childlike in Yvonne's presence, casting her as the mother he desires and Stephen as the father whom he must destroy in order to become her lover. Reynold Humphries suggests the image of Gogol palpating Stephen's newly unbandaged hands is of 'the son lovingly masturbating his father' (92) as he struggles with libidinal desires while trying to identify with and placate his father/rival. Later, Gogol mock-diagnoses Stephen's growing conviction that his hands possess 'a life of their own' as an 'arrested wish fulfilment', offering a hypothetical scenario of a childhood playmate throwing a knife so 'cleverly' that Stephen's inability to emulate it has 'festered deep' in his 'subconscious'. Of course, Gogol does not recognise that this dream image of boys comparing penises reveals his own phallic envy or stalled infantile development.

When Yvonne is disturbed while searching Gogol's chambers, she poses in the place of his waxwork of her, but a cut on her cheek betrays her. Gogol, confronted by the idealised image of her coming to life, complete with a bleeding wound, is unhinged by this sudden sex-ualisation of the maternal body and reminder of sexual difference. Deprived of the fantasy of blissful merger with the maternal, he takes on the role of the Grand Guignol's cuckolded husband, with Yvonne gasping in sexualised agony as he strangles her with her own hair. Arriving in the nick of time, Stephen becomes both Gogol-the-spectator and the absent lover Gogol could not play, killing Gogol and defeating his Oedipal challenge with a skilfully thrown knife, a legally sanctioned phallic penetration that enables the reunion of the heterosexual couple.[19]

The sexual anxieties evoked in *The Invisible Man* are primarily concerned with masturbation, a vice as solitary and thus 'unnatural' as the experiments Griffin conducts 'in secret', behind 'barred' doors and 'drawn' blinds. Indeed, the first thing Griffin does on obtaining a private lodgings in the Lion's Head pub is draw the curtains and ask for a key to lock the door. Jenny (Una O'Connor), the innkeeper's wife, is upset about the spillages and stained carpet in his room, and he explains, while anxiously pressing his palms together, that his work has 'affected his eyes'. He also complains that Jenny and her husband have 'driven' him 'near insane with ... peering through the keyholes and gaping through the curtains'. The sequence in which Griffin first reveals his invisibility even includes a shot of him, back to the camera, unfastening his trousers as he says 'this will give them a bit of a shock'. Other films about (in)visibility further develop this interconnection with sexuality. For example, during the final song in *Mr India* (1987), Seema Sohni (Sridevi) and invisible crime fighter Mr India (Anil Kapoor) declare their love for each other. Throughout the sequence, he phases in and out of visibility, careful to remain unseen by her since she does not know that he is actually her orphan-adopting landlord. Two kinds of screen substitute make evident the relationship between desire, fantasy, vision and cinema. When the couple dance together, the camera rotates around them, alternating shots in which only Seema is visible with shots of both characters silhouetted against hanging sheets of red fabric. The other screen substitute – a pane of glass – cannot actually be seen. To create the effect of Mr India kissing Seema, Sridevi leans forward so that her chin and lips press against the glass, implying his presence; later, after a storm has broken, Seema, her wet clothes clinging to her, presses her breast against the glass to indicate that Mr India is holding her to him.

Hollow Man (2000) is considerably less restrained. Preoccupied with making the visible invisible, and vice versa, its CGI effects repeatedly strip away the body, layer by layer, revealing fat, muscle, organs, tendons, cartilage, blood vessels and bones, and build up the body from (apparently) nothing. However, once arrogant, misogynist Sebastian Caine (Kevin Bacon) turns himself invisible, his predatory voyeurism transforms the film into an essay on cinema's scopophilic drive (see Mulvey). Having previously shown nothing but contempt for the research team's vet, Sarah Kennedy (Kim Dickens), Sebastian seizes the opportunity afforded by his invisibility to expose and fondle her breast while she sleeps. Sebastian's apartment is opposite that of an unnamed woman (Rhona Mitra) who he secretly observes since she frequently strips to her underwear before closing the blinds; once invisible, he sneaks into her apartment to watch her while she thinks she is alone before terrorising, raping and murdering her. Later, Linda McKay (Elisabeth Shue), the project's other key scientist and Sebastian's former lover, wakes from a nightmare of him undressing her while she sleeps. In each instance, just as the camera is already at its most scopophilic, the compulsion to look is heightened by the film's cutting-edge effects: the digital removal of hands unbuttoning garments; the digital manipulation of a CGI breast; the subjective steadicam viewpoint and the digital removal of its operator so that he cannot be seen in a mirror; and so on. The final example – Linda wakes up just as the invisible Sebastian she is dreaming about finishes removing her clothes – projects this rape fantasy into her consciousness in an attempt to disavow the film's prurience and the cinematic apparatus's masculine subject position.

In *The Invisible Man*, however, Griffin ostensibly desires invisibility so as to achieve 'something tremendous', 'to gain wealth and fame and honour, to write [his] name above the greatest scientists of all time', because he is 'just a poor struggling chemist' who has 'nothing to offer' his fiancée, Flora (Gloria Stuart), the daughter of his wealthy employer, Dr Cranley (Henry Travers). Social disempowerment and class anxiety produce his desire to detach from his origins and social position, to become the purified (because apparently disembodied) intellect. Consequently, from the moment that he becomes invisible on screen, sexual connotations fall away. But even Griffin must admit to the persistence of corporeality: food and drink remain visible for an hour after he has consumed them; rain and soot mark the outlines of his body, and mud his feet; even fog betrays him since he appears within it as a man-shaped fog-free space.[20] Furthermore, as with *Metropolis*'s Joh, Griffin's desire not to be seen and his desire for power are interconnected. Michel Foucault argues that the distributed power of the panopticon depends on both the visibility of the prisoners and the invisibility of the guard watching them so that the prisoners always behave as if they are under surveillance even when they are not. Griffin intends 'a reign of terror', beginning with 'a few murders here and there, murders of great men, murders of little men, just to show [that he] make[s] no distinction', and since 'the whole world' is his 'hiding place', people will fear that he is always potentially present.

In many films, though, scientists are content merely to cooperate with power. In *The Thing from Another World*, with the exception of Carrington, whose costume, appearance and manner connote a sophisticated, queer, Jewish, communist intellectual, the scientists are stolid and prioritise allegiance to military–corporate authority over their research. *This Island Earth*'s Dr Cal Meacham (Rex Reason) is at the heart of the military–industrial complex. After an opening shot from the top of the Washington Monument pans across the Mall until the Capitol is in the centre of the frame, the film dissolves to newspapermen posing Meacham next to the wing of a T-33A jet fighter. An electronics expert, he is on first-name terms with the journalists, who quiz him about the 'industrial application of atomic energy' conference he attended at the Committee on Atomic Power's behest. As he prepares to pilot the aeroplane to his West-Coast home, a journalist asks 'how long has the army been handing out jets' for personal use? Meacham replies: 'one of the boys at Lockheed handed me this one – I hope you taxpayers don't mind'. This scene presents as totally unproblematic the close relationships among government, military, industry and a complicit media happy merely to treat Meacham as a celebrity.

In contrast, in *Seven Days to Noon* (1950), Professor John Willingdon (Barry Jones), one of the Manhattan Project's British team and now the senior researcher at a government nuclear weapons establishment, can no longer accept the profound dissonance between his job and his personal/professional ethics. He threatens to detonate a nuclear bomb in central London if the prime minister does not announce unilateral disarmament. Although the film ultimately depicts Willingdon as having suffered a nervous breakdown, it insist that it stems from an irresolvable ethical dilemma rather than overwork.[21] *Quatermass 2* (1957) also critiques the gulf between corporate–state power and the interests of the people. Professor Quatermass (Brian Donlevy) discovers that establishment figures, possessed by an alien intelligence, have funded the covert construction of a massive industrial plant as an invasion beachhead. The film repeatedly points to the dangers of extending the wartime security state into peacetime and, by contrasting a derelict old village with a new housing estate policed by the plant's zombified security force, questions the postwar labour movement's willingness to exchange broader social transformations for an end to austerity.

A similar scepticism about state and corporate science becomes common from the 1970s onwards, in films such as *The Andromeda Strain* (1971), *Colossus: The Forbin Project* (1970), *Westworld* (1973), *The Terminal Man* (1974), *Scanners* (1981), *E.T.: The Extra-terrestrial* (1982), *Tron* (1982), *WarGames* (1983), *Short Circuit* (1986), *Gremlins 2: The New Batch* (1992), *Outbreak* (1995) and *Small Soldiers* (1998). However, regardless of such films' efforts to distance certain dissenting scientists from corporate–state–military interests, they generally remain conservative texts about individuals striving in exceptional or anomalous circumstances. Indeed, in *Primer* (2004), the whole purpose of scientific endeavour is to become part of the system. Aaron (Shane Carruth) and Abe (David Sullivan), who have devoted 30 hours of their spare time every week for two years to devising patentable tweaks to existing technologies in the hope of getting rich, inadvertently create a limited form of time travel (if one of them switches on the machine at time A and enters it later at time B, he can return to time A, but this means that between times A and B two versions of him exist simultaneously). However, Aaron and Abe are so profoundly woven into the fabric of late capitalism that they can only imagine using this fabulous new technology to leave everything – apart from their bank balances – exactly the same. They repeatedly travel back in time to sit in hotel rooms to play the stock market, using their knowledge of the very near future to enrich themselves without becoming visible. They reject taking advantage of lotteries because that would attract attention, and instead commit themselves even further to capital's appropriation of the future. In *Iron Man* (2008), the playboy-scientist-engineer-executive-celebrity Tony Stark (Robert Downey, Jr) might suddenly develop a conscience about arms dealing, but he is ultimately just a reactionary maverick; and both *Able Edwards* (2004) and *Iron Man 2* (2010) evoke the image of Walt Disney in an effort to make such conservatism more palatable. *I Am Legend* portrays its scientist protagonist, Robert Neville (Will Smith) as an airforce officer celebrated in such mainstream media as *Time*. The casting of a black actor as such an establishment figure, and of Smith in particular (in some respects the very image of supposedly 'post-racial' America) only serves to emphasise the extent to which science is assimilated into structures of power.

WOMEN IN THE LAB: BODY PARTS

The Bride of Frankenstein (1935) opens with Mary Shelley (Elsa Lanchester) announcing that the story of her creature did not end with the events depicted in *Frankenstein*, placing the previous film's conclusion under erasure and enabling the creature to return. This revision produces a curious effect. The title of the film presumably refers to the female creature (Elsa Lanchester) that Henry Frankenstein (Colin Clive) and Dr Pretorious (Ernest Thesiger) fashion as a mate for the unnamed monster (Boris Karloff), but the actual bride of Frankenstein is of course Elizabeth (Valerie Hobson). In *Frankenstein*, the creature attacks her before the wedding can take place and, although the coda in which Elizabeth nurses Henry while his father toasts a 'son for the House of Frankenstein' implies that she and Henry are married, it is unclear when precisely the ceremony occurred. The sequel effectively erases this scene (along with the baron, who is never mentioned), beginning instead with the lifeless Frankenstein being returned to Elizabeth. For a few moments, as he lies apparently dead, the film opens up the possibility that Elizabeth – the bride of Frankenstein – will be the protagonist, perhaps even repeating his experiments in order to restore him to life. That this possibility is immediately foreclosed – there is a flicker of life and Frankenstein is soon restored to the central narrative role – and that the film's title seems to refer, however inaccurately, to the female creature rather than to Elizabeth reveals a more general pattern in sf: it is far more common for female characters to be not scientists but objects of enquiry and experimentation, their personhood denied, their bodies subjected to cruel tortures. For example, Pretorius orders Elizabeth's abduction – she is kept bound, the threat of rape never far away – so as to force Frankenstein to assist in creating the monster's mate; and when the female creature is brought to life, she screams in wordless horror at the fate for which she has been built by men who fail to consider that she might have a will of her own.

This tendency to exclude women from science or treat them only as experimental subjects is evident in *Metropolis* and *Island of Lost Souls*, as well as in the multiple adaptations of Hans Heinz Ewers' *Alraune* (1911),[22] in which the daughter of a prostitute who was artificially inseminated with the semen of a hanged murderer grows up to be an emotionally cold, sexually obsessive woman, eventually murdering the scientist who created and raised her. *Four Sided Triangle* (1953) tells the story of three childhood friends: Robin Grant (John Van Eyssen), heir to the local manor; Bill Leggott (Stephen Murray), an orphan raised by Dr Harvey (James Hayter); and Lena Maitland (Barbara Payton). After graduating from Cambridge, Robin and Bill establish a research laboratory in the village, financed by Robin's industrialist father, with Lena as 'cook, nurse, confessor, chief bottlewasher and occasional mechanic'. Their experiments in matter transmission finally succeed, but before Bill can confess his love for Lena, she and Robin announce their engagement. After the wedding, Bill persuades Lena to let him duplicate her. He romances the newly created Helen, not pausing to think that, since she is a perfect copy of Lena at the moment of replication, she too loves Robin. Helen attempts suicide and threatens to keep trying, but eventually agrees to have her identity wiped: 'Yes, Bill, you're right, an empty mind and a new beginning'. Unable to address this scenario's fascinating possibilities or to reconcile its ideological contradictions, the film kills off Bill and Helen but cannot resist the (promptly quashed) suggestion that brainwiped Helen, rather than amnesiac Lena, survives the fatal blaze.

In *Les yeux sans visage/Eyes without a Face* (1960) and *Gritos en la noche/The Awful Dr Orloff* (1962), surgeons abduct and murder young women in order to obtain flesh to graft onto their recently disfigured daughters. Both Doctor Génessier (Pierre Brasseur) and Dr Orloff (Howard Vernon) seem as driven by the opportunity to break new scientific ground as by guilt over the accidents that caused their daughters' injuries, reducing their reluctant offspring to mere guinea pigs. In *Rabid* (1977), Dr Keloid (Howard Ryshpan) races to aid crash victims in order to get out of a meeting about developing his clinic into a 'franchised operation for plastic surgery resorts'; and then rushes into performing experimental surgery on the badly injured Rose (Marilyn Chambers) to prove he is more than just 'the Colonel Sanders of plastic surgery'. As a result, she becomes a blood-drinking plague carrier, but she is not wrong to protest: 'It's not my fault. ... I'm still me'. In *The Brain that Wouldn't Die* (1962), when Jan Compton (Virginia Leith) is decapitated in a car crash, her fiancé Dr Bill Cortner (Herb Evers) keeps her brain alive while searching among burlesque acts, nightclub hostesses and beauty contest entrants for a new body onto which to attach her head, finally selecting a glamour model with a disfigured face. Meanwhile, the bodiless Jan, her repeated pleas to be allowed to die ignored, develops telepathic powers. She commands the monstrous creation of an earlier experiment to destroy her tormentors and, as the laboratory burns down around her, to rescue the unwitting body donor. While it is problematic to claim that such moments of refusal – when female subjects reject interpellation as experimental subjects – are straightforwardly feminist, these films do expose male fantasies of power and control over women (and the natural world with which they are frequently conflated).[23]

The limits of such critique are indicated by *Daehakno-yeseo maechoon-hadaka tomaksalhae danghan yeogosaeng ajik Daehakno-ye Issda/Teenage Hooker Became Killing Machine in Daehakno* (2000). A teenage schoolgirl (So-yun Lee), who works as a prostitute specialising in pursuit-and-rape scenarios, admits to one of her teachers (Dae-tong Kim) that she is in love with him – she charges her biology and ethics teachers for sex, but not him – and dreams of having his baby. After cackling henchmen dismember her, she is reconstructed as a cyborg assassin. She kills her killers, but her programming forbids her to kill her teacher. When his promotion to principal removes him from this protected category, the schoolgirl stands, raises her skirt to reveal a huge robotic gun attached to her crotch and shoots him in the groin. He drops to his knees and she thrusts the barrel into his screaming mouth before firing again. However satisfying this conclusion might be, it fails to outweigh the film's sexualisation of the schoolgirl and its delight in her dismemberment.

Frankenhooker (1990) suffers from similar shortcomings but concludes in a more intriguing manner. When a freak lawnmower accident chops overweight Elizabeth Shelley (Patty Mullen) to pieces, her boyfriend Jeffrey Franken (James Lorinz) steals her head and, in his quest for 'just ... the right parts' to construct a new 'centrefold goddess' body for her, concocts rocks of supercrack that cause the prostitutes who smoke it to explode. He collects their scattered parts in order to construct a patchwork body, unaware that the prostitutes' memories and identities live on in their remains. Although the new Elizabeth feels 'so strange' at there being 'so many different women inside' her, she does not express horror or reject them. Indeed, when their pimp tries to claim her as his property, decapitating Jeffrey in the process, grotesque assemblages of the prostitutes' leftover body parts come to life and devour him in solidarity. Elizabeth attaches Jeffrey's head to a new body made from the prostitutes' remains. When he responds in panic and loathing to this feminisation, crying out 'Where's my johnson?', Elizabeth sardonically repeats his earlier self-justifications. The film ends as he realises that he is now just one of the people – and the only male one – in his body.

WOMEN IN THE LAB: SCIENTISTS

Such denials of female subjectivity recur throughout sf because the social relations of filmmaking are, like those of science, 'highly integrated with' and tend to reproduce 'the larger social relations of the societies that support' them (Harding 1986: 73–74). Indeed:

> the exclusion of the feminine from science has been historically constitutive of a particular definition of science – as incontrovertibly objective, universal, impersonal … and masculine: a definition that serves simultaneously to demarcate masculine from feminine and scientists from nonscientists – even good science from bad. In the past as in the present, the sexual division of emotional and intellectual labor has provided a readily available and much relied upon tool for bolstering the particular claims that science makes to a univocal and hence absolute epistemic authority … In turn, … the same authority serves to denigrate the entire excluded realm of the feminine – a realm which … invariably includes most women.

> (Keller: 241)

Consequently, women scientists have often seemed to be 'a contradiction in terms', and they have typically found themselves 'caught between two almost mutually exclusive stereotypes: as scientists they were atypical women; as women they were unusual scientists' (Rossiter 1984: xv). Therefore, 'the principal strategy employed by women seeking entrance to the world of science has been premised on the repudiation of gender as a significant variable for scientific productivity' (Keller 236). This, however, frequently reinforces institutional discrimination, translating 'difference into inequality, … otherness, and exclusion' and 'equality into sameness', thus 'guarantee[ing] the exclusion of any experience, perception or value that is other' while 'obscur[ing] the fact of that discrimination' (236). 'Others', such as women, 'are eligible for inclusion' in science 'only to the extent that they can excise' their 'differences' and eradicate 'even the marks of that excision' (236). This contradictory position is evident in the tendency, particularly in 1950s' US sf, for female scientists to have gender-neutral names or masculine nicknames, such as Dr Patricia 'Pat' Medford (Joan Weldon) in *Them!* (1954), but to be introduced into the narrative with an insistent masculine gaze – shared by the camera and male characters – that emphatically sexualises their bodies, particularly legs, hips and breasts.

Depictions of science are typically organised, often in complex ways, around such discursive and ideological binaries as scientist/woman, mind/body, subject/object, culture/nature and self/other. The female scientist struggles to be perceived in relation to the first term in each pair, while male characters (and the film more generally) align her with the second. For example, *Frau im Mond* implies that the relationships among industrialist Helius, his chief engineer Hans Windegger (Gustav von Wangenheim) and astronomy student Friede Velten (Gerda Maurus) were perfectly harmonious until Hans surprises Friede with a marriage proposal, which she accepts. This sudden reminder of her sexual difference makes Helius realise his own feelings for her, prompting him to undertake the lunar expedition so as to escape this painful situation. Protesting that he has always previously regarded her as his 'good comrade ... at work – in the laboratory – in this very room', she insists on joining the expedition, refusing to be treated differently just because he has begun to see her as a woman. However, as with *Contact*'s Eleanor Arroway (see note 19), Friede is disciplined into a more feminine role once her sexual difference has been unequivocally identified – neither woman is permitted to continue being as she was before and both must take up more 'appropriately' gendered roles.

Such insistence on sexual difference is common. In *Spaceways* (1953), when General Hayes (Anthony Ireland) is introduced to Dr Lisa Frank (Eva Bartok), he cannot resist saying 'a more charming mathematician I could not imagine'. In *Tarantula* (1955), when Professor Deemer (Leo G. Carroll) meets his new assistant, Stephanie 'Steve' Clayton (Mara Corday), his first words are 'I didn't expect to see a biologist that looked like you – oh, er, that was intended as a compliment'. In *This Island Earth*, Dr Ruth Adams (Faith Domergue), romantically involved with Cal Meacham three years earlier, feigns only a vague memory of him as someone she once met at a conference. She admits to being 'deeply flattered' by his interest, and perhaps even 'a little envious of the girl [he's] mistaken [her] for' but concentrates on the business at hand. Although the reason for her denials remains unclear, this exchange does suggest something of the sexual politics of the scientific workplace. Cal, an electronics genius, government advisor and manly celebrity, is unlikely to suffer from courting a playboy image. Ruth, despite her qualifications and expertise, has less reason to feel secure. Her rebuttals indicate the need to suppress or excise elements of her identity in order to secure advancement, and that she is unprepared to have her gender emphasised by a workplace romance. Nevertheless, the film repeatedly costumes her so as to display Domergue's body, a spectacular eroticisation that is perhaps most obvious when she dons one of the aliens' unisex jumpsuits, which has none of the bagginess of those worn by the men and is clearly tailored to accentuate her hips and breasts. Soon after changing into these uniforms, she, Cal and Exeter (Jeff Morrow) recline into almost-vertical seats to watch Zagon spacecraft attack on the flying saucer's viewscreen. Two almost identical setups position the cast in three-quarters shot, with Ruth in the foreground, positioned so that her breasts stand out, an effect emphasised by the pulsating purple light that heightens the contrast between her and the green background. During the attack, Ruth's bosom heaves and at one point she arches her back to cry out. Neither the character nor the actress are permitted to escape her physiology and the ideologies framing it.

The Strange World of Planet X (1958) reveals the aggression underpinning the insistent feminisation of female scientists. Whitehall official Gerald Wilson (Geoffrey Chater) relishes appointing a woman as the replacement computer operator for the research project run by the demanding Dr Laird (Alec Mango). Brigadier Cartwright (Wyndham Goldie), despite his own scepticism, derives as much pleasure from delivering the news. Laird protests that they 'must be joking', that it is 'preposterous' to assign such 'highly skilled work' to a woman. His assistant, Gil Graham (Forrest Tucker), insists 'I know the type: frustrated, angular spinster, very dedicated to her calling, without a sense of humour, bossy and infuriatingly right every time'. However, the moment Gil encounters Michele Dupont (Gaby André), who is introduced with his point-of-view shot of her legs, he finds this attractive French woman an 'agreeable' surprise. Laird's attitude changes the moment she explains how the 'yankee' computer he must use can be made safer and more efficient. Consequently, she is caught between Gil's desire for her to be more like a woman and Laird's desire for her to be indistinguishable from a man.

A similarly aggressive dynamic plays out in *Rocketship* X-M (1950). Talking to a male journalist, Colonel Floyd Graham (Lloyd Bridges) quips that his colleagues are 'the hottest crew I've ever worked with, especially' – indicating Dr Lisa Van Horn (Osa Massen), the lunar mission's chemist – 'in the brains department'. However, he adds, 'unless you look like a test-tube or a chemical formula you haven't got a chance'. After the launch, he criticises her for not laughing at a joke with the rest of the crew:

GRAHAM: Now don't get mad at me, but can't you ever relax? All these weeks, months, I've been watching you. Nothing but work, work, work. Now, I've been wondering, how does a girl like you get mixed up in a thing like this in the first place?
VAN HORN: I suppose you think that women should only cook and sew and bear children.
GRAHAM: Isn't that enough? There's such a thing as going overboard in the other direction, too, you know.

The low-key intimacy of Graham's voice and his rather more glamorous close-ups signify easy charm and good humour, especially when contrasted with Van Horn's furrowed brow and exasperated response. However, while his words suggest a kind of devotion to her, they also reveal him as a sexual predator who wishes to discipline her into 'appropriate' feminine behaviour – a task at which he eventually succeeds as she succumbs to his romantic attentions.

Van Horn faces a similar kind of gender discipline from the mission commander, physicist Dr Karl Eckstrom (John Emery). When a female journalist asks her to comment on the mission 'from a woman's angle', Van Horn replies, 'I never thought much about it'. When the journalist asks why one of the crew is female, Eckstrom insists that Van Horn earned her place through 'pioneering research with monatomic hydrogen that enabled her to develop the first rocket fuel powerful and concentrated enough to make this flight possible'. However, when the spaceship later loses power, and Eckstrom and Van Horn independently work through vital calculations so as to be able to confirm each other's results, he insists that the discrepancy between them comes from an error in her figures. Noting her chagrin at him discarding her work without trying to find which set of calculations actually contains the error, he chides her for becoming emotional. She argues that he should not arbitrarily impose his will when 'lives are at stake'. When he refuses to relent, she asks 'Aren't you human? Are you made of ice?' – the kind of charges more commonly levelled against women scientists. Adopting the kind of demure subservience he clearly expects, she apologises. 'For what?', he says, 'For momentarily being a woman? It's completely understandable'. However, he now calls her 'Miss' rather than 'Doctor'. This incident of gender disciplining is made more intriguing by two factors. First, Eckstrom's accusation of emotionalism is clearly an emotional response to a female subordinate questioning his results and insisting that they resolve the issue in a properly scientific manner. Second, Eckstrom is obviously in the wrong but the crewmen remain silent, even though his egotism jeopardises them.

Eve of Destruction (1991) makes the violent policing of gender even more apparent. The pre-title sequence opens with a man dressing in a hotel room, his manner rather odd. The viewpoint pulls back to reveal a team of scientists, headed by Dr Eve Simmons (Renée Soutendijk), monitoring him from behind a two-way mirror. Suddenly, in the middle of tying his tie, he seems to jam. Simmons orders him to shut down. Walls pull back and technicians rush in to disassemble the fake room and wheel the malfunctioning android Steve (Loren Haynes) away. Before Simmons can analyse the problem, she is hassled about likely delays and the upcoming budget review. She then watches on a monitor as Eve VIII

(Renée Soutendijk), an android double programmed with her memories and personality, finishes dressing for a test, seeking approval of her fashion choices from the male technicians circling her. Eve VIII's final 'How do I look?' is addressed directly to camera, implicating both Simmons and the viewer in the laboratory's – and cinema's – masculine surveillance. In a textbook example of the economy of the gaze described by Laura Mulvey, the viewer joins Simmons in not only watching a woman being displayed but also in watching her being watched – a stark contrast with the covert observation of Steve. The significance of this gendered distinction becomes clear as the film goes on to insist on sexual difference.

Simmons's young son, Timmy (Ross Malinger), points out to her the 'vagina', 'tits' and 'balls' in his schoolbook diagrams. This morphological dichotomy between women and men – that the film conflates with gender – is reiterated when McQuade (Gregory Hines) is briefed on Eve. He is shown footage of Project Rob, the first attempt 25 years earlier to construct an android that could pass for human. It has vaguely masculine features and looks like a robot, its stripped open chest revealing mechanical and electronic systems. He is then shown Eve, also bare-chested, and when one of her breasts is peeled away only organic systems are visible inside. This contrast reiterates the ideological associations of the male with the rational and the female with the irrational.

On field test in San Francisco, Eve is accosted by a man whose increasingly sexualised attempts to proposition her aligns the institutional surveillance of her handler with a more ubiquitous masculine surveillance of women. Eve twice refuses this stranger's attentions, even thanking him for the compliment in an attempt to diffuse potential aggression, but after damage disrupts Eve's programming her rejection of such interpellations escalates. She begins to explore and enact Simmons's suppressed memories and repressed desires, which enables the film to depict castration anxiety as a product of women's barely contained violent rage against men rather than of the male imagination. Despite traumatic flashbacks to Simmons's drunken father shouting at, beating and possibly killing her mother, and despite the near gang-rape of Eve, the film ultimately valorises male violence against women as a form of gender policing. Subjected to a crude, psychoanalytic interrogation by McQuade, Simmons – doubly rebuked by the ultra-conservative rhetoric of a successfully assimilated African American man – discovers that she just wants 'to be a good mother'. Allying herself with the state–corporate–military order McQuade represents, she contributes to the series of phallic thrusts that destroy Eve (she is shot through an eye-socket, hit by a subway train and finally despatched when Simmons punches a gun barrel into the empty eye-socket). Simmons at last achieves 'proper' femininity by refuting those aspects of herself that the rogue Eve played out and rejecting 'unnatural' technological creation (Eve, designed for battlefield combat, has a nuclear bomb instead of a womb) in favour of maternity and subordination to masculine authority.

After women began to receive scientific education and enter the scientific workforce in the late nineteenth century, a gender hierarchy was quickly established to police access through segregation: women could either 'hold auxiliary and subservient positions in the scientific fields where men predominated' (e.g., high school teachers, college instructors and assistant professors, laboratory assistants or technicians, journal editors) or 'practice science in such new "women's" fields as home economics or "cosmetic chemistry"' (Harding 1986: 62). These options are combined in the female protagonists of *The Wasp Woman* (1959) and *The Leech Woman* (1960), marginal, unqualified scientific practitioners who internalise the violent assertion of gender. In the former, cosmetics company Janice Starlin Enterprises has suffered a catastrophic drop in market share since Janice (Susan Cabot), knowing she could not be a 'glamour girl' forever, ceased – after 16 years – to appear in the company's advertisements. In a desperate bid to save her company, she finances the radical research of Professor Zinthrop (Michael Mark) into the rejuvenating powers of queen wasp royal jelly enzymes, even insisting that he conduct the first human trials on her. The film suggests that her impatience with the careful pace of Zinthrop's experiments stems from vanity, prompting her to take massive extra doses without his knowledge, which periodically transform her into a wasp-headed killer in a slinky black outfit; but it also lays bare the social structures and assumptions that constrain women's careers. No matter how successful Janice has been, even in middle age her career depends upon her appearing youthfully attractive.

The Leech Woman expresses these assumptions with remarkable bluntness. Dr Paul Talbot (Phillip Terry), an endocrinologist interested in retarding the ageing process, finds his wife June (Coleen Gray) repellent because she is ten years older than him (ironically, Gray was a dozen years younger than Terry so the make-up effects intended to convey how repellent June is to Paul merely make her look the same age as him). However, he abandons divorce proceedings and takes her on an expedition to find a remote African tribe who can reverse the effects of ageing. Only when he suggests that she undergo the procedure – which involves drinking the pollen of a rare orchid combined with male pineal hormones – does she finally realise that the hoped-for reconciliation was a sham and that he is only interested in her as an experimental subject. When the natives offer June the choice of any man from whom to extract – fatally – the needed pineal hormone, she has no hesitation in selecting him.

CONCLUSION

Setting aside the notion that scientific accuracy – or any other single arbiter – can define or delimit the genre, this chapter has explored some of the ways in which sf films utilise (pseudo)scientific and (pseudo) technological images, ideas and discourses to produce meanings and pleasures. Drawing on material from science studies, it explored the figuration of science in sf in relation to both science's self-image and the real-world compromises of scientific practice. It suggested that the contradictory demands that derange mad scientists create fictional figures who model the experience of all modern subjects, before tracing the more particular contradictions imposed on real-world and fictional women involved in science. The next chapter will reframe the question of the relationship between science and sf in terms of the relationship between cognition and affect, focusing on the genre's use of special effects and varieties of spectacle (the sublime, the grotesque and camp), as well as its tendency to use such technologically heightened moments to reflect upon the nature of cinema.

2

SF, SPECTACLE AND SELF-REFLEXIVITY

In *Love Story 2050* (2008), Karan Malhotra (Harman Baweja) travels into the future to find his dead lover, Sana Bedi (Priyanka Chopra), reincarnated as the multimedia celebrity Ziesha. One of several Indian sf films to build on the success of *Koi ... Mil Gaya* (2003), which reworked material from Spielberg's *E.T.* and *Close Encounters of the Third Kind* (1977), *Love Story 2050* alludes to such sf blockbusters as *Le cinquième element/The Fifth Element* (1997), *Artificial Intelligence: A.I.* (2001) and *I, Robot* (2004). Its depiction of mid-twenty-first century Mumbai's screen technologies draws explicitly, but less obviously, on *Minority Report* (2002), in the opening sequence of which John Anderton (Tom Cruise) stands before a wall-sized screen, manipulating image fragments and other blocks of data with hand gestures instead of a mouse or a touchscreen. *Love Story 2050*'s Karan navigates the internet and Ziesha's website using a similar gestural-interface technology. It seems entirely appropriate that one contemporary sf film should 'quote' from another when it comes to representing network technologies that themselves depend upon linkages between information. Indeed, when pushed to an extreme, as in *Southland Tales* (2006), contemporary films often seem less concerned with coherent, cause-and-effect classical narrative than with generating 'an affective constellation' through 'dispersed, ... indefinite and arbitrary' 'correspondences and connections'

(Shaviro 2010a: 72–73) – that is, through links whose affect depends as much upon intertextual knowledge as on intratextual relationships. However, *Minority Report*'s imaginary screen technology had an impact far beyond sf.

John Underkoffler designed the gesture-based interface, extrapolated from existing technology, as a 'diegetic prototype ... to demonstrate to the public, and potential funders, not only that [it] would work, but also that the technology would appear as if it were "natural" and intuitive for users' (Kirby 2011: 199–200). He developed a 'new gestural language based on American international sign language, SWAT team commands, air traffic control signals, and the Kodály hand system for musical notes' (200), even building a verisimilitudinous design flaw into the technology (when Anderton shakes hands with Danny Witwer (Colin Farrell), it mistakes the gesture for a command). This diegetic prototype attracted investment for the construction of a real-world prototype that utilises a system 'similar to motion-capture technology used in film animation' (Karp B1), which in turn caught the attention of a US military contractor, Raytheon, interested in developing a system to enable more rapid integration and analysis of multiply sourced battlefield data. Silicon Graphics, a computing solutions and special effects company whose credits include *The Lawnmower Man* (1992), *Johnny Mnemonic* (1995), *Jurassic Park* (1993), *Twister* (1996), *Men in Black* (1997), *The Relic* (1997), *Sphere* (1998), *Lost in Space* (1998), *Star Trek: Insurrection* (1998) and *Mission to Mars* (2000), worked 'with the Army to develop the computing firepower that [such] command centers will need' (B1). Meanwhile Underkoffler pursued commercial applications for his system, 'such as command-and-control operations for railroads and ports, ... virtual wind tunnels for industrial designers' and 'videogames' (B1), as well as working as a scientific consultant on *Hulk* (2003), *Æon Flux* (2005) and *Iron Man*.

This imbroglio – of national cinemas, of films and games, of military, industrial and commercial concerns – demonstrates the complexity of real-world scientific practice *and* illustrates an influential argument about the nature of sf cinema. Stephen Neale argues that even supposedly transparent classical cinema finds way to display, in '(regulated) forms of excess', the processes of its production (31). His examples include the musical's interplay of spectacle and narrative, film noir's often unmotivated use of light and dark and the epic's emphasis on costume and décor in widescreen colour. In sf, 'narrative functions largely to motivate the production of special effects, climaxing either with the "best" of those effects (*Close Encounters of the Third Kind*), or with the point at which they are multiplied with greatest intensity (*Star Wars*)', while 'a sophisticated technology of special effects and sound are introduced and displayed as and through' sf (31, 34). Garrett Stewart argues that sf is at its most self-reflexive when it deploys cutting-edge cinematic technologies to depict imaginary, futuristic technologies: 'Movies about the future tend to be about the future of movies', and sf cinema 'often turns out to be ... the fictional or fictive science of the cinema itself, the future feats it may achieve scanned in line with the technical feat that conceives them right now and before our eyes' (159).

This chapter will begin by considering sf as a cinema of attractions, paying particular attention to special effects and affect. It will then examine three varieties of sf spectacle – the sublime, the grotesque and the camp – before returning to the genre's self-reflexive explorations of cinema.

ATTRACTIONS

Perhaps 'the most common' complaint about contemporary sf 'is that it relies too heavily on ... expensive and essentially "empty" special effects' (King and Krzywinska 63). However, since the 1980s, a reconceptualisation of cinema's first decade has led to a more nuanced understanding of sf's spectacular imperatives. Traditionally, film histories privileged the Lumière brothers' *actualités* (short films recording real-world actions) over Georges Méliès' *féeries* (short fantasy or trick films that recorded profilmic illusions or created illusions through such camera-based and editing effects as slow motion, reverse motion, multiple exposures, substitution splicing and mattes).[1] However, both types of film should be seen as ways 'of presenting a series of views to an audience, fascinating because of their illusory power' (Gunning 1990: 57). This 'cinema of attractions', concerned with showing, presentation and exhibitionism, dominated film until 1907, when it was superseded by a system of narrative integration that emphasised telling, representation and voyeurism, culminating in feature films preoccupied with 'the narration of stories and the creation of a self-enclosed diegetic universe' (60). Nonetheless, despite narrative's ascendancy, attractions persisted 'as a component of narrative films, more evident in some genres (e.g., the musical) than in others' (57). Even classical Hollywood cinema was marked by a tension between narrative and spectacle,[2] with cinema's 'roots in stimulus and carnival rides' being reaffirmed 'in what might be called the Spielberg–Lucas–Coppola cinema of effects' (61).

Indeed, the spectacular blockbuster's apparent dominance of sf since the 1970s has fuelled many critics' indignation. Sean Cubitt, for example, describes films such as *Star Wars: Episode II – Attack of the Clones* (2002) in terms of a 'clothes-line model' of 'perfunctory narrative' along which 'effects sequences' are hung:

> Each set piece sequence acts to trigger a rush of emotions: putting a clock on the action, staging the spin-off computer game … The scream, the laugh, the tear, the white knuckles, the racing pulse: the stimuli are clichés because the emotions they elicit and that audiences seek are clichés. Market research ensures, as far as anything can, that expectations will be met. Of course, such expectations derive from the past, never from the future, and so the hectic overproduction of affects is only ever repetitive of old emotions. … each set-piece sequence miniaturizes the older classical plot into a few minutes of film, condensing as it simplifies the emotional content, delivering the intensified segment as an event in itself, and building, from the succession of events, a montage of affects.
>
> (238)

Echoing Freedman, Cubitt suggests that the 'awe at the majestic power of spectacle' produces in its audience 'self-subjugation' before 'the perfection

of the integrated spectacle' (264). This terminology implies a relationship between cinematic spectacle and the society of the spectacle – that
is, the world dominated by advanced capitalism and mass media and by
governments that perpetuate them (see Debord 1983, 1998). Indeed,
cinema emerged as 'part of the euphoria of modernity' (Paci: 125) in
which the society of the spectacle coalesced. The cinema of attractions,
like 'other fetish phenomena typical of modernity, such as billboards,
posters, expositions and store shelves', is 'merchandise that makes itself
visible, turning its presence into spectacle' (126). It is also related to

> exoticism (as found in the era's expositions and in the Paris arcades
> celebrated by Baudelaire and Benjamin), train journeys (and the new
> visions of the landscape in movement and the proliferation of per-
> spectives they offered), advances in the faculty of sight (from the air,
> for example, or with microscopes) and the improvements to fantastic
> images [that] had already fed the collective imaginative identity [and]
> extended new aesthetic habits.
>
> (125)

Leaving discussion of the nineteenth-century proliferation of image-
making technologies until later in this chapter, the remainder of this
section will consider sf in relation to the other phenomena Viva Paci
identifies.

The display of (authentic and faked) exotic people and locations was
a mainstay of *actualités*, but *féeries* also often featured fantastical versions
of foreign lands and arabesque design. Such exoticism typifies sf representations of other cultures (*Himmelskibet*'s and *Just Imagine*'s Martians, the
islanders of *Mosura/Mothra* (1961), the imperial court of *Dune* (1984),
the bustling Helion Prime of *The Chronicles of Riddick* (2004), the many
worlds of the *Star Wars* franchise (1977–)), often betraying assumptions,
shared with much actuality and anthropological filmmaking, regarding
non-Western peoples, places and cultures as raw materials for image
commodities. The clearest illustration of this is the sheer presumption
of Carl Denham (Robert Armstrong) in *King Kong* (1933), who assumes

that he has a right to film an indigenous ritual without the natives' knowledge or consent.

Although the train no longer seems a particularly futuristic or marvellous technology, it is represented as such in *Le voyage à travers l'impossible/ The Voyage Across the Impossible* (1904), *The Tunnel* (1936), *Vynález zkázy/The Fabulous World of Jules Verne* (1958), *Back to the Future Part III* (1990), *Moebius* (1996) and *2046* (2004). Since the mid-nineteenth century, the way in which trains throw 'people together both spatially and socially' has been both deplored and seen as a 'technical guarantor of democracy, harmony ... peace and progress' (Schivelbusch: 73). This association with democratising politics underpins New York commuters protecting the unmasked superhero's identity in *Spider-Man 2* (2004), the commitment of Bruce Wayne (Christian Bale) to building Gotham City's public transit system in *Batman Begins* (2005), and the chiding of anxieties about diverse strangers sharing confined social spaces in *Source Code* (2011).

In 1861, Benjamin Gastineau's described train travel in terms that evoke the shock of modernity in relation to variety theatre but seem also to anticipate the rapid succession of contrasting views early cinema audiences would experience 30 years later:

> Devouring distance at the rate of fifteen leagues an hour, the steam engine, that powerful stage manager, throws the switches, changes the décor, and shifts the point of view every moment; in quick succession it presents the astonished traveller with happy scenes, sad scenes, burlesque interludes, brilliant fireworks, all visions that disappear as soon as they are seen.
>
> (Schivelbusch: 63)

This relationship between train and cinema was made manifest by Hale's Tours, which existed from 1905–11. The audience would be seated by a conductor in an authentic railway carriage and watch 'filmed panoramic views shot from ... locomotives, which gave the viewer the illusion of being on a train – an illusion reinforced by the rocking back and forth of the train car and often by the blowing of a whistle' (Kirby 1997: 46).

A decade earlier, Robert Paul and H.G. Wells registered a patent application for a similar exhibition space cum attraction that would create the experience of a fantastic journey through time akin to that in Wells's *The Time Machine* (1895).

The train crash, which places fragile human bodies among velocities and masses they can neither control nor survive unharmed, is emblematic of the shock of modernity. While stories about audiences fleeing in terror from the Lumières' *L'arrivée d'un train à La Ciotat/Arrival of a Train at La Ciotat* (1896) are almost certainly untrue, there were cycles of films depicting trains travelling at rapid speeds (e.g., *The Black Diamond Express* (1896) and *Uncle Josh at the Moving Picture Show* (1902), in which a rube character panics at a screening of the former film) or crashing (e.g., *Railroad Smashup* (1904), which featured a staged head-on collision between decommissioned locomotives, with the footage reused in the fictional *Rounding up the Yeggmen* (1904)). Science-fictional rail crashes occur as early as Méliès's *Le voyage à travers l'impossible* and *Le Tunnel sous La Manche/Tunnelling the English Channel* (1907). In *Orlacs Hände/The Hands of Orlac* (1924), the nocturnal scene following a train crash – in which living and dead, dismembered and wrecked, mutilated and mangled, commingle in the darkness, obscured by clouds of steam and milling crowds, beneath a spotlight scanning the devastation like some mechanical eye – recalls a First World War battlefield, symbolic of the failure of modernity as a progressive force. In the train crash in *Spione/Spies* (1928), the camera adopts the viewpoint of a locomotive engine as it ploughs into the rear of another train; and King Kong's rampage across Manhattan catastrophically derails an elevated train.

Sf film relishes images of destruction. Dinosaurs and monsters wreck urban, and frequently iconic, locations in *The Lost World* (1925), *The Beast from 20,000 Fathoms* (1953), *It Came from Beneath the Sea* (1955), *Gorgo* (1961), *Gwoemul/The Host* (2006), *Dai-Nihonjin/Big Man Japan* (2007) and *Cloverfield* (2008), as well as numerous Japanese *kaiju eiga* and such *King Kong* variants as *Konga* (1961), *Kingu Kongu tai Gojira/King Kong vs. Godzilla* (1962), *Kingu Kongu no gyakushû/King Kong Escapes* (1967), *A*P*E** (1976), *King Kong* (1976), *Queen Kong* (1976), *Xing xing wan/The Mighty Peking Man*

(1978) and King Kong (2005). Similar damage is wrought by alien invaders and giant robots in The War of the Worlds (1953), Earth vs. the Flying Saucers (1956), Chikyû Bôeigun/The Mysterians (1957), Independence Day (1996), Mars Attacks! (1996), War of the Worlds (2005) and the Transformers (2007–11) and 20-seiki shônen/20th Century Boys (2008–09) trilogies. Earth is subjected to astronomical impacts and/or geological and/or meteorological upheavals in Verdens undergang, La Fin du Monde/End of the World (1931), Deluge (1933), Flash Gordon (1936), When Worlds Collide (1951), Nippon chinbotsu/Japans Sinks (1974), Armageddon (1998), Deep Impact (1998), The Day After Tomorrow (2004), Nihon chinbotsu/Japan Sinks (2006) and 2012 (2009), while such events form a backdrop for wry human dramas in Last Night (1998), Fisshu sutôrî/Fish Story (2009) and Melancholia (2011). Even the most jingoistic and triumphalist of these examples register, on some level, the cosmic insignificance of humanity, how easily our world might be swept away by forces that also often figure the return of capitalist modernity's repressed.

Paci also describes the 'proliferation of perspectives' and 'advances in the faculty of sight' as characteristic of modernity. Himmelskibet, Paris qui dort/The Crazy Ray (1925) and King Kong (1933) offer views from above of Copenhagen, Paris and New York previously accessible only to aviators and those constructing monumental modern architecture – and such aerial views lead to the recurring image of the Earth, floating in space behind departing spacecraft (which reaches an apotheosis in Contact's opening sequence), and to magnificent views of other worlds seen from space, such as Chesley Bonestell's astronomical paintings in Destination Moon (1950) and The War of the Worlds (1953). Alien or radically transformed terrestrial landscapes became increasingly common, whether constructed in a studio, shot on a location, or rendered by models and miniatures, conventional animation or CGI, or represented through a combination of these techniques (for examples, see Buck Rogers (1939), Der schweigende Stern/First Spaceship on Venus (1960), Robinson Crusoe on Mars (1964), Terrore nello spazio/Planet of the Vampires (1965), Tumannost Andromedy/Andromeda Nebula (1967), La planète sauvage/Fantastic Planet (1973), Outland (1981), Les maîtres du temps/The Time Masters (1982), Enemy Mine

(1985), *Kin-dza-dza!* (1986), *Pitch Black* (2002) and the *Star Wars* franchise).

Representing such spectacular places often involves the cutting-edge capabilities of cinematic technologies. For example, the title cards of *20,000 Leagues Under the Sea* (1916) state that '[t]he submarine scenes in this production were made possible by the use of the Williamson inventions, and were directed under the personal supervision of the Williamson brothers, who alone have solved the secret of under-the-ocean photography' before cutting to a shot of Ernest and George Williamson, bowing to the camera. *Tron* created a virtual world to showcase the capacities of computer-generated animation. In 'a moment of pure self-reflexivity' in *Star Trek II: The Wrath of Khan*, Captain Kirk watches a taped demonstration of the Genesis device, which transforms lifeless planets into habitable worlds, and simultaneously exhibits 'the potential of computer-generated imagery' (North: 127). *Renaissance* (2006) uses digital rotoscoping to depict a literally black-and-white noirish future, and *A Scanner Darkly* (2006) deploys it to create a jittery, unstable California for its tale of drugs and paranoia. The groundbreaking combination of live action and CGI in the same shot in *The Abyss* (1989) also marked existing technical limits. Throughout the film 'the 180-degree rule is flaunted constantly, and our orientation within the deep-sea station is never important to the editing', leaving the viewer 'to navigate a space established through mobile camera work, not through cutting'; but the film must jarringly 'resort to classical continuity editing' in combined live-action/CGI shots because, although the CGI liquid, alien pseudopod could have been rendered 'from any angle', 'the state of motion control in 1989 would not have allowed compositing on a constantly reframed shot' (Cubitt: 255).

Early sf was also fascinated with advances in the faculty of sight through new optical technologies. *Les rayons Röntgen/A Novice at X-Rays* (1897) and *The X-Rays* (1897) use multiple exposures and substitution splices to 'reveal' people's skeletons. In *L'éclipse du soleil en pleine lune/The Eclipse: The Courtship of the Sun and Moon* (1907), an astronomer observes a solar eclipse in which the sun and moon appear to have sex, filling the sky with a symbolic ejaculation of stars.

SPECTACLE, NARRATIVE AND AFFECT

Spectacle concerns the whole cinematic apparatus, not just special effects. Michele Pierson, for example, considers the spectacular consequences of switching from analogue to digital editing. Editors are now 'under much less pressure to conceptualize the film in its entirety every time a decision needs to be made' and the 'ease with which decisions can be reversed makes anticipating the consequences of any one decision less important' (143). Consequently, with 'enormous pressure on editors to reduce' post-production time, the 'editing of Hollywood movies' has become 'much less obviously motivated by the desire to maintain visual and narrative continuity' (144). Discussing the frenetic *Gamer* (2009), Steven Shaviro argues that 'contemporary film editing is oriented, not towards the production of meanings (or ideologies), but directly towards a moment-by-moment manipulation of the spectator's affective state … the frequent cuts and jolting shifts of angle have less to do with orienting us towards action in space, than with setting off autonomic responses in the viewer' (2010a: 118, 124).

There are three interrelated issues at stake in such discussions: the recurring sense that the nature of filmmaking has radically altered since either the 1970s New Hollywood or the digital turn; a tendency to treat spectacle as if it appeals only to the affective; and concern that the cinematic experience's embodied and affective dimensions necessarily threaten the rational subject. Undoubtedly, there have 'been changes in the precise relations between narrative and spectacle from one period to another' (King: 3), but criticisms of contemporary spectacle-driven blockbusters are typically constructed upon an ideal of classical narrative cinema that never actually existed. Moreover, denunciations of the apparent ascendancy of spectacle at the expense of narrative and character psychology normalise a specific 'politics of taste': 'An appreciation of "restraint", delayed gratification or the development of more complex, modulated narrative structures is the product of particular circumstances [and thus] built into the pleasures taken by those whose social, class or educational backgrounds provide a cultural capital that can be expended enjoyably in the celebration of such qualities' (King: 166–67). This socially constructed taste neglects the utopian feelings of abundance, energy, intensity, transparency and community that the social and aesthetic experience of mass-produced spectacular entertainment can generate (see Dyer 1992).

Rather than relying on sweeping generalisations, it is necessary to examine specific instances of the interrelationships between spectacle and narrative. For example, Charles Musser insists that Gunning's 'cinema of attractions' fails to take account of narrative elements within even single shot films, let alone a longer film such as *Le voyage dans la lune/A Trip to the Moon* (1902). Inspired by Jules Verne's *From the Earth to the Moon* (1865), Jacques Offenbach's operetta *Le Voyage dans la lune* (1875), Albert A. Hopkins's illustrated lecture *A Trip to the Moon* (1887), the 1901 Buffalo Pan-American Exposition's *A Trip to the Moon* cyclorama and H.G. Wells's *The First Men in the Moon* (1901), it was a massive international success that Méliès effectively remade twice, each time longer, with greater, if still relatively slight, characterisation and narrative complexity, and with more – and more complex – special effects, adding slapstick in *Le voyage à travers l'impossible* and anti-feminist satire in *À la conquêt du pole/The Conquest of the Pole* (1912). Each film repeats on a grander scale spectacular moments from its predecessor(s): for example, *Le Voyage dans la lune*'s famous shot of the moon growing larger as the spaceship approaches and then lands in its eye becomes *Le voyage à travers l'impossible*'s longer, more elaborate sequence in which the peculiar travelling machine flies towards and into the mouth of the sun; in turn, its briefly glimpsed octopus, combining costume and puppetry, becomes *À la conquêt du pole*'s massive, snow-giant puppet. This focus on developing and outdoing earlier effects betrays a preoccupation with spectacle over narrative, with Méliès himself reflecting in 1932 that 'the scenario constructed ... has *no importance*, since I use it merely as a pretext for the "stage effects," the "tricks," or for a nicely arranged tableau' (in Gunning 1990: 57).

Therefore, Gunning argues, it would be misguided to treat *Le Voyage dans la lune* as merely a precursor to 'later narrative structures' because its plot 'simply provides a frame upon which to string a demonstration of the magical possibilities of cinema' (58). Musser, however, contends that while Méliès might have considered narrative as just 'an excuse for his magical tricks', 'for his audiences it was a crucial one' (394). Gunning later acknowledged the impossibility of knowing whether 'audiences were mainly amazed by the sets, costumes and camera tricks ... or primarily drawn into its narrative of exploration' (2006: 38), but Musser insists that their cinematic pleasures need not have been derived from *either* spectacle *or* narrative but in the interaction of them both, not least because Méliès's spectacular devices are 'typically integral to the narrative' and give 'it substance' (395). For example, the 'scantily clad women' who 'load the huge gun and cheer as the space capsule is discharged into the sky' do not 'just display their sexuality' but help to lampoon 'certain kinds of public rituals ... in ways that cannot be fully appreciated if the intimate interrelationships between attraction and narrative action is not acknowledged' (395). Similarly, *À la conquêt du pole*'s caricaturing of suffragettes situates the polar expedition in a social context and introduces the narrative possibility of competing expeditions, culminating in scenes of countless rival flying machines. In turn, the whimsical design of many of these aeroplanes and dirigibles folds the film, purportedly inspired by Verne's *The Adventures of Captain Hatteras* (1864–66), back into European sf culture by alluding to the illustrations of Albert Robida and Jean-Marc Coté.

As Méliès's example suggests, cinematic narrative and spectacle have always 'existed in ... shifting relationships' (King: 3) and the appeal of spectacle – which draws, often self-reflexively, on cultural knowledge and contributes to narrative and thematic development – is not just affective. This is unsurprising if, as Laura U. Marks argues, '[f]ilm is grasped not solely by an intellectual act but by the complex perception of the body as a whole' (145). Since we 'hold knowledge in our bodies and memory in our senses' (xii), although cinema 'only directly engages two senses', it 'activates a memory that necessarily involves all the senses' (22).

To help understand that one cannot really distinguish between mind and body, cognition and affect, individual and society or culture and nature, Elizabeth Grosz introduces the Möbius strip, a three-dimensional figure of eight created from a two-dimensional strip with a twist in it so that 'tracing the outside of the strip leads one directly to the inside without at any point leaving its surface' (1994: 116–17): the 'inside flips over to become the outside, or the outside turns over on itself to become the inside' (160). The Möbius strip shows that the terms in each of these pairs 'are not two distinct substances or two kinds of attributes of a single substance' but something 'in between' (xii), that 'there can be a relation between two "things" … which presumes neither their identity nor their radical disjunction', and that 'while there are disparate "things" being related, they have the capacity to twist one into the other' (210).

Brian Massumi makes an analytical distinction between affect and emotion: the former is an 'intensity', the latter an inevitably reductive attempt to understand and describe that intensity through 'the conventional, consensual systems' of language and expression (27–28). Affect is troubling and has a utopian potential because it always exceeds and escapes the emotions by which we reduce and misname it, and because it does not have a goal other than itself: 'It is enjoyable to enjoy. It is exciting to be excited. It is terrorizing to be terrorized and angering to be angered' (Sedgwick: 99–100). Moreover, affect is not merely a response to 'distinct transitory physical or verbal events'; rather, it 'already … reflects the complex interleaving of … causes, effects, feedbacks, motives, long-term states such as moods and theories', undermining analytical distinctions between stimulus and response (104). Finally, affect is synaesthetic – that is, the experience of all the senses 'become flesh together, tense and quivering' (62). Synaesthesia remains the norm of human experience because we continue to encounter the world through all our senses at once – for example, 'we can see texture. You don't have to touch velvet to know that it is soft, or a rock to know that it is hard' (Massumi: 157)[3] – although as infants we learn to draw retrospective and artificial distinctions between the optical, the tactile and the kinaesthetic (Grosz 1994: 67). Consequently, it is imperative when considering spectacle not to lose track of its affective impact; but it is equally important to recognise that: first, a film cannot trigger uniform affect in its audience, and that even if it could, that affect would be experienced and understood differently by each viewer; and, second, that cognition/affect distinctions drawn for analytical purposes can only ever be arbitrary since memory, knowledge, sensation and affect are equally embodied and thus present, active and activated during the cinematic experience.

SPECIAL EFFECTS AND IMMERSIVITY

Michele Pierson describes the spectator as constantly 'combining, overlapping, and alternating between consciousness of the illusion of reality produced by the film and surrender to the aleatory play of fantasy and remembering that the film's illusionistic effects invite' (20–21), with sf in particular offering 'experiences in which we do, and do not, believe our eyes, simultaneously' (Tuck: 250).[4] Dan North considers 'every film in which special effects play a significant part' to be about 'illusionism' – 'about special effects', 'techniques of visualisation' and 'the real and its technological mediation' (2). For example, the travelling matte shots in *The Incredible Shrinking Man* (1957), which combine moving images of the ever-diminishing Scott Carey (Grant Williams) with shots of the world in which he no longer fits, 'declare themselves tricks through their sheer impossibility' (Pierson: 10). They are moments of 'mediated ostentation', when 'capital-intensive special effects production' is 'dedicated to "fetishising innovation and difference, pointing out the fallacy in mimesis to the audience as part of its product differentiation"' (North: 13, quoting Miller and Stam: 97). The sense of wonder such moments generate depends, at least in part, on the doubly conscious spectator 'speculating about how they were achieved or alternatively, and more satisfyingly, ... being able to identify their improvement on older methods of combining images filmed at different times' (Pierson: 10). Similarly, the sequence in *Godzilla* (1998) when Victor (Hank Azaria) films the giant reptile on the loose in Manhattan reminds us that we, too, are seeing spectacular images ... , that Godzilla owes its existence to an act of representation. But the insertion of the act of representation within the narrative space ... also ... naturalizes the production of spectacle, decreasing the distance between the spectator-as-consumer-of-spectacle and those depicted on screen. The spectacle of Victor standing before the giant lizard with a video camera ... draws our attention away from the fact that he, the camera and Godzilla occupy different levels of fictional construction: the actor and camera are substantially real and present, [the CGI] Godzilla is not. The presence of the camera, in a world in which so many events are mediated through television, acts paradoxically as a signifier of the reality at which it is pointed. We watch the view through a camera pointed at an elaborately staged spectacle, but watch another camera pointed at part of the same spectacle taken by that cameraman to be reality.

(King 162–63)

However, while the foregrounding of film technologies within the diegesis might take the viewer 'further into the fictional space' (163), it might also draw attention to the filmic construction of the fictional space, pushing the viewer out of it.

A similar tension registers whenever special effects – as is always their eventual fate – become visible in ways that undermine illusion. However, it is important also to recognise that many effects are not concerned with producing 'absolute simulation and imperceptible illusion' (North: 2). For example, films from *Invasion of the Saucer Men* (1957) to *Kataude mashin gâr/The Machine Girl* (2008) embrace an anti-illusionist aesthetic, relishing a 'low-budget insubordination' whose 'steadfast refusal to observe ... rules of decorum' is 'a useful corrective to the expectation that special effects must be state-of-the-art in order to contribute to a text's communicative operations' (North: 106, 105). Moreover, contemporary 'digital imaging techniques' seem either to 'remake film in [a] mode ... closer to traditional feature film animation' (Pierson: 132), as in the *Star Wars* prequels or *Avatar*, or as a more painterly medium, as in the long shots and broad landscapes of *Jurassic Park* (1993), *King Kong* (2005) and *The Road* (2009).[5] Furthermore, the becoming-visible of special effects provides 'points of access for the spectator's critical engagement with the film on a technical level', negotiating between affect and cognition on diegetic, intertextual and speculative levels as the special effect 'portrays a kind of fictional event occurring within a self-contained narrative space', 'invites comparison with other portrayals of similar story events' and 'suggests the eventuality of even more astonishing illusions using the same technology' (North: 5, 6). This complexity is perhaps most evident in the case of a remake and its original.

King Kong (1933) is a self-conscious development of its director's spectacular, exotic documentaries, *Grass: A Nation's Battle for Life* (1925) and *Chang: A Drama of the Wilderness* (1927), which like those of its diegetic director, Carl Denham (Robert Armstrong), were successful but lacked a crowd-pleasing romance angle; and of *The Lost World*, which eight years earlier showcased Willis H. O'Brien's stop-motion animation effects. The intertextual relationship with the latter extends beyond narrative similarities. For example, the thoroughly decontextualised test footage Denham shoots of Ann Darrow (Fay Wray) screaming in response to an unseen threat, rework the close-up reaction shots of the earlier film's Paula White (Bessie Love), which have no discernible background but are intercut with detailed special effects shots. Indeed, *The Lost World's* screenplay was structured so as to 'be coherent and entertaining should there have been a need to abandon the animation and leave out the dinosaurs', a structural segregation of elements 'still evident' inasmuch as 'the actions of the monsters never affect the humans irreversibly' and 'technological limitations [prevent] actual physical contact between human actors and miniature models' (North: 80). *King Kong*, by foregrounding the absence of something for Ann to react to, emphasises its spectacular difference to *The Lost World* – the apparent diegetic co-presence and interaction of previously segregated elements.

North suggests that the 'impossibility of the image and the discrepancies of scale and mannerism between Kong and Wray compel the spectator to inspect the frame for the disjunctures that reveal the joins between composited elements, even as the narrative presumes acceptance of their unity' (67). At the same time, stop-motion animation 'preserves the textural or anthropomorphic attributes of a model or puppet, but renders the resulting figure distinctly "othered", sometimes uncanny' (66). In contrast, Peter Jackson's King Kong remake exemplifies the growing tendency to use digital technologies not to create special effects that intrude into the analogue real but 'as the ground for all cinematic figuration' (Pierson: 132). Consequently, it makes sense to replace the test footage sequence with Denham (Jack Black) filming scenes between Ann (Naomi Watts) and Bruce Baxter (Kyle Chandler) that reconstruct scenes between the original's Ann and John Driscoll (Bruce Cabot), abandoning an uncanny frisson for the pleasures of intertextuality. Similarly, while the digital figuration of the diegetic world robs the monsters of uncanniness,[6] it instead offers the possibility of affective excess by restaging familiar sequences on an even more spectacular scale. Not only does Kong fight more Tyrannosaurus rexes and withstand more volleys from swooping biplanes, but the film also includes the chasm sequence that the original was forced to abandon, in which Kong's pursuers fight off a giant bug attack, and does so on such an absurdly excessive scale as to imply that the original version really would have been as spectacular as fans have for decades imagined.

For Greg Tuck, Kong's fight with the Tyrannosaurus indicates further differences in the nature of the special effects and spectacle these two versions display. In the original's three-minute sequence, Kong perches Ann in a foreground tree so as battle the dinosaur in the background, reasserting the size difference between humans and monsters while establishing Ann as an audience surrogate watching, in effect, a screen behind her. Even when the tree is knocked over, this spatial segregation in depth is maintained. In Jackson's eight-minute sequence, Kong fights three Tyrannosauruses, plunging over a cliff with them to continue the fight while suspended from lianas, before finding a clear arena on a lower ground level in which to dispatch the last of his foes. Ann is integrated into the action, repeatedly snatched from the jaws of one dinosaur or another, falling through space to be caught by vines or in an extended paw or on a dinosaur snout, and ultimately retreating between

Kong's feet as he faces down the last dinosaur. When the original Kong kills the Tyrannosaurus, a self-reflexive joke sees the ape animate the dinosaur, opening and closing its jaw. This gesture is

> a strange mixture of childlike curiosity, clinical examination and sheer brutality, confirming his power yet hinting at his intelligence. We cannot be certain *what* this gesture means, but *that* it means seems certain. It suggests Kong is not simply a dumb beast but has interiority, one we cannot imagine as content although we can perceive it as form.
>
> (Tuck: 260)

In Jackson's version, its meaningfulness is diminished by 'so much spectacle' preceding it (260). However, the film does then attempt to demonstrate Kong's interiority: when he turns his back on Ann for having fled from him, there is an ambiguity as to whether he is not merely sulking but performing sulkiness so as to discipline her into submitting to him. In the original the segregation of elements allowed Kong a subjectivity-for-himself, but the remake's integration of elements constructs Kong's interiority entirely in relation to Ann.

Initially, sf used digital effects to indulge in 'self-conscious showcasing of a new type of effects imagery' (Pierson: 125), with The Abyss (1989), Terminator 2: Judgment Day (1991), The Lawnmower Man (1992) and Johnny Mnemonic (1995) 'exhibit[ing] a mode of spectatorial address that – with its tableau-style framing, longer takes, and strategic intercutting between shots of the computer generated object and reaction shots of characters – solicits an attentive and even contemplative viewing of the computer-generated image' (124). However, there was already a special effects tradition – exemplified by Douglas Trumbull's work on 2001: A Space Odyssey (1968), Silent Running (1972), Close Encounters of the Third Kind (1977), Star Trek: The Motion Picture (1979), Blade Runner (1982) and Brainstorm (1983) – that sought to 'integrate the virtual space of the spectacle with the physical space of the cinema' (Pierson: 126–27). In Bukatman's words: 'A Trumbull sequence is less the description of an object than the construction of an environment ... the wide-screen effect becomes an enveloping thing' (2003a: 94). With the development of digital technologies, this aesthetic has become more common.

For example, *Avatar*, which eschews opening credits so as to minimise pronouncements of its own artefactuality, utilises new 3D technologies alongside cutting-edge CGI, motion capture and digital sound, as well as alternate widescreen formats to suit specific kinds of screening venue, in order to create the alien world of Pandora as a total, 'immersive' environment. Bioluminescent flora and fauna light up the screen, reducing 3D's distracting low-luminence levels. Rapid motion, precipitous action and vertiginous perspectives combine to evoke embodied, kinaesthetic responses in the viewer. *Avatar* even turns immersivity and embodiment into key themes. In the corporate beach-head's control centre, administrators sit before an array of holographic computer screens, many of which curve around the user, recalling the curvature of the Cinerama screen (which accentuated the format's effect on peripheral vision, creating a kind of kinaesthetic 3D effect). This immersivity effect contrasts with the link system that enables humans to remote-operate physical avatars – genetically engineered bodies of the indigenous N'avi – and experience their entire sensory input. The exhilaration of avatar embodiment is emphasised by a paraplegic protagonist, Jake Tully (Sam Worthington), once more capable of running and jumping, and of riding the Pandoran equivalents of horses and dragons. However, *Avatar*'s immersive aspirations are undermined by the very 3D system upon which they depend, from the irritation of the 3D glasses to sequences in which the apparent projection of depth of field out into the auditorium resemble layered stage flats (when this occurs, the image recalls the flattened depth of Méliès's *féeries*, in which the locked-off camera focuses square onto a stage in which foreground and mid-ground props are decorated in the same 'illustrated' manner as the painted flats forming the background and edges of the [re]presented space).

There is nothing necessary or inevitable about using digital technologies to produce immersive cinematic experiences. *Stingray Sam* (2009) – an ultra-low-budget space-western-with-songs, composed of six ten-minute instalments and designed to be watched on screens of all sizes, from an

iPhone upwards – utilises digital technologies to rather different ends.
It premiered on 15 September 2009 as an online live-streaming event
and as a 35mm print projected at Los Angeles's Downtown Independent (followed by an online Q&A session with the director,
projected live) and simultaneously became available to purchase online
as a download and a DVD. It cuts between black-and-white live-action
HD footage and colour, computer-animated collages; and between wry,
expository voice-over narration by David Hyde Pierce, dialogue scenes
and musical numbers. The animation favours still collages animated by
virtual rostrum zooms, tracks and pans, and the live action continues
this presentational – rather than representational – style through lateral
tracking shots and static shots that are face on or at 90° to the action,
which is often arranged in tableau. The techniques flatten the depth of
field, an effect also achieved by sparse sets and retro décor, by arranging
figures to create graphic compositions and by the dancing styles of
Stingray Sam (Cory McAbee), which typically contain movements
designed to be seen sideways-on. The camera is usually static, but it
does track around Sam when he sings more intimate numbers, slipping
from the presentational to the representational; nonetheless, but it
tends to emphasise Sam's stillness rather than suture the spectator into the
diegesis. As this contrast with *Avatar* suggests, cinematic attractions can
offer very different experiences, and so this chapter will now consider
in turn three varieties of sf spectacle: the sublime, the grotesque and
the camp.[7]

THE SUBLIME

As 'part of the euphoria of modernity', cinema exploited and contributed
to the technoscientific extension of 'the realm of what could be seen and
understood by measuring, representing and revealing through the use of
telescopes, microscopes, thermometers, X-rays' (Paci: 125–26). Cameras
could bring into the realm of representation phenomena that were too small
or too large, too fleeting or too slow, to register in normal perception:

cheese mites filmed through a microscope could be projected on a monstrous scale, while time-lapse photography could capture the opening of a flower.[8] André Bazin described the 'miracle' and 'inexhaustible paradox' of the science film:

> At the far extreme of inquisitive, utilitarian research, in the most abso-lute proscription of aesthetic intentions, cinematic beauty develops as an additional, supernatural gift. What cinema 'of imagination' could have conceived of and produced the bronchoscope's fabulous descent into the hell of bronchial tumors … What special effect could have produced the magical ballet of freshwater microorganisms, arranged miraculously under the eyepiece as if in a kaleidoscope? What brilliant cho-reographer, what delirious painter, what poet could have imagined these arrangement, these forms and images?
>
> (2000: 146)

However, from the earliest days of photography, some deployed cameras in attempts to see even further into the world invisible to the eye. For example, photography pioneer Henry Fox Talbot speculated in 1844 about recording images with light from beyond the visible spectrum:

> I would propose to separate these invisible rays from the rest, by suffering them to pass into an adjoining apartment through an aperture in a wall … This apartment would thus become filled (we must not call it illuminated) with invisible rays … If there were a number of persons in the room, no one would see the other: and yet nevertheless if a camera were so placed as to point in the direction [of one of them] … , it would take his portrait, and reveal his actions. … the eye of the camera would see plainly where the human eye would find nothing but darkness.
>
> (quoted in Krauss: 40–41)

While such a proposal concerns the materially real (if invisible), 'scientist-turned-mystic' Emanuel Swedenborg's influence was such that many thought of light as 'the conduit between the world of sense impression and the world of spirit': 'Beginning from Newton's view of light as corpuscular – made of infinitely small particles – and adding to this the Cartesian notion that matter consists of particles that are indefinitely divisible, it was possible to think of light as a spectrum that begins in the world of the senses and shades off into the world of spirits' (Krauss: 37, 39). In nineteenth-century séances, 'the departed chose to put in their spectral appearances' as 'luminous image[s]', and 'it required only a baby step in logic to conceive of recording these apparitions photographically' (37).

This kind of logic – in which technological enhancement enables vision to extend so deeply into the world that it starts to perceive something beyond, something sublime towards which the subject is drawn and from which the subject also recoils – recurs in sf. The sublime has been described in terms of this 'contradictory' sensation since the eighteenth century: it 'raises the mind to fits of greatness and disposes it to soar above her mother earth', it 'dilates and elevates the soul', but at the same time 'fear sinks and contracts it' (Baillie: 88, 97); it is 'a pinnacle of beatitude, bordering upon horror, deformity, madness! An eminence from whence the mind, that dares to look farther, is lost! It seems to stand, or rather to waver, between certainty and uncertainty, between security and destruction. It is the point of terror, of unde-termined fear, of undetermined power!' (Reynolds: 126). In X: The Man with the X-Ray Eyes (1963), Dr Xavier (Ray Milland) develops chemical eyedrops that give him x-ray vision. He goes into hiding, financing further research first by working as a sideshow attraction and then by providing 'mystical' diagnoses for the urban poor. The bullying avarice of his seedy business partner, Crane (Don Rickles), and having constantly to peer into the diseased, decrepit bodies of an endless succession of hopeless, but hopeful, slum dwellers, confront him daily with human moral and physical finitude. Xavier's pursuit by police through the Californian desert recalls the sublime vistas of Jack Arnold's 1950s sf films; and Xavier's viewpoint as his silvered eyes begin to see through the fabric of reality – distorted monocular shots, accompanied by an eerie theremin – recall the 3D point-of-view shots attributed to the aliens in It Came from Outer Space (1953), while mildly psychedelic colour effects evoke an emergent countercultural mysticism. Xavier wanders into a revivalist tent meeting, looks up, his eyes now completely black, and says: 'I've come to tell you what I see. There are great darknesses, further than time itself, and beyond the darkness, a light that glows and changes. And in the centre of the universe, the eye that sees us all'. The film's final shot, momentarily freeze-framed, is of the bloody sockets from which Xavier has plucked his own eyes.

Classical writers associated the sublime with the poet's ability to evoke awe, but in the eighteenth century it was increasingly linked to the natural world. Edmund Burke located the sublime in 'whatever is in any sort terrible … or operates in a manner analogous to terror', adding that, 'at certain distances, and with certain modifications', it can be pleasurable (36–37). Immanuel Kant considered the sublime's pleasure to derive not from the security offered by distance but from human reason, which overcomes an initial inability to comprehend the sublime by substituting a concept for the raw experience. For example, while The Incredible Shrinking Man is unable to descend into the submicroscopic realm into which the endlessly miniaturising Scott Carey is propelled, it does end with him looking up at 'God's silver tapestry' of stars as he disappears into the 'infinitesimal'. Carey recognises his 'presumption' in thinking only 'in terms of man's own limited dimension', displacing and mastering his terror by comparing the endless depths of scale he faces to the endless depths of space, whose incomprehensible vastness is conceptualised in terms of 'the infinite' and through religious sentiment: 'All this vast majesty of creation had to mean something. And then I meant something, too. Yes, smaller than the smallest, I meant something, too. To God, there is no zero. I still exist.'

The Fantastic Voyage (1966) features a similarly religiously inflected manoeuvre. A miniaturized submarine and its scientist crew are injected into a patient's bloodstream so that they can operate on an otherwise inaccessible brain injury. Their reduction in scale is, of course, accompanied by an increase in scale as the patient's body is transformed into sublime landscapes for the scientists to contemplate and traverse.

Kim Sawchuk compares these Oscar-winning effects to nineteenth-century landscape paintings that

> tried to render in art the feeling of the sublime found in man's encounter with nature. They often included a small figure of a human being who is shown looking upon a scene, obviously overshadowed by its enormity and implied power. While the figure ... is enveloped by these forces, the viewer who looks at this transformed nature in the work of art is once again made triumphant. It is *we* who look upon both the landscape and the tiny human figure, giving us as spectators a gratifying omniscient, omnipotent point of view. The awe we feel standing next to these paintings is surmounted by our relationship, in scope, to them.
>
> (14–15)

The viewer's experience of the patient's inner body is mediated by the contrasting attitudes of Dr Duval (Arthur Kennedy), who repeatedly invokes the divine, and the remorselessly materialist Dr Michaels (Donald Pleasance). When Duval describes the oxygenation that they witness as 'one of the miracles of the universe', Michael retorts that it is merely a natural process, 'a simple exchange'. On reaching the brain, Duval states that 'all the suns that light the corridors of the universe shine dim before the blazing light of a single human thought', a sentiment echoed by Grant (Stephen Boyd), who rhapsodises about the 'incandescent glory that is the mind of man'. When Michaels mocks them – 'Very poetic, gentlemen: tell me when we pass the soul' – Duval responds: 'The finite mind cannot comprehend the infinite. The soul that comes from God is infinite'. In this manner, the 'discourse of biotourism maintains "the sacred" within the technological experience' (Sawchuk: 16), while aligning the film with a Kantian perspective (18).

For Kant, the sublime is found in formlessness (e.g., a storm at sea) or in things that so exceed our ability to perceive their form that they are effectively formless (e.g., a mountain range). We cope with 'this *unboundedness*' by conceptualising 'its totality' (98). He distinguished between the mathematical and the dynamical sublime.[9] The former concerns the overpowering of human imagination by spatial or temporal magnitude: any attempt to enumerate the 200–400 billion stars in our galaxy is confronted with what feels like an endless series that extends towards infinity; faced by this scale and number, reason introduces a conceptual totality – the idea of a galaxy as a singular thing – and thus masters the threat. The dynamical sublime concerns the natural world's overwhelming power:

> bold, overhanging … and threatening rocks, thunderclouds piling up in the sky and moving about accompanied by lightning and thunderclaps, volcanoes with all their destructive power, hurricanes with all the devastation they leave behind, the boundless ocean heaved up, the high waterfall of a mighty river. Compared to the might of any of these, our ability to resist becomes an insignificant trifle [but such a sight] becomes all the more attractive the more fearful it is.
>
> (Kant: 120)

David Nye argues that, in the twentieth century, the sublime has been found in technological objects – bridges, skyscrapers, space rockets, atomic bombs – and that rather than implying human limitations, the technological sublime builds on a positive pleasure by representing humanity's apparent 'ability to construct an infinite and perfect world' (287). Although Nye fails to treat such popular spectacular forms as panoramas, dioramas and landscape painting that 'frequently evoked the rhetorical figure of the sublime' (Bukatman 2003a: 82), or indeed cinema, his language is suggestive of the digital simulations and immersive effects of contemporary blockbuster sf. Arguably, if one responds with awe to the natural and artificial heights to which Peter Jackson's Kong ascends or the vast and luminous sunsets he contemplates, or kinaesthetically to Avatar's precipices and vertiginous plunges, one is experiencing something of the sublime, whether through the cinematic evocation of natural magnitudes or through the impressiveness of the technologies displayed and on display.

2001: *A Space Odyssey* utilises an array of effects to evoke the sublime. The luminous skies and distant mountains that appear as the backdrops for the 'Dawn of Man' sequence recall the landscape paintings of Frederick Edwin Church and other luminists. The triptych of white panels in front of which Floyd stands to address the Clavius meeting recall Cinerama's widescreen system, an effect exaggerated through the curvature of the wide-angle lens's barrel distortion. Long shots of distant space vehicles emphasise the vastness of the lunar surface. The apparent immobility of the *Discovery* speeding towards Jupiter for months on end, and the tedium of its crew's activities, demonstrate the cosmic insignificance of a space mission that is the pinnacle of human technological development. However, 2001 also 'adheres so rigorously' to a mathematically sublime aesthetic 'that its sf content can be read as the pretext for the representation of the sublime' (Csicsery-Ronay 2008: 163). The film proliferates geometrical images: circles and rectangles hint at an endless series extending towards infinity; the bone thrown into the air that cuts to an orbiting weapons platform four million years later is in turn replaced by Heywood Floyd's (William Sylvester) pen, floating in free-fall, which gives way to the elongated *Discovery*. 2001's wide-angle lenses, allowing greater depth of field while magnifying the distance between objects, again suggests a potentially infinite series of things, while the complete absence of shot/reverse-shots between close-ups of human characters reduces humans and elevates all other elements of the mise-en-scène to an equivalent thing-ness. 2001 rejects conventional continuity editing so as to emphasise the 'brutal rupture' of the cut, often underscored by 'strong contrasts in brightness' between shots (Chion: 81). Michel Chion describes this as a commutative style, in which 'where there was nothing, suddenly there is something [that] can itself disappear in an instant', giving 'us the feeling that there is no build-up of the information supplied in the shots, no memory of each shot in the one that comes after' (112). To the extent that 2001 eschews conventional connections between shots, it too becomes a potentially infinite series of things – as the climactic stargate sequence, racing headlong through patterns of light and over colour-filtered landscape, without any clear goal or obvious meaning in sight, further emphasises. 2001 thwarts the viewer's ability to determine its meaning, while repeatedly insinuating through its apparent artistry – its careful patterning, doubling and rhyming – that it must mean something, that there must be some way in which reason can recontain its sublime excess.

Most films that aspire to replicate 2001's sublime affect – *The Black Hole* (1979), *Star Trek: The Motion Picture* (1979), *Petlya Oriona/Orion's Loop* (1982), *The Abyss* (1989), *Contact* (1997), *Mission to Mars* (2000), *Solaris* (2002), *Sunshine* (2007) – fail because competing demands push them towards spectacles of action and melodrama or insist upon explaining the depicted events, often in a relatively unimaginative and banal manner. As Philip Shaw notes:

> In a very strong sense the sublime does indeed verge on the ridiculous; it encourages us to believe that we can scale the highest mountains, reach the stars and become the infinite when all the time it is drawing us closer to our actual material limits: the desire to outstrip earthly bonds leads instead to the encounter with lack, an encounter that is painful, cruel, and some would say comic.
>
> (10)

The combination of aspiration and failure, of the comic and the cruel, can be seen in Steve Spielberg's sf films, which evoke and then retreat from the sublime. This manoeuvre simultaneously articulates the gendered oppositions around which conceptualisations of the sublime are often constructed: for Longinus, 'sublime speech "ravishes" or rapes the listener'; for Burke, it is a 'virile masculine power ... contrasted with its passive feminine counterpart, the ... beautiful'; and Kant distinguishes 'between the depth and profundity of the masculine sublime and the shallow, slight nature of the feminine beautiful' (Shaw: 10). An Oedipal scenario is evident in these distinctions. For example, Burke's sublime is 'embodied in the "authority of a father", venerable and distant', evoking a 'masculine realm' of 'pain and terror', whereas the beautiful is associated with the feminine, the maternal, 'friendship', 'love', 'pleasure and compassion' (Kramnick: 96–97), and the drama is concluded when 'the excess of the sublime' is converted 'into a principle of internal discipline' in which the erring son must learn to become a father himself by 'symbolically' appropriating 'the authority of the unfathomable' (Shaw: 59). Consequently, the threat 'to which we are exposed and from which we are then released in the sublime moment is an unconscious fantasy of parricide' (Weiskel: 92), as is played out in *Close Encounters of the Third Kind*.

Roy Neary (Richard Dreyfuss) flees from adult responsibility and from his wife, Ronnie (Teri Garr), who is mother to his children but refuses to mother him and expects him to act like a father. When he eventually enters the alien mothership, a spectacular cathedral of light, he abandons the phallic Devil's Tower and re-enters the womb, thus 'revers[ing] the three determining moments in Lacan's account of childhood development. He regresses through the Mirror Phase, subsuming his identity to transcendental unity; he fulfils desire symbolised by the *fort-da* game, escaping from positionality in language; and in breaking family ties and defying authority to get there, he overturns the Oedipus complex (submission to the law)' (Morris: 17). A similar Oedipal drama occurs on the sublime, frozen landscape of *Artificial Intelligence: A. I.*'s future Ice Age. The android child David (Haley Joel Osment) is obsessed with his mother, Monica (Frances O'Connor), upon whose breasts – comfortingly maternal, dangerously sexual – the film pointedly lingers. The traumatic moment of separation, in which the infant recognises its existence as an individual distinct from its mother, takes the exaggerated form of Monica abandoning David in a fairytale-gothic forest, prompting his quest to return to the maternal body. When the far-future aliens temporarily reconstruct Monica, David hesitates between replacing his father or reverting to infancy, settling on the latter: 'Monica declares her love and David sheds a further tear as she returns to bed. Eventually he closes his eyes voluntarily for the first time – a real boy, he believes – and the camera tracks discreetly back, leaving him sleeping with his Mummy' (Morris: 310–11).

Films that hint at the sublime but only evoke it in their closing moments tend to be more effective. *The Quiet Earth* (1985) opens with a two-minute-and-40-second shot of the sun rising above the ocean, slowly separating from the optical illusion of what appears to be another sun. In New Zealand, failed suicide Zac Hobson (Bruno Lawrence) wakes in a deserted world – depopulated, perhaps, by the US Project Flashlight, which was attempting to tap into the planetary energy grid. He meets two other survivors, first Joanne (Alison Routledge) and, later, Api (Pete Smith), who both also died at the moment the event – whatever it was – occurred. Intermittently, the characters experience periods of disorientation (visual flashes of what appears to be a black sun – or a pupil – against a blue background, or of a star pulsating and shattering; superimposed shots of a room rotating in different directions; track-zoom vertigo effects; rippling superimpositions; apparent changes in the orientation of gravity, so that walls become floors), leading Zac to surmise that the altered fabric of the universe has become unstable and that the sun will soon collapse. The only solution is to destroy the Project Searchlight installation in which he used to work so as to crash the global network. Zac dies in the explosion. A viewpoint races through a stream of white particles, through a red-walled tunnel, towards a point of light, imagery that previously accompanied Joanne and Api's recollections of dying. Zac awakes on a beach, beneath a blue sky in which strange cloud formations hang. A giant ringed planet rises over the horizon. The final shot freezes on his face as he looks on in wonder, the lapping of waves the only sound in this new world. In contrast to *Mission to Mars*, which culminates in a prolonged, if spectacular, illustrated lecture about the fate of the Martians and the seeding of Earth with life, *The Quiet Earth* is reticent about exposition, stepping sideways into the unexpected and unexplained. Zac admits to only guessing about what is happening, the film neither confirming nor refuting him, leaving questions unanswered: was the solar implosion averted? Are Joanne and Api returned to a populated world? Where exactly is Zac? In Chion's terminology, relocating Zac – who may or may not be dead (again) – to this alien beach is an act of commutation. It creates an epistemological gulf, a gap without determinate meaning, a sublime rupture.

The Wild Blue Yonder (2005) achieves its sublime affect by manipulating the gaps between its found footage, its interviews and the commentary provided by an alien (Brad Dourif) living on Earth, who is depressed about the failings of his own species and of humanity. When real-life mathematician Martin Lo attempts to explain how gravitational tunnels and superstring theory might enable cheap, fast travel throughout galaxy, his inarticulacy – and the cheesy artist's illustration of gravity tunnels – open up the possibility of imagining something inexpressible. Similarly, the closing aerial footage of towering plateaus rising above the clouds, described as a view of the Earth in 820 years, no longer inhabited by humans or scarred by the traces of human civilisation, restores a sense of the sublime to the actually existing world by representing, but obviously not being, what the narrator claims. This technique is also deployed throughout a sequence in which astronauts explore beneath the frozen sky of the alien's long-deserted homeworld. This found footage, actually shot beneath Antarctic ice, reveals a luminous blue, fluid, alien environment here on Earth, full of peculiar fish-like darting shards of glass and strange, rippling, translucent lifeforms with ambiguous shapes that defy inside/outside distinctions; and it hints at a different physics as divers stand upside down on the underside of the ice ceiling. The alien's sardonic commentary becomes less frequent as our world becomes more sublime.

Stalker (1979) uses the smallest of actions to imply an awful strangeness behind the surface of the world. Twenty years prior to the story, something uncanny fell from space. Troops sent to investigate did not return, and so the authorities cordoned off the impact area. However, rumours circulate of a room inside the Zone where wishes come true. The Writer (Anatoli Solonitsyn) and the Professor (Nikolai Grinko) hire Stalker (Aleksandr Kaidanovsky) to guide them through the Zone. Stalker's Wife (Alisa Frejndlikh) protests that he has only recently returned from prison for the same crime, to which he retorts: '[I]t's prison everywhere': they subsist on the edge of a grim industrial city, its decay emphasised by monochrome cinematography, which foreground the textures rather than the boundaries of people and objects. In contrast, the Zone is shot primarily in muted colour, with lighting changes and areas of darkness that push some of the interiors towards a monochrome look, suggesting the extent to which the mundane hedges in the marvellous. Indeed, the Writer even insists on the impossibility of marvels: 'our world is hopelessly boring. Therefore there can be no telepathy, or apparitions, or flying saucers, nothing like that. The world is ruled by cast-iron laws and it's insufferably boring. Alas, these laws are never violated. They don't know how to be violated. So don't even hope for a UFO, that would have been too interesting … '. Nonetheless, the Zone is imbued with strangeness. Direct routes are traps. The room must be approached circuitously. When the Writer disobeys Stalker and heads straight for the derelict building containing the room, the wind picks up gently. As he approaches, a shot from within the doorway captures his sudden uncertainty, and something formless – perhaps a shadow, perhaps a dark fabric – falls down from the framing darkness. Later, it starts to rain indoors. Such elliptical effects, and equally elliptical dialogue, imply something beyond, something sublime, but the trio return from the Zone, their wishes apparently unmade and Stalker bemoaning intellectuals for lacking belief.

On the night before the expedition, as Stalker and Wife sleep, their daughter, Monkey (Natasha Abramova), between them, the camera pans from a bedside table on which a glass begins to move because of the vibration of a passing train, over their sleeping faces and back again. At the end of the film, Monkey, who is rumoured to have been born mutated because of Stalker's exposure to the Zone, sits by a table, in the background of the shot. In a line in front of her, extending into the midground, are a half-filled tea glass, a jar containing a broken egg and an empty milk glass. She looks at the tea glass, which slides past the other objects, across the table into the foreground, as out of shot the dog Stalker brought back from the Zone whimpers. Monkey turns her attention to the jar, which glides past the milk glass and comes to a halt. Then, as the camera tracks out slightly and as Monkey rests her head on the table, the milk glass glides forward and off the end of the table. Only then, as the camera tracks back in, does the sound of a train approaching become audible, shaking the table, but not enough to move the objects standing on it. As the camera tracks in on Monkey's impassive face, Beethoven's 'Ode to Joy' is briefly heard. Throughout the scene, the air has been filled with drifting seeds, dandelion, perhaps, or milkweed. The screen fades to black, Monkey's implied-but-deniable telekinesis evoking a sublime fullness beyond – and capable of transforming – the mundane world. In Slavoj Žižek's words: '[T]he spiritual and material spheres are intertwined: the spiritual emerges when we become aware of the material inertia, the dysfunctional bare presence, of the objects around us' (2003: 13).

THE GROTESQUE

At the end of 2001, a foetus – possibly astronaut Dave Bowman reborn as a more highly evolved being – floats in space above the Earth, its intentions unfathomable, utterly sublime. *Innerspace* (1987) offers a similar image to rather different effect. Hotshot navy pilot Tuck Pendleton (Dennis Quaid), in a miniaturised one-man submarine, is accidentally injected into hapless Jack Putter (Martin Short). When Putter kisses Pendleton's former girlfriend, Lydia Maxwell (Meg Ryan), Pendleton is unintentionally and unknowingly transferred into her body. Finding himself in a warm, orange, glowing space, he gazes in awe at the embryo floating above him. 'Lydia,' he whispers, 'I'm in a Lydia. Oh, Lydia. I'm a dad'.

Representations of the foetus during pregnancy establish both a bond and a separation between mother and embryo, with anti-abortion discourses using such images 'to privilege the autonomous personhood of the fetus', 'obliterating' the woman 'from the picture' and 'leaving as the focal point the fetus floating in a vacuum rather than a body, like a little tiny spaceman' (Sawchuk 20). Similarly, medical imaging technologies used to monitor pregnancy, and associated discourses, tend to reduce the 'female body' to 'a mere vessel for the fetus' (Smelik: 137). Consequently, *Innerspace*'s reactionary conclusion – Pendleton, restored to normal size, abruptly mends his ways and marries Lydia – is unsurprising.

Because masculine identity, and thus patriarchy, typically conceptualises itself as rational, proportionate and complete, and female identity as irrational, irregular, fragmentary and incomplete, male bodily fluids must be both denied and controlled. This is often achieved by

> representing the flow as a mark of appropriation, as the production of a solid, with all its attendant rights and occasional responsibilities, [enabling men to] demarcate their own bodies as clean and proper. Moreover, through this ... transmission of possession men take on the right of the proprietors of women's bodies too insofar as women's bodies are conceived as the receptacles of men's body fluids and the nesting place of their product – the fetus.
>
> (Grosz 1994: 201–2)

The foetus that Pendleton presumes is his – as both a biological product and a patriarchal possession – secures his masculinity by ensuring that his bodily excrescences (here, semen) are productive. Both he and the film ignore Lydia's contribution, rights and wishes, denying her subjectivity while imagining her body as an empty space, a marvellous cavern, a grotto. Before turning to the grotesque's 'low, hidden, earthly, dark, material, immanent, visceral' connotations (Russo: 1) in relation to wombs, pregnancies and birthings, this section will begin with the grotesque in the sense of the bizarre or fantastically distorted.

The grotesque shocks the subject into realising 'that objects that appear to be familiar and under control are actually undergoing surprising transformations', and that despite being 'near and intimate, ... prove to be strange' (Csicsery-Ronay 2008: 146), both attractive and repellent. The grotesque's anomalousness stems from the inadequacy of rationalised systems to account for the material fullness of the universe, reminding us that the universe consists not of bounded objects – individual, monadic, distinct – but of endless processes and interrelations; not of nouns or being, but of verbs and becoming. The grotesque calls into question the distinctions 'between the body and the world and between separate bodies' (Bakhtin: 315), offering a utopian prefiguration of 'the free and happy interflow of human carnal processes and the removal of boundaries between bodies' (Csicsery-Ronay 2008: 185).

However, sf typically portrays such somatic unboundedness as horrifying or dystopian, turning the viewer's 'arrested attention intensely toward things, in which it detects a constant metamorphic flux, an intimate roiling of living processes that perpetually change before understanding can stabilize them' (190). For example, The Thing's metamorphic alien survives by infecting host organisms and replacing them, cell by cell, until all that is left is the alien replica. Its presence is only revealed when a husky from a neighbouring Antarctic research base is placed in a kennel with other dogs, who immediately sense the interloper's strangeness. The husky hisses menacingly and its muzzle splits open four ways, like a bloody orchid. A thick tentacle emerges from its throat, thrashing violently, blindly, across the floor. Whiplike flagella extrude through the husky's back, followed – with a horrendous cracking noise – by arachnoid-crustacean legs. It hoses one of the dogs with an obscene jet of translucent fluid that becomes viscous on contact. When MacReady (Kurt Russell) comes running, he is confronted by the husky, now a mound of flesh and organic extensions from which the deformed, gloopy musculature of a flayed dog's head turns to him, howling discordantly. Flagella engulf a dog cowering nearby, choke another. As Childs arrives with a flamethrower, two grey, muscular arms, terminating in three-clawed hands, extend from within the mass of flesh and pull part of the alien, all twitching flagella and arachnoid legs, through a hole in the roof. An eye, possibly human, can be discerned within the writhing mound. A sac forms, and bursts open to reveal another flesh-orchid that races through the air, prompting Childs at last to trigger the flamethrower, engulfing the alien in fire.

The Thing seems designed to illustrate the Bakhtinian grotesque, but stripped of its positive social and political connotations. For Mikhail Bakhtin, the grotesque body expresses the 'fertility, growth, and ... brimming-over abundance' of 'the collective ancestral body of all the people' that exceeds 'the isolated biological individual' and the 'private, egotistic "economic man"' (19). The grotesque sets out to degrade 'all that is high, spiritual, ideal, abstract' so as to insist on the materiality of life, on the 'bodily' and the 'erotic' (19, 20). The grotesque body is 'unfinished and open', blending 'with the world, with animals, with objects' (26, 27); it is 'a body in the act of becoming. It is never finished, never completed; it is continually built, created, and builds and creates another body ... [it] swallows the world and is itself swallowed by the world.' (317). In its openness, protrusions, irregularities, secretions, multiplicity and constant change, it contrasts with the 'transcendent and monumental, closed, static, self-contained, symmetrical, and sleek' classical body associated with high culture and 'the rationalism, individualism, and normalizing aspirations of the bourgeoisie' (Russo: 8). The Thing's grotesque spectacle is predicated upon hyperbolic processes, treating the alien as flesh-without-boundaries, being-without-form, so as to confront the subject with the material embodiment that constitutes, rather than merely houses, the subject.[10] As Julia Kristeva argues, the grotesque undoes 'narcissism' and 'all imaginary identity' by bringing the subject to 'the edge of non-existence and hallucination', to 'a reality that', if acknowledged, will annihilate it (208, 2).

The brief glimpse of an eye in the Thing's roiling flesh is unsettling because eyes 'express an individual ... self-sufficient human life', while the grotesque prefers eyes that protrude or bulge, replacing individuated consciousness with 'a purely bodily tension' (Bakhtin: 316, 317). When Norris (Charles Hallahan), apparently dead from a heart attack, is defibrillated by Copper (Richard Dysart), his chest cavity opens up into a monstrous mouth that bites off the doctor's arms. For Bakhtin, the mouth is the most grotesque of human facial features, a 'wide-open bodily abyss' that, like the bowels, genital, anus and other bodily 'convexites and orifices', overcomes the separation between body and world:

> Eating, drinking, defecation and other elimination (sweating, blowing of the nose, sneezing), as well as copulation, pregnancy, dismemberment, swallowing up by another body – all these acts are performed on the confines of the body and the outer world, or on the confines of the old

and new body. In all these events the beginning and end of life are closely linked and interwoven.

(317)

As Norris rapidly transforms, his neck stretches and tears, revealing complex inner cordage that lowers his head to the floor before snapping free of his torso. A fleshy cord whips out from the open mouth to pull the head clear of the chaos surrounding the abandoned body. Legs erupt out of the skull, turning the upturned head into a crab-spider that sprouts a pair of comically fleshy eyestalks from the multiple folds of its throat. Norris's own eyes are irrelevant to this combination of elements drawn from the Thing's history of encountering and incorporating the world. Just as Norris's inverted head suggests the overturning of reason, the protruding eye stalks – along with Norris's form becoming two separate entities – suggest an end to individuated subjectivity. Identity is replaced by a restless, material becoming that 'signals the precarious grasp the subject has over its identity and bodily boundaries, the ever-present possibility of sliding back into the corporeal abyss from which it was formed' (Grosz 1992: 198).

Grosz relates 'the fear of being absorbed into something which has no boundaries of its own' (194) to the viscous, to the kinds of glutinous fluid – 'half-way between solid and liquid' (Douglas: 39) – that coat the transmuting Thing's unstable body, seeming to defy gravity's pull. An 'aberrant fluid or a melting solid' (39), the viscous simultaneously clarifies 'the outline of the set in which it is not a member' and demonstrates that 'life does not conform to our most simple categories' (39). The epistemological and ontological crisis it poses often manifests as disgusted recoil from proximity and contact, as felt both by character and viewer when, in *Bad Taste* (1987), Barry (Peter O'Herne) shoots an axe-wielding alien-in-human-form in the head: blood splatters on Barry's face, shredded brain flies through the air, gouts of blood spurt from what remains of the alien's head as it stumbles towards Barry, its outstretched and blood-stained hands sliding down his jacket and, as it falls forward, the bloody remnants of its exposed brain rubbing against his jeans and slurpily spilling out onto his trainers. The revulsion produced by this and other moments – Frank (Mike Minnet), undercover as an alien in human form, drinking bright green, chunky vomit; Derek (Peter Jackson) replacing a chunk of his missing brain by mushing an over-large handful of a dead alien's brain into the gap beneath his skull – depends not merely on the threat of proximity but also on 'the perception that something is illegitimately in something else', the grotesque 'sense that things that should be kept apart are fused together' (Harpham: 11).

However, as Sara Ahmed argues: 'borders need to be threatened in order to be maintained, or even to appear *as* borders' (87). This border 'maintenance-through-transgression' requires the production of 'border objects' that the subject expels because they are disgusting and which become disgusting because they are expelled (87). For example, such abject phenomena as saliva, urine, semen, faeces, menstrual blood and vomit blur the distinctions between inside/outside and subject/world. They are separable from the body, 'but there is still something of the subject bound up with them' (Grosz 1994: 81), and this ambiguity 'offends against order', marking the limits to rational, or supposedly rational, efforts to 'organise the environment' and impose structure and meaning upon it (Douglas: 2). The abject is evidence that the body is permeable, as likely to leak out into the world as to be infiltrated by it. Consequently, the abject undermines any aspiration towards being a unique, monadic, autonomous individual, and because these are relentlessly reproduced ideological norms, the abject is typically cast as horrific and dystopian rather than euphoric and utopian.

The Thing's computer simulation shows the abject's threat to the monadic subject: like a virus, the alien cells come from outside, but once inside they are like a cancer, identical to bodily tissue and voracious. As Jackie Stacey notes (in language that seems equally to describe the Thing), the malignant cancer cell, 'produced by the body', is 'Neither self nor other' but 'both the same as and different from its host':

> The cancer cell is just a self-serving replicant … It should be an expelled object, but it remains part of the system. Its facility for

self-replication brings it more allies until they outnumber the cells of the organs which house them. The tumour which these rogue cells come to form is part of the body and yet separate from it. … it can enlarge organs and protrude from the body. It can even transgress bodily boundaries and break through the skin, bringing the inside into the outside. … It impersonates the subject long enough to establish the power of its real difference, often until it can overpower its host body.

(1997: 77–78)

However, since pregnancy, like cancer, is an abject condition (89), sf more frequently generates grotesquerie through imagery related to the condition to which only women are susceptible. Bakhtin describes grotesque terracotta figurines of laughing, 'senile pregnant hags' in terms of 'a death that gives birth'; they disturbingly combine 'a senile, decaying and deformed flesh with the flesh of new life, conceived but as yet unformed' (25–26). This image emphasises the cultural abjection of the female body as that 'which leaks, which bleeds', as that 'which is at the mercy of hormonal and reproductive functions' and as 'a vessel … lacking in itself but fillable from the outside' (Grosz 1994: 204, 206). The ways in which such interlocking connotations determine female subjectivity is demonstrated in sf, which struggled to reconcile second-wave feminism and the sexual revolution even as a reactionary backlash gathered, in such films as *Shivers* (1975), *The Stepford Wives* (1975), *Rabid* (1977), *Coma* (1978) and *The Brood* (1979), and such sexploitation, sex comedy and pornographic sf as *Zeta One* (1969), *The Nine Ages of Nakedness* (1970), *Percy* (1971), *Flesh Gordon* (1974), *Percy's Progress* (1974), *Queen Kong* (1976), *Rollerbabies* (1976), *The Sexplorer* (1976), *Cinderella 2000* (1977), *Sexworld* (1978), *The Satisfiers of Alpha Blue* (1980) and *Outer Touch* (1981).

In *Inseminoid* (1981), an archaeological expedition to an apparently deserted alien world is plagued by fatal outbreaks of madness and violence. When Sandy (Judy Geeson) and Mitch (Trevor Thomas) venture out from the base, a fleetingly glimpsed alien dismembers Mitch and disables Sandy's air supply. She wakes, naked, on a table lit from beneath. It is unclear whether this is an actual location, a nightmare or a hallucination.

As she writhes in torment, the expedition's aloof doctor, Karl (Barrie Houghton), looming over her – and breaking spatial continuity – injects her with a syringe of green liquid. Sandy grimaces and turns away, cuts overlapping on the action so as to further undermine conventional continuity. A superimposed shot of her lying on the table whirls over her naked body, which then seems to recede into blackness beneath a shower of glitter, the electronic score suggesting a discordant dis-embodiment. Eventually the whirling table comes to a rest. The camera tracks in over Sandy as her raised knees part and the alien's phallic head rises into view. Unable even to scream, she turns away as the alien lowers a glass pipe between her legs, pouring a green, egg-bearing fluid inside her. Her distraught face is slowly occluded by the shadow of the alien, turning the screen black. Cut to Sandy safely back inside the base, being tended by Karl and others.

This rape and its consequences condense many of the film's anxieties. One of Karl's duties is to administer contraceptive injections to female expedition members. Despite the liberal mores implied by admitting to and enabling sexual activity among expedition members, the system of policing reproduction reinforces heteronormativity and a gendered hierarchy: all women, regardless of their sexuality, must be rendered incapable of conception, because patriarchal discourse pathologises female bodies as the cause of reproduction. Furthermore, since Sandy is sexually involved with Mark (Robin Clarke), the monstrous pregnancy that results from her rape can be seen as 'natural' maternity rebelling against technological intervention in order for the 'empty vessel' to be filled. As Sandy's pregnancy proceeds, she becomes murderously deranged, attacking, killing and eating her colleagues. This development abjects and dehumanises Sandy in two ways: it reduces her to an animalistic drive to survive and reproduce; and it suggests that her consciousness has been suppressed and her body possessed by that which is inside her but should not be there.

Even under normal circumstance, the 'pregnant body … defies … ideals of masculine individuation since it is more than one, but not yet two people' and disturbs 'the conventional categories of subject and object, of self and other' (Stacey 1997: 87).[11] *Inseminoid* exaggerates this disturbance through the repeated suppression of Sandy's agency: her fertility is subjected to institutionalised management, and her rape makes her a mere incubator for psychically conjoined, flesh-eating alien twins. Ultimately, of course, it is Mark who must kill the murderous Sandy. Not only has her subjection to the contraceptive regime prevented her transformation into his possession (the receptacle for his offspring), but that proprietorship has been asserted by an alien other. Injured by and fleeing from Sandy, he falls through a damaged floor and is doused by a broken sewage pipe. Only after this cloacal rebirth is he able finally to brutally assault and kill his lover, whose gasps and screams parody orgasm, and to return, coated in blood and fecal matter, to the children that are not his – and who immediately kill him.[12]

Alien similarly plays out the abjection of pregnancy and birth. Kane (John Hurt) finds the hold of a derelict alien vessel packed with knee-high eggs, one of which opens up like the petals of a leathery plant. A creature resembling an arachnoid-crustacean hand leaps out, melts through his space helmet visor, attaches to his face and wraps its whip-like tail around his throat. Defying forcible detachment, it keeps him alive until it dies and falls off. The crew gather with the recovered Kane for a meal. Parker (Yaphet Kotto) jokes with Lambert (Veronica Cartwright) about cunnilingus as a form of consumption while Kane stacks his plate with food – he is, albeit unknown, eating for two now, the face-hugger having deposited an embryonic lifeform inside him. In an obscene parody of birth, the alien – a monstrous spermatozoön, a feral penis – punches its way out through his chest. The horror of this scene depends not only on Kane's uncontrolled thrashing, the spurting blood, the unseemly alien or the mere fact of birthing – which in another context, Kristeva describes as 'the ultimate of abjection', 'the height of bloodshed and life, the scorching moment of hesitation (between inside and outside, ego and other, life and death), horror and beauty, sexuality and the blunt negation of the sexual' (155) – but also upon its unexpectedness. As in *Inseminoid*, the alien has raped, impregnated and reduced a human to an incubator; but it has also, with cavalier disrespect for human reproductive physiology, done so through the mouth of a male body. While the agonising visibility of this birth contrasts with the crew's earlier, cleansing awakening from suspended animation, it also resonates with the later assault on Ripley (Sigourney Weaver).

After Ripley discovers that the Company is more interested in bringing back samples of the alien than in the safety of the *Nostromo* crew, science officer Ash (Ian Holm) implacably sets about killing her. As they square off, blood runs from Ripley's nose and a bead of white fluid trickles down Ash's brow, emphasising sexual difference through connotations of menstruation and semen. Having thrown Ripley into a sleeping alcove decorated with pornographic images of women, Ash roles up a pornographic magazine and, echoing the oral rape of Kane, rams it into Ripley's mouth to suffocate her. Parker hits Ash in the head with a fire extinguisher. White fluid spurts from Ash's mouth, he loses control of his body and, thrashing around the alcove, spurts more and more fluid. Parker hits Ash's head so hard that it comes off, hanging by the flesh of his throat, revealing that he is an android. White fluid coats Ash's innards and spurts from tubes in his neck. Thrown to the floor, Parker holds Ash's torso away from him while wrapping his legs around Ash's waist to hold him in place. Both are now covered in Ash's ejaculate and this parodic pornographic scenario is brought to a climax as Lambert steps in and penetrates Ash from behind with an enormous metal rod. The sheer excessiveness of Ash's money shot further undoes patriarchal distinctions between male and female bodies since the most coldly rational of the crew seems to consist of nothing but 'the hydraulics of male ejaculation' (Williams 1990: 94).

Just as sf usually depicts the corporeal abyss as horrifying rather than utopian, so its frequent mapping of the body and society onto each other tends to represent a reactionary attempt to police difference by associating the grotesque with 'non-normative' others (women, homosexuals, peoples of colour, the working class, foreigners and so on) and by depicting triumph over the grotesque as the salvation/restoration of 'natural' social relations. However, the grotesque, by its very nature, tends to leak out of control, signifying – albeit ambiguously or ambivalently – different ways of being in the world. For example, *Phase IV* (1974) pits humans against a super-intelligent ant collective, which not only defeats the monadic individualism of the film's rather detached protagonists but also absorbs a pair of humans, transforming them into ant-human hybrids, a posthuman Adam and Eve. In sf conflicts with hive minds – troubling figurations of totalitarian hierarchy *and* of distributed intelligence – victory is more commonly ceded to the humans, but not before drawing parallels between the antagonists, as with *Starship Troopers'* alien bugs and fascist humans, or demonstrating the attractions of the hive. In *Star Trek: First Contact* (1996), the seductive appeal of the collective is embodied by the Borg Queen (Alice Krige), and in *Pandorum* (2009), the posthuman 'savages' are the product of artificially accelerated evolution to fit their new environment. In both cases, inhuman others bear subcultural markers – S&M costumes and paraphernalia, tribal markings, piercings – which suggest that their collective identities are accessible to humans even as heteronormative, possessive individualism marginalises and denigrates them.

Society (1989) provides a more sustained, if equally ambivalent, example. Bill Whitney (Billy Warlock) is disturbed by the abnormal, perhaps incestuous, closeness between his parents, Jim (Charles Lucia) and Nan (Connie Danese), and his older sister, Jenny (Patrice Jennings). His paranoia is fuelled by strange goings-on: glimpses of female bodies rippling, twisting and distorting hint at morphological instability; an illicit audio recording of Jen's coming-out party suggest an upper-class bacchanalia, with Jen's ritual deflowering followed by an intergenerational and incestuous orgy. After their deaths are faked, Bill and David Blanchard (Tim Bartell) are presented to Beverly Hills's high society for a bizarre ritual of discorporation and ingestion. The rich, it seems, are 'a different race ..., a different species, a different class' who have evolved along-side humans, and Billy – who was adopted and raised especially for this ritual – is simply 'not one of' them. Stripped to their underwear, the gathered white elite begin to 'shunt' – to secrete a gelatinous fluid that desolidifies David's body, and to lose their own solidity. Faces elongate into snouts that meld with David's melting flesh. Fingers dig into – sink into – his buttocks. Judge Carter (David Wiley) thrusts his fist up David's arse until it emerges from David's mouth, and then reaches for David's scalp to pull his face off his head. Hitherto, *Society* has repeatedly alluded to films noir about Los Angeles's webs of financial and sexual corruption, such as *Murder My Sweet* (1944) and *Chinatown* (1974); but this sequence's use of 'The Blue Danube' waltz alludes to 2001, simultaneously mocking sublime aspiration and implying that such material excess might itself be edged with the sublime.[13]

While David's assailants melt into an elaborate, interlocking array of lascivious body parts, Billy escapes upstairs, only to find Jen, Jim and Nan shunting together. Nan has arms instead of legs, from between which Jen's head emerges to suggest that 'if you have any Oedipal fantasies you'd like to indulge in ... now's the time'. Meanwhile, Jim's face appears, farting, between his buttocks, embodying both Billy's earlier 'butthead' insult and Bakhtin's description of the grotesque body in which 'the buttocks persistently [try] to take the place of the head and the head that of the buttocks' (353).

Back downstairs, the writhing mesh of body parts is surrounded by carousing, caressing bodies, to the extra-diegetic strains of the 'Eton Boating Song'. Revellers pluck David's remaining eye and pass it from mouth to mouth; another eats his matted hair. Obviously intended to repel, the prosthetic and makeup effects also compel the viewer. In this oscillation, it is possible to perceive *Society*'s fleshy others as a polymorphous alterity, a plenitude without borders, a utopian drive 'toward gaining more intensive and extensive pleasure, toward the generation of libidinous ties with one's fellow men, the production of a libidinous, that is, happy environment' (Marcuse 1970: 19). This is also suggested by the film's conclusion, which implies the ongoing sexual relationship between Billy and the non-human Clarissa (Devin Devasquez). They are accompanied by Billy's friend, Milo (Evan Richards), who has spent most of the film acting like a stereotypical jilted girlfriend, fulfilling the role of the 'effeminate rival or confidante' who serves 'to authenticate the virility and normality of the leading man' (Cohan 1997: 290). The queer possibilities presented by this cross-species trio are, of course, neither mentioned nor explored, and Milo merely hovers on the periphery of the action, a spectral trace of the 'ghost that haunts heterosexuality': 'the illicit desire needed to define legitimacy' (Merck: 233).

God Told Me To (1976) offers a similar utopian trace, self-consciously blasphemous and queer. Detective Peter Nicholas (Tony Lo Bianco) investigates a series of spree killings, after each of which the perpetrator explains 'God told me to' then commits suicide. He discovers that the killers were in telepathic thrall to the apocalyptic Bernard Philips (Richard Lynch), and uncovers two accounts of alien abductions and impregnation. The first victim, in 1939, was his own mother, taken by an alien force from the New York World's Fair; the second, in 1951, was Philips's mother. They are in fact half-siblings. Philips – born neither male nor female to a virgin mother – is aware of Nicholas's grief and sense of failure over his wife's multiple miscarriages (her womb refused to host such alien otherness), and he offers to be impregnated by Nicholas and bear his child. While the film treats Nicholas as inhuman and this offer as obscene, it also relishes casting Philips not merely as a sexless fallen angel but as a hermaphrodite Christ capable of incestuous, 'homosexual' reproduction.

The queerness of Philips, and of his offer, is calculated to offend, and thus exposes the ways in which discourses of normativity – around sexuality and Christian mythology – serve to discipline human bodies and behaviours. This queerness offers a glimpse of a sublime utopian possibility that counters the 1939 World's Fair's propagandist celebration of corporate America as the utopian future (see Franklin). By utilising the grotesque's oscillation between fascination and repulsion, Society and God Told Me To refuse, or at least cultivate ambivalence towards, the normative framework within which they otherwise operate. In this way, they 'live inside straight time and ask for, desire, and imagine another time and place', 'represent[ing] and perform[ing] a desire that is both utopian and queer' and 'participat[ing] in a hermeneutic that wishes to describe a collective futurity, a notion of futurity that functions as a historical materialist critique' (Muñoz: 26). That such films are incapable of treating such queerings of normativity as utopian rather than merely grotesque is disappointing, but 'disappointment … is part of utopia – the hangover that follows the hope' (111). The next section will explore traces of this hopeful utopian futurity, and its concomitant disappointments, in camp sf.

CAMP

Matthew Tinkcom suggest that camp occupies those moments 'when narrative fails as an explanation for how a given text is formally and aesthetically conceived', especially when 'one senses that the film image has diverged from *narrative* expectations' into a 'bad taste' visual excess (28).[14] Since 'narrative is a comparatively demanding formal structure for organizing the cinematic image', such 'divergences … always beg explanations' (29). Unlike the sublime and grotesque, camp does not demand 'wonder at the magnitude of the project's undertaking' (85) but instead reveals cracks in spectacle's totalising authoritarianism.

Camp sf movies can be divided into five broad (and overlapping) categories, and examples identified with each might also belong, in part or as a whole, to one or more of the other categories. First, there are badly made efforts that nonetheless fascinate and entertain, often because of the dissonance between aspiration and accomplishment, self-regard and ineptitude or straightfacedness and silliness, such as *Red Planet Mars* (1952), *Robot Monster* (1953), *Plan 9 from Outer Space* and *Santa Claus Conquers the Martians* (1964). Similar to more mainstream Hollywood productions, these examples indicate the limitations of a commercial production model of 'efficiency and standardization' by not 'taking the time, having the resources, having the ability' (Tinkcom: 89). Indeed, the persistent 'failure' of directors such as Ed Wood, Jr 'to succeed in conventional terms, to find a way to adjust to the boredom and alienation of everyday life, to insist on doing something else, even if it means doing it badly but in one's own peculiar style' (99) can be understood as a camp utopian critique of the heteronormative, capitalist social order – the 'determined negation of that which merely is' (Adorno and Bloch: 12).

The passage of time and different viewing contexts often amplifies such films' dissonances. This is evident, for example, in superhero movies in which Hollywood norms collide with local norms, traditions, aesthetics and production regimes: the masked wrestling matches interspersed through the Mexican *Santo en el museo de cera/Santo in the Wax Museum* (1963) and *La mujer murciélago/The Bat Woman* (1968); the narrative verve and pop cultural cannibalism of the Turkish *3 Dev Adam* (1968) and *Yilmayan seytan/The Deathless Devil* (1973), which appropriate Sherlock Homes, Captain America, Spider Man and Santo; the French opposition to American imperialism in Vietnam in *Mr Freedom* (1969); the *wuxia* martial artistry of Hong Kong's *Dung fong saam ha/The Heroic Trio* (1993); the Japanese punk weirdness of *Electric Dragon 80,000 V* (2001); the broad Filipino humour of *Volta* (2004); the song and dance sequences in the Indian *Krrish* (2006); or even the American independent style of *Special* (2006). However, this variety of camp often involves condescension, exacerbated by ignorance of the ways in which these films were produced, circulated and consumed.[15]

Second, 'naïve' camp is to be found in the film that 'does not mean to be funny' but suffers from 'a seriousness that fails' (Sontag 1994b: 282–83). There is far less consensus about this category, not least because such judgments, which can seem merely subjective, constitute overt expressions of cultural capital – of the critic's kind and degree of social power. For example, treating Mimi Leder's *Deep Impact* as camp (because of the overblown family melodrama through which its story of averting/surviving an impending asteroid impact is told) but not Michael Bay's *Armageddon* (despite its overblown mapping together of patriotism and patriarchy through the (re)constitution of families) privileges the male-authored text by denigrating the female-authored text. Failed serious sf films are typically those that are overtly political or issue oriented, which mistake sentimentality or the obvious for the profound, which clumsily fall back into formulaic material or are driven by a creative force (writer, producer, director or star) who misunderstands or diverges too far from the genre's – or narrative film's – norms and capabilities. A list of such films might include *Things To Come* (1936),

One Million B.C. (1940), *The Creation of the Humanoids* (1962), *The Mind Benders* (1963), *The Omega Man* (1971), *Slaughterhouse-Five* (1972), *Z.P.G.* (1972), *Zardoz* (1974), *Quintet* (1979), *Star Trek: The Motion Picture* (1979), *Altered States* (1980), *Dune* (1984), *Communion* (1989), *White Man's Burden* (1995), *The Island of Dr Moreau* (1996), *The Postman* (1997), *Bicentennial Man* (1999), *It's All About Love* (2003), *The Island* (2005), *The Fountain* (2006) and the *Matrix* trilogy (1999–2003).

A third kind of 'deliberate' (Sontag 1994b: 282) camp is found in those films that self consciously replay, play on and play up hackneyed conventions and formulas, whether to mock earlier films that depended upon such clichés, to reiterate earlier films' mockery of those clichés or to negotiate between what the story demands and the budget allows. Examples include *Sins of the Fleshapoids* (1965), *Batman* (1966), *The Craven Sluck* (1967), *Flesh Gordon* (1974), *Doc Savage: The Man of Bronze* (1975), *Big Meat Eater* (1982), *The Adventures of Buckaroo Banzai Across the Eighth Dimension* (1984), *The Return of Captain Invincible* (1984), *Wild Zero* (2000), *Captain Eager and the Mark of Voth* (2008) and the *Austin Powers* (1997–2002) trilogy.

A fourth 'deliberate' kind of camp is the pop camp sf movie, such as *Il Pianeta degli Uomini Spenti/Battle of the Worlds* (1961), *La decima vittima/The Tenth Victim* (1965), *Dr. Who and the Daleks* (1965), *Billion Dollar Brain* (1967), *Casino Royale* (1967), *Barbarella* (1968), *Diabolik* (1968), *The Final Programme* (1973), *Flash Gordon* (1980), *CQ* (2001) and the *Man from UNCLE* (1964–68), *Derek Flint* (1966–67), *Matt Helm* (1966–69) and *Dr Phibes* (1971–72) series.

The fifth 'deliberate' kind of camp is to be found in more or less overtly queer sf movies, such as *The Bride of Frankenstein* (1935), *Flesh for Frankenstein* (1973), *The Rocky Horror Picture Show* (1975), *Jubilee* (1978), *Poison* (1991), *Flaming Ears* (1992), *Gayniggers from Outer Space* (1992), *Orlando* (1992), *Vegas in Space* (1992), *Nowhere* (1997), *Velvet Goldmine* (1998), *The Sticky Fingers of Time* (1997), *Dakota Bound* (2001), *Hey, Happy!* (2001), *Tian bian yi duo yun/The Wayward Cloud* (2005), *Socket* (2007), *Horror in the Wind* (2008), *Post-Apocalyptic Cowgirls* (2008) and *Xingxing xiangxi xi/Star Appeal* (2008).

The distinction between naïve and deliberate camp is, however, problematic because of the homophobia and heteronormativity of the essay in which it was introduced. Susan Sontag equates camp with a 'love of the unnatural' (1994b: 275), repeatedly depicts homosexuals as mendacious narcissists and consistently downplays the role of queer individuals and communities in the development of camp tastes and practices. She is anxious that her affinity for camp might be misread as queer: she is 'strongly drawn to Camp, and almost as strongly offended by it'; her 'deep sympathy' for camp is 'modified by revulsion' (276). In this context, her insistence on naïve/pure camp's superiority over deliberate camp imposes a heteronormative conceptual framework. While the camp of the 'small urban cliques' (275) to whom she refers is self-conscious, performative, deliberate and most likely queer, she instead privileges the consumer who, overwhelmed by the mass cultural representations circulating in a media-saturated environment, responds to his or her resulting experience of 'detachment' (288) by developing ways in which to derive 'ingenious pleasures ... in the coarsest, commonest ... arts of the masses' (289). Through camp, the modern bourgeois subject 'transcends the nausea of the replica' (289). Thus Sontag celebrates Oscar Wilde because his belief 'that a door-knob could be as admirable as a painting' anticipated camp's 'democratic *esprit*' by proclaiming 'the equivalence of all objects' (289), not because his persecution outed the queerness of his camp style. By recovering camp for the straight dandy, Sontag seeks to liberate bourgeois subjects from 'the constant exercise ... of good taste' (291) in a culture of mass production. By adopting a camp posture, one can replace judgement with 'a daring and witty hedonism' and a 'mode of enjoyment, or appreciation' (291) that enables the subject to deplore commodity culture without feeling compelled to do anything about it.

Therefore, Sontag's model of camp as a (straight) mode of consumption strips it of any political function, and her indicative canon of camp not only articulates a popular intellectual's cultural capital but also serves to reinforce middlebrow tastes, as inverting her valorisation of naïve over deliberate camp demonstrates. Deliberately camp, *Flash Gordon* (1980) is constructed around the sustained, ironic enjoyment of a half-century-old, gorgeously executed but ideologically problematic comic strip. It knows such material cannot be taken seriously, but embraces the artifice this distancing offers. It is brazen about its psychedelic, sequined shallowness and the erotically charged, sensuous surfaces of its excessive, tasteless mise-en-scène. In contrast, Blade Runner is naïve/pure camp, insisting on its own seriousness through constant allusions – to William Blake, John Milton, Frank Lloyd Wright, film noir, Christ – which distract from its lazy dystopianism (darkness, rain, ethnic others, urban decay) and worn-out plot (world-weary ex-cop brought out of retirement one last time to pursue killer robots falls in love with a woman he is supposed to be investigating/killing). Such painstaking efforts simulate, but do not produce, significance; yet the simulation is so effective that many perceive Blade Runner as too good and important to be anything other than good and important. However, if the camp sensibility is alive to 'the difference … between the thing as meaning something, anything, and thing as pure artifice' (Sontag 1994b: 281), surely one must celebrate the artistry and relish with which Flash Gordon insists upon its unimportance and be amused by Blade Runner's desperation to mean something, anything, to be important, to be properly appreciated only by those with appropriate cultural capital. In contrast, Flash Gordon not only demonstrates that it knows what it is doing but also insists on the viewer knowing that it knows what it is doing. By shamelessly performing and thus foregrounding its immoderate recycling of popular culture, it democratically dissolves the distinction between the hidden 'private zany experience of the thing' and its '"straight" public sense' (281), and invites the audience in.

The purpose of such an exercise in transvaluation is not to persuade anyone of Flash Gordon's superiority to Blade Runner, but to illustrate the political limitations of Sontag's treatment of camp as a kind of consumer skill, which overlooks questions of production and erases the queer subjects responsible for much camp cultural production. Moe Meyer defines camp in opposition to Sontag as 'the strategies and tactics of queer parody' (9). For him, camp is 'political' and 'solely a queer … discourse', embodying 'a specifically queer cultural critique' (1). All 'un-queer activities' described as camp are 'appropriation[s] of queer praxis' that – because they interpret camp 'within the context of compulsory reproductive heterosexuality' – do not 'qualify' as camp (1). However, Fabio Cleto argues that by imposing a distinction between queer camp – 'the original/originary, fundamental, political and intentional parodic practice' of enacting a socially visible queer identity (16–17) – and pop camp, Meyer reiterates Sontag's naïve/deliberate binary and essentialises queer as an ahistorical, unraced, ungendered identity (i.e., the white male bourgeois homosexual). Consequently, Meyer's position reinforces heteronormative hierarchies – the very opposite of a queer politics and critique.

Tinkcom suggests that many critical–theoretical treatments of camp concern the 'pleasures unleashed in the sphere of consumption of popular culture' by objects that do not warrant such attention because the camp sensibility is often, whether it realises it or not, attuned to 'the labor of queer intellectuals who produce the camp object' (13). This claim represents a powerful utopian fantasy of reconstituting social relationships between people that have been replaced by the capitalist market place; but it also indicates the need to rethink camp in relation to the entire cycle of production, including distribution and exhibition, as well as consumption. For Tinkcom, camp is 'a form of queer labor that has shaped a way of knowing capital in its lived dimensions' (2), but also a specific case of the way 'that many members of contemporary human societies invent representational sleights of hand to signify their social presence' (5). Such prestidigitations occur because of contradictions within capitalism and the systems of social regulation that support it.

Under capitalism, one's 'social worth' is predicated upon one's labour, but to survive under heteronormativity's 'censorious regulation of sexuality' one must 'ensure one's habits of desire fail to signify' (6). Capitalist production requires diverse and specific skills of its workers, but also 'seeks to treat all labor as undifferentiable' (10) – it is indifferent to workers as full human beings, concerned only with exploiting their labour power so as to maximise the extraction of surplus value (profit). Onto these contradictions, Tinkcom maps Hannah Arendt's distinction between 'labour' and 'work': the former is 'the ongoing, repetitive, dull task of scratching out a life from the world' performed in exchange for a wage; the latter describes human creativity, which might be channelled into but always exceeds labour, and which capitalism denigrates as play, recreation or loafing (11). In work-as-play, we might discern 'a horizon imbued with potential … that lets us feel that this world is not enough', that rejects the 'here and now' and insists on the 'concrete possibility' of 'another world' (Muñoz: 1). The playful traces, and their deniability, that queer subjects inscribe in the mass cultural products on which they labour can therefore be understood as the utopian '"preappearance" in the world of another mode of being', one that is neither dominated by capital nor by its disciplinary regimes of social regulation and 'that is not yet here' (147). Such glimpses of utopia – the 'alternative visions of the modern world' to which camp devotees 'attach themselves' with unusual 'devotion' – are then taken up in other cultural productions that may not involve the labour, or work, of queer subjects but which resonate with, and perhaps amplify, the 'affectively necessary' work as play that they do involve (Tinkcom: 29, 25).

Tinkcom illustrates the distinction between 'labour' and 'work' in a film by treating the 'production of narrative' as labour and 'the extra-added exertions, say, in the excessive forms of performance, lighting, mise-en-scène' as 'work' (28). In such a film,

> the structure of the commodity remains relatively intact, but many of its outward stylistic flourishes offer a clue to the additional efforts of camp as work-as-play. In this regard camp reveals itself as a luxuriance in the inefficiencies of capital's modes of production, because despite the insistence … that capital is a wholly more streamlined way to organize human labor, within the lacunae of its modes of production, camp filmmakers find the opportunities to press the cinematic commodity into a new form of service that expresses their presence within the domain of production.
>
> (28–29)

This distinction can be traced in *The Abominable Dr Phibes* (1971). Robert Fuest, who complained that films 'are not art anymore' but mere 'product' into which 'you have to smuggle art', was presented with a script that was 'dynamite, but totally serious' as well as three times longer than needed; it was rewritten 'as a send-up' while the film was being shot (Sothcott). Dr Phibes (Vincent Price), believed dead, avenges himself on the people he holds responsible for his wife's demise, staging elaborate murders that allude to the plagues of Egypt. The 1920s mise-en-scène presents the period's art deco, art nouveau and African primitivist art and design, simultaneously signifying ideologies of progress and representing the fetishisation of signification, or style, itself. Sontag writes that 'stylization in a work of art, as distinct from style, reflects an ambivalence (affection contradicted by contempt, obsession contradicted by irony) toward the subject matter' that is 'handled by maintaining, through the rhetorical overlay that is stylization, a special distance from the subject' (1994c: 20). While the *moderne* artefacts that populate the mise-en-scène are themselves stylised in this sense, it is also imperative to note the film's own stylisation.

Fuest typically utilises an array of unusual camera angles, accentuating spatial distortion with wide-angle lenses. Transitions between scenes often involve graphic matches and associative editing but – as when he cuts from the headlights of Phibes's limousine to the bedside light of Phibes's first victim – the associative chain is not directed towards the creation of meaning: it is a flourish, expressing pleasure in 'rhyming' shapes and functions. Likewise, Fuest's use of depth of field does not construct meaning through the interplay between foreground and background but takes delight in the plays of scale enabled by the flattening of three dimensions into two. For example, when Phibes considers a pair of plucked daisies, Vulnavia (Virginia North), visible in the background through a hole in Phibes's carved chair back, plays the violin, providing diegetic mood music for her master. Soon after, Fuest offers an even more exaggerated composition, in which the left foreground is dominated by a telescope on a tripod; behind and to the right of it, the seated Phibes watches his next victim's demise through its eyepiece; Vulnavia is now playing in the left background, visible between the tripod's legs. By this juncture, such a visually extravagant statement of their relative power is utterly superfluous. A similar composition follows, with Phibes standing in the centre of the screen, behind the telescope, and Vulnavia in the background to his right. The film cuts to this shot just as Phibes spins the telescope away from his eye in triumph. As it rotates, the eyepiece rises and the lens drops so that the telescope momentarily forms a perfect top-left-to-bottom-right diagonal across the screen, briefly concealing Phibes's face from view. The telescope stops rotating just as he becomes visible once more, neatly segmenting the screen as he raises his hands to applaud his latest murder. Although the order in which these shots appear is not necessarily the order in which they were filmed, the second shot's elaboration upon – and clearer depth-of-focus than – the first creates a strong sense of filmmakers trying to outdo themselves; likewise, the precision with which motion is introduced into the third shot. While this might merely be the discipline of labour, there are two other possibilities to consider.

First, José Esteban Muñoz's treatment of queer art's utopian aspects indicates the importance of the 'gesture' as 'a cultural supplement that, in its incompleteness, promises another time and place', 'a moment when that overwhelming frame of a here and now, a spatial and temporal order that is calibrated against one, is resisted' (162). Fuest's retention of the first, least accomplished and narratively superfluous shot and his inclusion of the second shot (even though it retrospectively underscores the shortcomings of the first) emphasises the labour of production (so many pages of script to be filmed each day) and the economics that determine that less-than-ideal footage is good enough, thus 'betray[ing] the knowledge that' as a commodity the film is 'destined to become "useless"' (Tinkcom: 9). However, at the same time, the similar but more accomplished shot also suggests work-as-play, human creativity for itself, refusing to be merely good enough for the commodity system. This is reiterated by the grand flourish within – and of – the third shot. Second, Muñoz argues that virtuosity – demonstrated in the first shot until the even more virtuoso second and third shots outdo it – 'offers an escape from a systemic mandate within capitalism to labor in order to produce a product', a 'going off script' that 'debunks production-based systems of value that make work and even cultural production drudgery and alienated debasement' (178)

As well as smuggling in art through visual excess, *Dr Phibes* introduces a 'playful corporeality' (Tinkcom: 28) that mocks decorum. For example, when Inspector Trout (Peter Jeffrey) is stopped in the corridor and berated for his investigation's lack of progress, he is clearly en route to the lavatory; but rather than leaving this implicit, the scene concludes with him being forced to announce his destination. In an earlier scene, Dr Longstreet (Terry-Thomas) seizes the opportunity presented by his housekeeper's night off to watch dirty movies. With a glass of brandy in one hand and the other out of shot, hand-cranking the projector (suggesting masturbation), he watches enthralled as an exotic dancer lowers the head of a snake into her mouth. Suddenly, he stops in surprise. A reverse shot reveals his housekeeper's sensible shoes and wrinkled stockings beneath the bottom edge of his screen. Mortified, he stops the film. The next reverse shot shows her head above the screen, her body unexpectedly sexualised by the dancer's body projected in front of her torso. She chides Longstreet for his naughtiness but, to his relief, she is referring to his failure to eat the supper of 'cold brawn' she prepared for him. This playfulness around fantasy and frigidity, desire and denial, is further developed after she retires. Struggling to get the projector working properly again, Longstreet looks up to find that the screen has disappeared, replaced by the beautiful mute Vulnavia, dressed in stereotypical white Russian furs. As she advances upon him, the dancer is projected onto her torso, replacing a two-dimensional fantasy with a real woman, while reducing her to a fantasy image, combining hot and cold. She is, of course, not there to seduce Longstreet but to assist in his murder.

This accumulation of playfully excessive, self-referential and corporeal moments add a dimension of pleasure to the narrative demand for a fixed number of set-piece killings predetermined by the premise, showing work-as-play alongside the labour of production. This distinction is most pronounced in the opening ten-minute sequence. The film begins with a tilt up from a pink marble floor, past stairs to a dais, behind which a cowled figure in a black robe – it is Phibes, but he is not identified in this sequence – plays, with grandiose flourishes, an organ rising up through the floor. Cut to a shot, taken with the camera on its side alongside the organ, so vertical movement appears as horizontal movement. The next shot, from just below the level of the dais, is dominated by red Perspex fins – the organ pipes – strongly lit from behind, as they continue to rise into the room like some tacky, retrofuturistic radiator grille. A longer shot reveals dead trees on either side of the organ, populated by stuffed owls; the organ seat's plastic cover glistens. The credits play out over another three shots, culminating in a low angle shot of Phibes, the foregrounded breast, throat and beak of a stuffed bird of prey matching the curve of the tops of the organ pipes in the background. Three minutes into the film, the credits end, along with the organ music, and Phibes descends from the dais between two wing stages on which are arranged Dr Phibes Clockwork Wizards, a mechanical seven-piece band, which he mock-conducts. The screen blazes with light as a door is thrown open and a woman in a white, feather-trimmed gown and elaborate headgear appears, pauses and then descends to join Phibes (it is Vulnavia, but she too is not identified in this sequence). High-angle and low-angle shots with a wide lens, shots framed by the mechanical pianist and shots from the floor level capture their dance. Abruptly, Vulnavia moves away, leaves via the balcony – part of the consciously flattened and unconvincing creation of a theatrical space – and Phibes lowers, from nowhere, a shrouded cage down through a hole in the floor. Vulnavia, now in a translucent blouse and dark fur hat, loads the cage into a car, and climbs into the driver's seat. Phibes seats himself in the back and raises the opaque window, on which is a picture of his profile. There follows the first of Phibes's murders. He returns home, switches off the mechanical band and reseats himself at the organ, which sinks back into the floor. We have still not seen his face.

Lasting over a tenth of the film's running time, this remarkable sequence holds the viewer suspended, with no clear sense of what it all means; even the murder occurs without context, rendering it meaningless yet in some way meaningful. This denial of narrative signifies a refusal of labour-as-production in favour of work-as-play; and even though these opening ten minutes do also represent labour-as-production, they encourage the viewer to find pleasure not in narrative or star/ character but in the giddy mise-en-scène and costuming struggling, fabulously, against obvious budgetary constraints.[16] Consequently, the sequence prompts the 'astonished contemplation' that 'helps one surpass the limitations of an alienating presentness and allows one to see a different time and place' (Muñoz: 5).

While *Dr Phibes*'s witty excesses displace the viewer's focus from narrative to design-based pleasures, from labour to work, their sensuous appeal is only tangentially concerned with sexuality (although 'Over the Rainbow' accompanies the end credits). This does not however prevent the film from being camp, or indeed queer. Herbert Marcuse (1955) distinguishes between 'the pleasure principle, which represents Eros and play; the reality principle, which stands for labor; and ... the performance principle', which dominates and orders the relationship between the other two (Muñoz: 134). This distinction allows us to see moments of camp excess as fleeting refusals of the performance principle, in which the pleasure principle escapes regulation by the reality principle, and links such moments to a queerness that 'is more than just sexuality': a 'great refusal of a performance principle that allows the human to feel and know not only our work and our pleasure but also our selves and others' (135).

Flash Gordon (1980) opens up the possibility of wider sensual engagement as a source of pleasure, creating a sumptuous world in which surfaces and textures, as in Alex Raymond's comic strips, are saturated in an eroticism that extends to and flows from bodies: from silks and satins to scenes of bondage and flagellation, from Max von Sydow's magnificent Ming the Merciless and Ornella Muti's fabulous Princess Aura, from Brian Blessed's booming, bombastic King Vultan to the rich, brown dissolute voice of Jason Wyngarde's Klytus. By rejecting *Star Wars*' *faux naïve* style in favour of a pantomimic sensibility, costume designer Danilo Donati's camp taste and the queer associations of

Queen's soundtrack, *Flash Gordon*'s tone mitigates against certain budgetary constraints and the source material's colonialist imaginary. Flash's (Sam J. Jones) near-naked body is subjected to the kind of eroticising gaze normally attributed to the masculine spectator. For example, after his 'execution', he lies unconscious, clad only in glossy black hotpants. The doubled image of his body, reflected in his open coffin's mirrored lid, invites contemplation as Princess Aura (Ornella Muti) kisses him and runs her fingers over his reviving body. Reassuring him that she will not watch him change into a pilot's uniform, she turns away, only to watch his reflection as he starts to pull down his shorts. This moment, teasingly cut just as he notices Aura's covert gaze, is on the cusp between the era of sexual liberation and the era of reactionary backlash.

Richard Dyer argues that in colonial adventure narratives, the muscularly 'built body ... speaks to the need for an affirmation of the white male body without the loss of legitimacy that is always risked by its exposure' (1997: 146–47). Sam J. Jones lacks the bulky upper body of Raymond's comic-strip Flash, and is less obviously athletic than Larry 'Buster' Crabbe's movie-serial Flash; nor is he on the same scale as the bodies displayed in 1980s action cinema. He has neither Arnold Schwarzenegger's clean-edged mass nor Sylvester Stallone's work-until-you-burst bulk nor Jean-Claude Van Damme's buffed tone nor Bruce Willis's or Mel Gibson's masochistic endurance. Such hypermasculinised Hollywood male bodies typically valorise the forces of reaction, reinforcing corporate, military and commodity systems and racial, sexual and gendered hierarchies. In contrast, Jones's physique and the ways in which it is displayed for the viewer's pleasure suggest that the anxieties that they represent (about the vulnerability of Western patriarchal capitalist hegemony) are not yet dominant. For example, when Flash is brought to his knees in a duel with Prince Barin (Timothy Dalton), he blurts: 'Promise me if you kill me you'll team up with Vultan and fight Ming'. This moment situates the film among and against the narratives Dyer discusses of muscular white male bodies in colonial settings. The heroic possessor of such a body usually 'sorts out the problem of people who cannot sort things out for themselves', performing 'the role in which the Western nations liked to cast themselves in relation to their former colonies' (1997: 156). *Flash Gordon*'s hilarious overstatement of this self-serving delusion rejects the reactionary politics of the decades to come and instead embraces libidinal energy, placing Flash in the 'discothèque in the sky' (Kael 1986: 124) where he always belonged − a poly-morphously perverse, queer utopia of primary colours and painted skies, lip gloss and pillow fights, whips and black leather hotpants.

A similar queer utopianism − that moves beyond the kind of 'identity politics built around set categories' that enable 'the mainstream … to contain the threat' the queer poses to 'the "natural" order of society' (Wyatt: 25−26) − can be found in *CQ*, a film that mediates and remediates cinematic technologies and 1960s pop-camp and arthouse cinema. Paul (Jeremy Davies), an American film editor in Paris who des-perately, and with self-destructive self-absorption, wants to be Jean-Luc Godard, finds himself directing the conclusion of *Codename: Dragonfly*, a Dino De Laurentiis-style French-Italian sf movie that owes even more to *Diabolik* than it does to *Barbarella*. In this film-within-the-film, Mr E (Billy Zane) is the louche leader of a lunar revolution, dressed and accoutred as a cross between Che Guevara and Huey P. Newton. In his personal quarters, relaxed but earnest in a golden, satin Cuban military uniform, set off by a maroon-and-ochre paisley neckerchief, a beret and a comically full head of hair, he broadcasts his revolutionary credo, pausing between sentences as if he is only discovering it as, with passion, he articulates it: 'We will soon be ready to leave our lunar domes, to descend and bring change to Earth. We need to be free. To make love all day. Every day. Must be free.'

Billy Zane later appears as the actor who plays Mr E. Dressed in a white tuxedo, white ruffed shirt and brown-and-crème paisley neckerchief, he bursts in on Paul in the bathroom to discuss the film's final scene. His dandy outfit and unconcern about lavatorial etiquette − and the whining, preening boyfriend trailing round behind him − signify homosexuality. However, the fact that, in contrast to Mr E, he appears only once works to include, but not subsume, his gay identity into Mr E's utopian revolu-tion, which consequently is just that 'bit queerer, which is to say more expansive and including various structures of feeling and habits of being that the relatively restrictive categories of gay and lesbian identities are incapable of catching' (Muñoz: 115). By making queerness more than just an 'identitarian marker', CQ begins to restore camp's 'political resonance' (86).

SELF-REFLEXIVITY: INANIMATING THE ANIMATE, ANIMATING THE INANIMATE

As CQ's films-within-the-film, foregrounded intertextual allusions and archaeology of cinema movements and technologies suggest, sf's self-reflexive engagements with cinematic apparatus, culture and experience can take many forms. For example, at the climax of *Frankenstein*, windmill sails rotate like a film-reel on a projector as the scientist confronts his creation across a rotating drum, its vertical struts briefly obscuring the creature's face, which repeatedly reappears as if in a series of film frames; and in E.T.: *The Extra-terrestrial*, Elliott (Henry Thomas) stages his first encounter with the alien as if he is sitting in a cinema, the porch light behind him like a projector and the shed door through which E.T. emerges as the screen. In *The Man Who Fell to Earth* (1976), if the stranded alien Thomas Jerome Newton (David Bowie) paid more attention to the televisions with which he surrounds himself – one shows *The Third Man* (1949), 'the great cinematic tale of betrayal', and another, *Billy Budd* (1962), in which a 'young man [is] annihilated because his innate goodness is too unguarded' (Stewart: 203, 205) – he might have been more aware of his looming fate; while in *Reign of Fire* (2002), Quinn (Christian Bale) and Creedy (Gerard Butler) entertain children born after the apocalypse by re-enacting *Star Wars: The Empire Strikes Back* (1980). The tone of *Repo Men* (2010) abruptly changes during its climax to one of cartoonish, visceral violence, finally fulfilling the promise of its organ-harvesting premise; but the revelation that this denouement is part of a seamless, virtual reality experience into which the protagonist has been placed without his knowledge goes beyond alluding to the conclusions of *Brazil*

(1985) and *Minority Report* (2002) to critique contemporary blockbuster narrative norms and to question the viewer's desire for and complicity in such violent spectacle.

While all films are capable of such self-reflexivity, sf differs in two key respects. Because of its overlap with big-budget filmmaking, sf drives the development and use of new cinematic technologies; and because of its subject matter, sf frequently envisions future screen technologies. For example, *La charcuterie mécanique/The Mechanical Butcher* (1895) represents a technological marvel whose physical appearance alludes to the camera/projector and whose function suggests cinema's transformative capacities and ability to reconstitute temporality: four men load a live pig into a crate, behind which a hand-cranked wheel rotates, and then remove sausages and various cuts of pork from the other side of the crate and place them on display. Among this short film's imitators are *Making Sausages* (1897), *Fun in a Butcher Shop* (1901) and the longer, more elaborate *Dog Factory* (1904), in which a Patent Dog Transformator turns dogs into strings of sausages and vice versa. While none of these films contain any special effects, merely recording profilmic trickery, *Dog Factory* builds on the then-common audience experience of seeing films projected in reverse as they were rewound (creating such marvels as a demolished wall flying back together from a pile of rubble), thus extending its precursors' self-consciousness about cinema's potential.

In *Paris qui dort*, a scientist develops a device that places the city – possibly the entire world – into stasis, with only the Eiffel Tower's night watchman and half a dozen aeroplane passengers remaining conscious and mobile. Writing about the watchman's descent from his lofty station, Annette Michelson describes the 'constantly shifting position' of the camera that transforms the Tower into a viewfinder, 'varying angle and height and distance, making every shot and sequence of action dynamic through the powerful, changing asymmetry of its framing girders' and 'provid[ing] a range of low- and high-angle positions, a vocabulary of movement, a play of light and shadow, of solid and void, which generate visual tension, a range of kinetic responses' (39). The Tower, she argues, is thus transformed from 'décor and actor ... into a complex optical instrument, a filmic apparatus ... a camera' (39). This transformation has already been suggested. When the watchman looks over the platform's railing, the film cuts to a shot of the formal gardens at the Tower's base, which appears to represent his viewpoint until the camera's downward tilt eventually reveals him at the bottom edge of the frame, implying that the Tower itself is contemplating the scene and presenting, through the projector, 'the magnificent urban views opened up by new constructions in iron' that were previously available only to 'the workers and engineers' (Benjamin: 160) who built them. Indeed, *Paris qui dort* insists upon making the viewer see – not just Paris but the cinematic image itself, repeatedly 'play[ing] upon the relation of still to moving image' (Michelson: 43). Shots of the watchman's progress through the dormant city are intercut with freeze frames of the streets through which he passes; but one of these shots turn out not to be a freeze frame at all as, after a moment, the watchman walks through it. Similarly, when the aeroplane passengers drive into Paris, a figure sitting on the kerb, head bowed, apparently frozen in place, suddenly leaps up, revealed as the watchman. When Professor Ixe (Charles Martinelli) switches off the ray, carefully poised, motionless actors spring into action, freeze frames suddenly animate and even briefly accelerate into fast motion, increasing the city's precipitous bustle.

The nineteenth-century expansion and intensification of industrial capitalism 'reified, standardized, stabilized, and rationalized' time, transforming it from 'a medium in which the human subject is situated' into something 'externalized' (Doane: 5, 7). In 1880, for example, the desire to schedule rail travel saw London time imposed over local time throughout the UK; in 1884, the 24 international time zones were established; and in 1913, 'the first regulating time signal transmitted around the world was sent from the Eiffel Tower' (5). In the 1890s, US factories introduced time cards to record workers' arrivals and departures, and soon the principles of 'scientific management' broke down production line activities into efficient sequences of movements so as to reduce wasted time and energy and thus increase productivity (reducing workers to mere components in a system, further alienating them from their labour and its products, while maximising the extraction of surplus value). The protagonist of *Onésime horloger/Onésime Clock Maker* (1912), unwilling to wait 20 years for his inheritance, interferes with Paris's central clock so as to accelerate the passage of time. Undercranked footage projected at regular speed shows a series of remarkable scenes: pedestrians and vehicles race through Paris; department store customers try on garments at breakneck pace; workers construct a wall in seconds; newlyweds rush into the bedroom, emerging moments later with a baby that grows into an adult while being bounced on its father's knee. An intertitle claims that Onésime's intervention has made life 'more beautiful', but the accelerated footage produces a clear sense of harried Parisians subjected to the domination of an indifferent, irresistible external force.[17] *Paris qui dort* contains similar footage, the film's interplay of stasis/action or inanimation/animation similarly addressing both the the cinematic apparatus and the experience of modern temporality.

Mary Ann Doane notes:

> the pressure of time's rationalization ... , and the corresponding atomization that ruptures the sense of time as ... continuum, produce a discursive tension ... embodied or materialized in film form itself. For film is divided into isolated and static frames – 'instants' of time, in effect – which when projected produce the illusion of continuous time and movement.
>
> (9)

Some pre-cinematic experimenters used still cameras specifically to capture and observe bodies in motion, reducing the passage of time to a succession of frozen moments. Eadweard Muybridge would trigger a series of cameras in rapid succession, later displaying the consecutive images in linear strips; Étienne-Jules Marey would record multiple images on the same plate, producing a single 'chronophotograph' showing several distinct stages of a complete movement. Both methods indicate the lost intermediate moments between the recorded instants, but cinema *appears* to replicate 'time perfectly, without loss' (62). This is, of course, an illusion; film 'conceal[s] the division between frames' and cinema 'refuses to acknowledge the loss of time on which it is based' (62).

The 'bullet-time' effect introduced in *The Matrix* (1999) recalls Muybridge's and Marey's experiments. In the opening sequence, police attempt to apprehend Trinity (Carrie-Ann Moss). As one officer reaches for her, the camera seems to track around behind him at a 'normal' pace as, in slow motion, she turns, leaps into the air and hangs there, suspended, until the camera returns to an optimal position from which to admire her immaculate aerial pose and the kick she delivers to her would-be captor. Later, Neo (Keanu Reeves), confronted by one of the Matrix's agents, leans backwards from his knees, his coat streaming behind him as his torso becomes parallel with the rooftop on which he stands. The viewpoint, starting from behind his left shoulder, swirls more than 360° around the slow-motion action at a 'normal' pace, rising up to look down at him, descending to parallel his extended torso as the agent's bullets whizz past, and ending up behind his left shoulder in time to intersect a bullet's trajectory. The effect 'mixes analogue camera techniques (Muybridge style)' – 'still cameras take multiple images within a fraction of a second from several perspectives' – with 'digital interpolation and virtual camera techniques' (Røssaak: 323–24). Digital manipulation of the images works, like Marey's inclusion of multiple exposures in a single image, to erase the sense of discontinuity between sequential images. Simultaneously, though, by moving around a (more-or-less) still image, bullet-time creates the illusion of overcoming the camera's fixed perspective that can only ever capture one side of the object upon which it is focused. Unlike photography, which 'stills time', the effect shows 'the images of *frozen time* sequentially, as film', apparently spatialising time and making it available for exploration (324). Simultaneously, however, the spectacular inflation of these sequences emphasises the discontinuous stream of images upon which film is based.

Because film appears to record/project a continuous reality, it has long been compared to Zeno's Paradox: 'At any given moment, [an] arrow [in flight] occupies a space equal to its volume and simply is where it is. Therefore, at any moment it is at rest. Therefore, it is always at rest and never moves. At each point of its course, it is motionless; hence it is motionless during the entire time it is allegedly moving' (Doane: 173). More recently, Brian Massumi has used this paradox to expose the supposedly binary thinking underpinning cultural theory's tendency to imagine subjects as occupying externally determined positions – 'male versus female, black versus white, gay versus straight, and so on' (2) – on the cultural grid.[18] Understanding humans in terms of the external determinants of subjectivity renders them immobile, like the arrow in flight, but the subordination of the arrow's motion to its position obscures the fact that the arrow 'was never in any point' but 'in *passage* across them all' (6). Likewise, the subject moves through multiple, complex and contradictory positions on the cultural grid – never being, always becoming – and only subsequently can the subject be back-narrated into a determinate position. Massumi's description of this dynamic in terms of 'indeterminacy and determination, change and freeze-framing' (8) indicates the extent to which cinema inflects his understanding of subjectivity. He later describes President Reagan in similar terms as interrupting and decomposing movement, cutting

> continuity into a potentially infinite series of submovements punctuated by jerks. At each jerk, … the potential is there for the movement to veer off in another direction, to become a different movement. Each jerk suspends the continuity of the movement, just for a flash, too quick really to perceive but decisively enough to suggest a veer.
>
> (40)

Similarly, the production of each individual frame cuts into the motion of the profilmic world; contingent fractions of time are recorded, and the rest are forever lost, but the smooth projection of these frames in sequence conceals this loss. However, the use of freeze frames, altered rates of motion or static simulacra of living beings (photographs, statues, mannequins, robots, androids, replicants) reflect upon film's inanimation of the animate (when filming) and subsequent animation of the inanimate (when projecting), upon film's material substrate of still images (photograms) and lost moments brought illusorily to life, upon the potential to veer off on other trajectories and upon the nature of memory, subjectivity and affect.[19]

In *Paris qui dort*, the transition from stasis to motion 'restores the moment when the photographic image, after sixty years of existence, leaped into action' with the motion picture (Michelson: 44). In 'the sequences of arrest and release, of retard and acceleration', Michelson writes: 'we experience the shock and thrill, the terror and delight' and the intoxications of a modernity that promises 'the control of temporality itself' (44), while 'the precipitation of stasis into a choreography of frenzy, the general revival by reinscription of the temporal flow within the dozing world' also 'declare[s] the demiurgic powers of the filmmaker' (45).

A similar declaration of cinema's power to animate the inanimate occurs in *The World, the Flesh, and the Devil* (1959). African-American mining engineer Ralph Burton (Harry Belafonte) emerges from a collapsed mine to find a post-apocalyptic world devoid of animal life – not even corpses remain – and makes his way to an eerily silent Manhattan. Extreme high- and low-angle shots, long shots and extreme long shots utilise the CinemaScope widescreen to emphasise his isolation and diminution, dwarfed into insignificance by monumental architecture and a stillness that 'mock[s] animate existence' (Sobchack: 119). Alluding to *Bronenosets Potyomkin/Battleship Potemkin* (1925), the film demonstrates the power of animation while drawing attention to the photograms upon which the moving image depends. In a final effort to signal his presence to any survivors in the city, Burton tolls St Patrick's Cathedral's bells. The film cuts to five brief shots of lion statues – sleeping; waking; head raised; sitting up; standing and roaring – which creates the impression of a creature coming to life, and simultaneously fails to do so, drawing attention instead to the stillness of the individual shots. Sergei Eisenstein used a similar montage to suggest a slumbering proletariat waking into revolutionary action; Ranald MacDougall's reworking implies, intertextually, the passing of an old order and indicates, intratextually, the emptiness of the world it left behind, which nothing but cinematic trickery can bring to (the semblance) of life. This rather forlorn prognosis is underlined moments later when, in another *Bronenosets Potyomkin* allusion, a pram rolls by the doorway in which Burton shelters from a downpour.

However, between these two intertextual allusions, the audience learns that Burton is not alone. Exiting a building, he tosses a coin and lets it fall to the ground. It lies on the pavement after he walks off, the focus of attention as the shot drags on for half a dozen seconds, with nothing apparently happening. (But a tossed coin must land on one side or another, collapsing indeterminacy into a position, an outcome that determines future action. A still image – whether the photogram itself or a freeze frame or an image devoid of movement – is full of potential to veer, to become something else, to take on life and meaning, to establish the trajectory of subsequent images.) And then a woman – a white woman, Sarah Crandall (Inger Stevens) – steps into the shot. Cut to a long shot of Burton, his gait awkward, his body huddled against the cold, as he approaches crashed vehicles blocking the unpeopled street; and then the cut to the pram, folding intertextuality back into the text. It is raining because Burton is at his most despondent, but for the viewer, who knows that Burton is no longer alone, the pathetic fallacy becomes ironic. The pram's emptiness implies the possibility of perpetuating the species, of renewing the world, but for Burton it is merely a reminder of his isolation; and it also reminds the viewer of the racism of the world that had to be destroyed to make interracial union possible.

The film explores the cinematic potential for inanimation/animation in other ways. Burton returns from one of his forays for supplies with a pair of elegantly dressed, white mannequins with which to amuse himself. His interactions with 'Betty' – he flirts with her, telling her she is too good for 'Snodgrass' – and her positioning within the frame create the sense that she might suddenly come to life, while Snodgrass's more stylised features imply distance and disapproval (foreshadowing the arrival of the white Benson Thacker (Mel Ferrer), who will eventually try to kill Burton in order to win Susan). On the night Burton restores power to his street, Susan, who has still not revealed her presence, darts out of sight around a corner. Behind her, a shop window cobbler's dummy springs to life, repeatedly hammering a heel back onto a shoe. When Burton rushes into the street, his shadow precedes him into the shot, cast onto the theatre façade opposite, expanding and coming to life. Noticing his shadow, he joyfully pretends that he might catch it moving independently of him. He exits the shot but turns to face his shadow again, dancing a jig for the sheer pleasure of watching movement restored to the city. The sequence ends with a long shot of the street: in the foreground, a white woman in dark clothes stands motionless in front of a lighted window in which a dummy performs limited, repetitive actions; in the background, a black man dances with joy as street lights illuminate the night and bring the semblance of life to the theatre's screen-like façade. This image is densely packed with meaning – about race, about the cinema's flickering images, about frozen moments of time that seem to take on life and about the flash of atomic light, haunting Cold War sf, that reduced Japanese people to shadow imprints on walls.[20]

Eventually, Burton throws the supercilious Snodgrass from his apartment balcony, prompting the watching Susan to scream in horror at what she imagines is Burton's suicide; but by the time Burton gets down to the street, she has gone. The tracking camera follows him as he backs dejectedly across the sidewalk to a storefront, before which Susan stands, immobile as a mannequin, until he turns and notices her. She comes to life, flinching from his touch – a movement that establishes a narrative trajectory of growing intimacy and proximity as well as physical, social and cultural distance and separation. Her stillness and sudden motion, her step away – she closes her eyes, pleads 'don't touch me' – and her immediate pause, her refusal of outright flight, recalls the photogram, a static moment snatched from and then returned to motion, bestowed with illusory life. Simultaneously, the uncertainty of her recoil also demonstrates the relationship between embodiment and the social, between affect and emotion.[21] Inger Stevens's performance captures the inner conflict between Susan's hopes and fears, and the difficulty of transforming that complex affect into an expression, a socially readable response that draws on the repertoire of emotions and their physical expression, which somehow communicates a relative unconcern about race nonetheless shaped by a culture laden with stereotypes of violent black male sexuality. Burton, raised in the same culture, responds by maintaining careful distance between them, becoming even more static, and thus unthreatening, than her. The film charts their tentative, awkward relationship in the aftermath of the white-supremacist culture that complexly shaped their subjectivities, emphasising the disjuncture between experiencing one's self as a full human subject and being unable to escape the fact that, for other subjects, one is an object. For example, Susan's frustrated protest that she is 'free, white and twenty-one' is intended to legitimate her desire, as an adult women, for Burton; but for him, her unthinking repetition of this cliché indicates that he is neither white nor free in a world in which other survivors might be committed to restoring the pre-apocalyptic social order.

La Jetée (1962) starts with a shot of Orly airport's main pier, an emphatic diagonal receding from foreground bottom left to background top right, emphasising perspective. The rostrum zoom out momentarily creating an illusion of movement within the image despite the insistent immobility of the figures it depicts. Indeed, with one exception, the entire film is composed of photographic stills – held for varying lengths before cutting or dissolving to the next – which a voice-over connects into a narrative of love, death and time travel. A male child, who sees a man being shot on the pier, also notices the face of a woman (Hélène Chatelain) in the crowd. Years later, after the Third World War, he (Davos Hanich) is recruited as a subject for time-travel experiments because men with strong mental images of past moments seem particularly suited to temporal displacement. He repeatedly travels to the period of his childhood, where he meets and falls in love with the woman from the pier. He also travels into the future, securing a power plant that will enable human civilisation to be rebuilt. He convinces the people from his future to return him to his past, to the woman he loves. As he runs to meet her on the Orly pier, an assassin from his own time kills him in front of the child version of himself.

This photomontage emphasises two aspects of cinema: the relation between sound and image, and the photogrammatic base upon which the illusion of cinematic movement – and, here, stillness – is based. The narrator (Jean Négroni) connects the images into a narrative, with no obvious dissonance between audio and visual components, but there are also elements within the images that the narrator cannot (or does not) explain, emphasising the viewer's role in negotiating between sound and image.[22] For example, when the man and the woman look at a sequoia cross section against the rings of which historical events are mapped, the viewer is invited to recognise an allusion to Hitchcock's *Vertigo* (1958), and such recognition reconfigures several earlier shots as intertextual references to the same film: the woman's gathered-up hair recalls the distinctive coil that Judy (Kim Novak) sports when posing as Madeleine/Carlotta; the man's necklace recalls the one that betrays Judy's deception; the shots of the man and the woman in front of and reflected in a department store mirror next to a bouquet recall the shot when Scottie (James Stewart) spies on Judy in a florist; and images of stuffed birds perhaps allude to *Psycho* (1960) and *The Birds* (1963). Such allusions develop the film's treatment of time, memory and desire, transforming moments extracted from earlier films and the viewer's experience of them into memories – in the narrator's words, 'nothing tells memories from ordinary moments, only afterwards do they claim remembrance on account of their scars'. At the same time, these inter-textual resonances extract moments from *La Jetée* and transform them into memories.

This process is extended in *Twelve Monkeys* (1995), an adaptation of *La Jetée* that makes more overt Hitchock allusions when James Cole (Bruce Willis) and Kathryn Railly (Madeleine Stowe) hide out in a cinema showing *Vertigo*, *Strangers on a Train* (1951), *North by Northwest* (1959), *Psycho* and *The Birds*. Among the Hitchcock footage interpolated into *Twelve Monkeys* is *Vertigo*'s sequoia sequence, and when Kathryn returns, transformed into a blonde, to collect Cole, their embrace takes on the lighting effects and music from the scene in which Judy, transformed once more into the image of Madeleine, returns to

Scottie. It comes as both a delight and no surprise, then, to see *La Jetée*'s stuffed museum animals brought startlingly to life during *Twelve Monkeys*' conclusion, transforming the vaguely remembered giraffes of the earlier film into a concrete memory and giving them a significance that they did not previously possess.

In *La Jetée*, at the end of a three-quarters-of-a-minute sequence consisting of a dozen shots of the woman's face as she sleeps, she opens her eyes. The preceding sequence of fades between shots have, at times, come close to animating the image, suggesting the languid motion of a dreamer; but the final shot brings her both to consciousness and to life, as if the cinematic pressure towards motion has finally burst through the threshold of stasis. This celebrated moment sees an idealised Woman once more constructed as an image and as an object of the Man's gaze – entirely, as the film's *Vertigo* allusions suggest, in terms of her 'to-be-looked-at-ness' (see Mulvey). This gendering is reiterated when the pressure towards motion almost animates the man, not in passive and oblivious repose but in action, almost brought to life by the quick cuts between static shots as he runs along the pier.

Blade Runner's persistent probing of the similarities and differences among mannequins, automata, replicants and alienated humans reflects upon cinematic (in)animations. Rick Deckard (Harrison Ford) is employed by the police to 'retire' replicants – androids designed for labour in the off-world colonies – who have illegally returned to Earth seeking a 'cure' for their fixed lifespans. He uses an Esper machine to scan a photograph belonging to the replicant Leon (Brion James), enabling him to search it more thoroughly for clues. When the Esper zooms in on selected parts of the image (revealing more visual information than could possibly have been recorded on the photograph), it does so in discontinuous jumps. This flicker effect – between image detail and a bright blue screen, accompanied by a sound similar to photos being shot in rapid succession – recalls cinema's animation of photography even as it draws attention to the limitations of both in recording the entirety of a single moment and the passage of time. The Esper attempts to restore the photograph to a three-dimensional space-time, to make the absent (recorded) past present in the now and – like *The Matrix*'s bullet-time – to spatialise time, so that Deckard can prowl around in the recorded moment and, through the fortunate placement of mirrors in the photographed space, see around corners to unearth a valuable clue: right at the limits of the Esper's enhanced resolution, he discovers the face of a sleeping woman, the replicant Zhora (Joanna Cassidy).

When Deckard examines a photograph belonging to Rachel (Sean Young), who has just discovered she is not human, this image of a young girl and her mother sitting on a front porch seems to come to life as the shadows of branches swaying in a breeze momentarily play across their faces. This can be understood in relation to Méliès's response to leaves rustling in the background of *Repas de bébé/Baby's Dinner* (1895). For an audience accustomed to theatre's 'painted backdrops', the motions of 'photographed people were accepted ... as performance, as simply a new mode of self-projection; but that the inanimate should participate in self-projection was astonishing' (Vaughan: 65). However, *Blade Runner*'s animation of an inanimate photograph also reflects upon the affective relationship between memory and its prosthetic enhancements and substitutes. The photograph is a residual trace of 'a cut into the movement' (Massumi: 40) of the world, supplanting the moment itself and becoming memory by reducing the moment's totality into a legible, reproducible fragment – just as affect gets reduced to categories of emotion and the full person becomes an interpellated subject position. The animation of Rachel's photo under Deckard's gaze represents his own desire for that which is lost and which, if he is a replicant, he never had.

After a chase through crowded streets, Deckard shoots Zhora. She crashes, in slow motion, through five plate-glass windows before collapsing, dead. Artificial snow from a shop window display falls on her corpse. Just minutes before, casually changing from her exotic dancer costume to street clothes, she possessed the matter-of-fact materiality of a real person, somehow exceeding the reduction of her to a semi-naked body; but as her transparent plastic rain shawl implies, Zhora is merely a doll, an erotic image destined to stillness and death. Later, the replicant Pris

(Daryl Hannah) poses as a mannequin beneath a diaphonous shroud, concealing herself from Deckard among the dolls and automata littering the apartment of J.F. Sebastian (William Sanderson). Her deathlike inanimation prompts Deckard to get too close, and she erupts into violent, gymnastic action, crushing his neck between her thighs as if in a sexual frenzy. When he shoots her, she thrashes uncontrollably, spasming and screaming as a light source strobes through the shot. This combination of hyperbolised motion and rapid visual intermittence introduces a powerful cinematic flicker, rendering the illusory continuity of cinema's discontinuous images visible while reducing the female to an eroticised image intimately related to death.

SELF-REFLEXIVITY: SURVEILLANCE, INTERPELLATION, REIFICATION, DEATH

In Méliès's *Photographie électrique à distance / Long Distance Wireless Photography* (1908), an inventor demonstrates to a dignified elderly couple a marvellous device for transmitting images in real time. He projects an allegorical painting of three gauzily dressed women representing stars onto a screen – although the screen version shows, courtesy of a double exposure, real women posed like the painting briefly coming to life before the image fades. Next, the projected image of a young woman cavalierly disregards the posture of its source. When the elderly woman poses for the device, the screen shows a close-up of a toothless old crone's gurning face. Next, the old man's close-up takes the form of a tonsured, bewhiskered monkey head, prompting an outraged assault on the inventor's equipment. Méliès's embrace of artifice satirises the notion that by capturing the surface of the world the camera not only reveals things indiscernible to human perception but also shows the 'truth' of the world. At the same time, the satirical portraits of the elderly couple suggest artifice's ability to project truths that elude the camera's photochemical recording processes. Furthermore, in the elderly couple's response to being reproduced as images, and in the contrast between them and their images, Méliès introduces two interrelated concerns – surveillance and interpellation – that recur in sf's imaginary technologies of vision and representation. While feigning neutrality, the imaginary device reproduces the couple as objects of technoscientific observation, and as technological reproductions the portraits, however distorted, gain pseudo-objective weight.

The Invisible Ray (1936) further explores this dialectic of observation and interpretation, of surveillance and interpellation. Janos Rukh (Boris Karloff) has completed an invention that will prove correct his discredited belief that in prehistoric times 'a great meteor bearing an element even more powerful than radium struck an uncharted spot somewhere in the continent of Africa'. Rukh believes that 'everything that ever happened has left its record on nature's film, every sound since eternity began still vibrates, recorded somewhere in outer space'. In a remarkable presentation to sceptical representatives of the scientific community, he projects onto his laboratory's domed roof a viewpoint that accelerates back along a ray from the Andromeda Nebula, racing away from the Earth, past the moon, Saturn, the Orion Nebula, until it approaches Andromeda. He then halts the movement and – with a strobing effect like a zoetrope's spinning drum – turns the viewpoint back onto the Earth in order to witness the meteor impact. This fantasy of universal surveillance, that information can always – with the appropriate technology – be recovered, recurs in the film.[23]

Rukh joins an expedition in search of the meteorite, but is poisoned by the Radium X he extracts from it, causing his skin to glow in the dark and his touch to become fatal. Dr Benet (Bela Lugosi) produces a counteragent to manage these symptoms, and the obsessive Rukh remains behind in Africa. When he eventually returns to Europe, he finds his young wife, Diane (Frances Drake), in love with the explorer, Ronald Drake (Frank Lawton), and Benet fêted for his Radium X treatments. Rukh begins to murder the expedition members who have, he thinks, betrayed him. When Sir Francis Stevens (Walter Kingsford) is found dead, Benet photographs his eyes with an ultraviolet camera 'before the eye tissues glaze'. The developed plate captures the image in Sir Francis's eyes of Rukh, reaching out with his deadly touch. This pseudoscientific process derives from Dr Vernois's 1870 announcement that under microscopic observation the retinas of murder victims held 'an imprint of the victims' last sight – an image of their murderers':

> the optogramme produced a fantasy scenario of guilt involving a number of powerful condensations. The body of the victim becomes a photographic apparatus at the moment of death. For the murderer, the act of being seen collapses into the act of being identified by producing ineradicable evidence, both indexical and iconic, of his guilt. The very act of murder produces its own record. And the instant of death fixes a final, latent image as a mute testimony, one which only modern science and medical technology can bring to light, analyze, and circulate.
> (Gunning 1995: 37)

The implication of Rukh's invention that the universe records itself in recoverable forms of information is confirmed, on a more intimate scale, by Benet's optogramme.[24] The irony, of course, is that images can only record externalities, moments extracted from spatial and temporal contexts, encouraging (mis)interpretations. This is emphasised by Rukh's deranged identification of his betrayers with statues adorning a church. After each murder, he destroys a statue with a Radium X ray gun, reducing each character to a plot function in his own psychic drama, making them mere images.

Although the optogramme was never accepted as a forensic technique, photographic methods of detection were used by the police before the invention of cinema. For example, the Bertillon system photographed, sorted, codified and displayed on comparative charts numerous individual examples of physical features, such as kinds of ear, against which suspects could be compared. This made the body 'a sort of unwilled speech, an utterance whose code is in the possession of a figure of authority rather than controlled by its enunciator' (Gunning 1995: 32–34). This systematisation of somatic data brought 'order and control to the chaos of circulating bodies, tamed through the circulation of information' (32). Such methods were also deployed in the suppression of political dissent, a function extended to advanced satellite surveillance technology and facial recognition software in the *Resident Evil* franchise (2002–) and genetic sampling in *Gattaca* (1997) and *Code 46* (2003). The interweaving of state power and capitalist interests remains a feature of real-world surveillance technologies, as satirised in *Minority Report*, in which precognitive surveillance prevents murders before they are attempted and shops combine facial recognition software, credit records and purchase histories to pitch individually tailored advertisements at passersby. On the run, Anderton avoids detection by hiding out in a run-down neighbourhood where there are few cameras since incomes are so low that corporations are uninterested in tailoring adverts to the locals.

In *Looker* (1981), a film concerned with the body's dual existence as a material phenomenon and as a signifier in systems of representation, the body's 'unwilled speech' interferes with the perfection of the human form. Lisa (Terri Welles), a model for television adverts, explains to cosmetic surgeon Dr Larry Roberts (Albert Finney) that she is not beautiful: 'I have lots of defects ... my nose is 0.2 millimetres too narrow and my cheekbones are 0.4 millimetres too high and my chin has a little 0.1 bump here and my areola distance is 5 millimetres and I have a mole here on my ribs, so I need plastic surgery'. She is not the first model to approach him with such a precise list of requirements, and when they begin to die under mysterious circumstances, he uncovers Digital Matrix's lethal scheme involving new advertising technologies. Because viewers tend to fixate visually on the bodies of models in adverts rather than the products being sold, Digital Matrix created 'a group of actors with the exact specifications for visual impact' through minor surgical tweaks – before surgery, Lisa scored 92.7, after surgery 99.4, 'which is the video scan registration limit, so she's perfect'. However, the moment she started to move, her score dropped back down to 92.9. Unable to discipline their models into maximum productive efficiency, Digital Matrix opted instead for automation – scanning and mapping the actresses to create virtual models that can be inserted into advertisements with precisely controlled visual impact – and murdering the originals. Real, material bodies can no longer live up to the virtual ideal: the body in motion must be reduced to a position, or series of positions, designed to maximise the asymptotic approach to an unattainable, abstracted perfection. The female body can be reduced to its labour power and purged of the abject.[25]

In *Metropolis* (1927), the perfect knowledge required to command the city efficiently eludes Joh Fredersen, but the connection between communication and control is evident in the screen technology he utilises to communicate with foreman Grot (Heinrich George), which is 'crisscrossed with a wire mesh', exemplifying 'optical science sold out to surveillance and enforcement' (Stewart: 167) – processes linked even more overtly to capitalist industry in *Modern Times* (1936). The opening sequence shows workers subjecting themselves to a system of surveillance and control as they clock on. The factory is shot so as to emphasise the extent to which workers are dwarfed – made anonymous and thus interchangeable – by the machines they operate. Later sequences demonstrate the tyranny of Fordist methods over the body and subjectivity of the Factory Worker (Charles Chaplin) as he is forced to subordinate himself to the production line's relentless pace, eventually deranging him. In contrast to the scurrying workers, the President of the Electro Steel starts his day in the office working on a jigsaw puzzle and reading the funny pages before turning to the screen that provides him with surveillance footage of the factory floor. He uses the same technology to communicate with key workers via view screens, ordering speed ups and so on. This surveillance system extends to workers having to clock off – i.e., not be paid – when they go to the bathroom, encouraging them to further subordinate their bodies and subjectivities to the dominance of the factory system. (Later, Electro Steel experiments with a machine for feeding workers so as to eliminate lunch breaks and thus maximise the proportion of the shift spent producing surplus value.) The Factory Worker, reprimanded by the president via a viewscreen for using a toilet break to relax and smoke a cigarette, clocks back on but then dawdles back to the production line, demonstrating tactics developed within strategies of control to avoid their complete domination of the subject.

1984 (1956) opens with a demonstration of this politics of evasion. In a dystopian future London, Winston Smith (Edmond O'Brien) returns to his rundown flat with a package containing contraband – an old, blank diary in which he wishes to record his thoughts. As with all members of the dictatorial party, he has a wall-mounted surveillance device in his room, positioned adjacent to the door at head height on the wall above a dresser. Through a series of carefully planned movements, he sneaks the diary past the camera eye even as he follows a well-established, compulsory ritual of subordination: he removes his ID badge and holds it up for inspection, places it on the dresser, steps back and holds open his jacket to show that he is concealing nothing inside it, pats down his hip and breast pockets to show that they are empty, takes the papers from his briefcase and holds it up for inspection before fanning through the papers to show nothing is concealed among them. This outward display of conformity and innocence concluded, he sits down with his back to the device at the periphery of its field of vision, ostensibly to work on his papers while covertly retrieving the diary. As he writes in it, his voice-over starts, evoking the full-person who evades surveillance while simulating the obedient subject the state's panoptical vision is designed to interpellate. A similar dialectic occurs when Winston and Julia (Jan Sterling) join in with a hate-filled crowd calling for the execution of enemy prisoners while simultaneously using it as a cover to secretly arrange a forbidden assignation. After this pair of unlikely dissidents have been captured, tortured and broken, they meet again one last time and each admits to betraying the other: 'later, you tell yourself you just said it to make them stop' but 'at the time, when it happened, you meant it'.

Ironically, the freedom for which Winston and Julia crave turns out to be a nostalgic vision of 1950s consumerism and gender roles, as indicated by Julia's surprise makeover and change of costume just before they are captured. In *Colossus: The Forbin Project* (1970), in order to coordinate resistance to the megalomaniacal supercomputer, Dr Charles Forbin (Eric Braeden) persuades Dr Cleo Markham (Susan Clark) to pose as his lover so that Colossus will allow them periods of privacy in the bedroom, free from surveillance. Like the prisoners in Foucault's panopticon, they are never absolutely certain whether or not they are being observed. Furthermore, their simulation of bourgeois coupledom soon overtakes reality, and they become a bourgeois couple indistinguishable from the one they simulated. While films such as *A Clockwork Orange* (1971), *The Parallax View* (1974) and *Cypher* (2002) see individuals subjected to brainwashing and behavioural modification by overpowering, cinema-like technologies, *Looker*'s John Reston (James Coburn) identifies the everyday potency of a less spectacular screen technology as a structure of interpellation:

> Television can control public opinion more effectively than armies or secret police because television is entirely voluntary. The American government forces our children to attend school, but nobody forces them to watch TV. Americans of all ages submit to television. Television is the American ideal. Persuasion without coercion. Nobody makes us watch. Who could have predicted that a free people would voluntarily spend one fifth of their lives sitting in front of a box with pictures? Fifteen years sitting in prison is punishment. But fifteen years sitting in front of a television set is entertainment. And the average American now spends more than one and a half years of his life just watching television commercials. Fifty minutes, every day of his life, watching commercials. Now, that's power.

In order to illustrate the process by which ideology interpellates subjects, Louis Althusser conjures up the scene of a busy street in which a policeman calls out 'Hey, you there!' and 'the hailed individual ... turn[s] round', becoming in this 'one-hundred-and-eighty-degree physical conversion' the subject of the hail (163).[26] A similar scenario is played out in *Fahrenheit 451* (1966). Montag (Oskar Werner), a fireman in a dystopian future in which books are banned and his job is to burn them, returns to his suburban home to find his wife, Linda (Julie Christie), absorbed by a programme on the wall screen. When she finally tears herself away from it, she tells him that she has a part in a play to be broadcast that night. They sit together on cushions in front of the screen, and watch an extraordinarily stilted conversation between two men about seating arrangements for a large dinner party and bedroom arrangements for the guests. Charles (uncredited) turns to look out of the screen and asks, 'What do you think, Linda?', at which point a flashing red light and a beep signal that she should respond. Linda hesitates uncertainly, and just as she finally begins to formulate an answer, Charles turns back to Bernard (uncredited) and says, 'You see? Linda agrees with me'. After further discussion, Charles turns to Linda once more, and asks if he is right, to which she responds enthusiastically, 'Absolutely'. Charles turns to Linda one more time for advice, and both men approve of her strongly steered but tentatively offered suggestion, much to her delight. Hours later she is still chattering about her acting abilities, prompting the disgruntled Montag to point out that all of the 200,000 Lindas in the country, not just her, would have been invited to play the role. This extrapolation of Althusser's scenario – and its anticipation of supposedly interactive media – emphasises not merely the banality and massification of ideological hailings, but also the speed with which Linda is disciplined into, and then takes pleasure in giving, the expected responses, embracing her own conformity to a discursive hierarchy over which she has no power. It does not even matter whether she responds, whether she ignores, resists or dissents.

Le couple témoin/The Model Couple (1977) elaborates extensively on the interpellative scenario. The Ministry of the Future selects Claudine (Anémone) and Jean-Michel (André Dussollier) to represent 'typical users of the year 2000' in an experiment to determine the suitability of an urban development to its future inhabitants (and vice versa). Their new apartment is under constant surveillance and they are subject to endless and frequently absurd tests. In one scene, a female psychosociologist (Zouc) enquires: '[I]f I asked you point blank, "Are you happy?", what would you say? Very happy? Mostly happy? Happy? Mostly unhappy? Very unhappy? No opinion?' Claudine responds: 'We're mostly happy' but under pressure decides, 'maybe that's too strong. Maybe just "happy"'. Pressed further, she protests: 'It's not like we're unhappy!'

and admits 'it's not always easy', concluding: 'put "slightly unhappy" if you want'. Chided for their apparent unwillingness to cooperate, Jean-Michel insists that their answers shift because they do not know what the pyschosociologists want to hear – that is, they actively desire interpellation.

Claudine's enquiry as to why 'fairly happy' was not an option, since it best described their condition, indicates her existence as a subject who cannot be reduced to a determinate subject position; but at the same time it indicates both a willingness to comply with such inter-pellation *and* her conformity to another ideological hailing, unnoticed throughout this scene, that positions her and Jean-Michel as a couple, each of whom can also answer for his or her partner and for the couple as a whole (and thus marginalises those elements of their selves that cannot be homogenised into this larger unit of observation, measure-ment and control). The psychosociologists warn the couple that they were selected because they 'were 76 per cent average' but 'after just a few days' of tests they are 'barely 44 per cent average'; if they 'don't stay above 50 per cent', they will be thrown out of the experiment, wasting all the resources that have been spent on it and letting down their country and themselves. Jean-Michel begins to question the seriousness of the research, unaware that the psychosociologists – bored, frustrated and underpaid – are in this instance merely exercising their power because they have it. The disconcerted couple, meanwhile, have strayed so far from norms and expectations that their speech goes out of synch with their lip movements. This disjuncture, of which the couple are aware, suggests the gulf between the person and the ideological subject, between the materiality of embodied existence and the body's appearance as a signifier within representational and ideological systems.[27]

In *The Final Cut* (2004), people can be fitted with 'Zoe implants' that record everything they see and hear, but which can only be accessed posthumously. On the death of a loved one, it is customary to hire a cutter, such as Alan Hakman (Robin Williams), to comb through the recorded material and produce a 'rememory', a memorial film of treas-ured moments, or as renegade former cutter Fletcher (Jim Caviezel) puts it, to 'take people's lives [and] make lies out of them'. Children grow up unaware of whether or not they have such an implant so as not to inhibit their development, and some are transformed when they grow up and discover 'that someone would one day watch' what they did; but others, such as EYEtech corporate executive Charles Bannister (Michael St. John Smith), act with impunity because cutters are forbidden implants and cannot share recovered material. Alan stumbles upon a late-night scene in which Bannister invites his young daughter, Isabel (Genevieve Buechner), into his study, where he sexually abuses her. Intriguingly, although Alan deletes the scene, his rough cut of the rememory includes the footage of Bannister approaching Isabel in her bed, saying 'Daddy loves you so much, you know that?' and Isabel blearily responding, 'I love you, too, Dad'. However, he cuts from this to Isabel's violin recital, intending to alter the meaning of the dialogue by changing the context in which it appears, but the depiction of incest is so clichéd that one must question the effectiveness of this juxtaposition in misleading diegetic viewers.

Bannister's implant and all the footage is destroyed before the rememory can be constructed, but it is clear that guests at the rememory service would have been complicit in believing the counterfactual image of Bannister. While EYEtech typically insist on ownership of its executives' implants in order to protect corporate secrets (and, it is implied, conceal malfeasance), Bannister's widow, Jennifer (Stephanie Romanov), success- fully fought for possession of his implant so as to cover up his incestuous assaults on their daughter. While this is mostly conveyed through Jennifer's physical and social awkwardness around Isabel, when Alan questions Isabel about her memories of her father, she has obviously been coached to say: 'My daddy is the best daddy in the world. He had a really big meeting one day, but instead he took me horseback riding. He would read me stories before bed every night. Sometimes he would make it up as he went along, and I knew, but I didn't care'. These formulaic senti- ments and scenarios, designed to portray an ideal, bourgeois family, are undermined by Isabel's affectless, rote recital, the only resource she has to resist the rewriting of her memory and identity to suit her mother's purposes. The brutality of the environment in which Isabel lives is hinted at by her confused request that Alan make her 'daddy forget that [she] drew on his contract with crayon ... and ... pulled Dottie's hair so hard that she cried'.

The repressive, alienating function of the Zoe technology, subordinating human memory and history to mediatised fragmentary images edited to conform to particular narrative and ideological requirements, is perhaps best captured by Garrett Stewart's reading of a similar technology in *Zardoz*. Zed (Sean Connery), a Brutal warrior in a post-apocalyptic future, breaks into an enclave of the jaded Eternals whom he serves as an Exterminator, where he is subjected to a process by which his captors

> parasitically feed off his memories, projecting them on a giant viewing screen. That this ... reflects back on [the voyeurism of] movies ... is underscored by the nature of these involuntary projections. We see Connery's violent warlike forays against his enemies not as he would have seen them at the time, or remembered them [but] visually recast as a narrative *film*, Connery himself in the picture ... His body, his very being, is objectified as a visual scapegoat for those his cinematized recollections now entertain. By a future refinement of media technology, his own subjectivity is not only transgressed, violated, and conscripted, it is transformed and effaced ... as public spectacle.
>
> (Stewart: 194)

Whether the subject's interiority is exteriorised as a public spectacle in this way, or as a commodity text (e.g., *Strange Days* (1995), *eXistenZ* (1999)) or for therapeutic or forensic reasons (e.g., *Dreamscape* (1984), *Abre los Ojos/Open Your Eyes* (1997), *The Cell* (2000), *Eternal Sunshine of the Spotless Mind* (2004), *Papurika/Paprika* (2006)) or for the overt manipulation of the subject (e.g., *Videodrome* (1983), *Inception* (2010)), this transgression and transformation interpellates the subject into structures of domination and frequently, through processes of memorialisation, serves to reify experience and to supplant social and natural worlds, often conflating the fixity of the subject with a deathlike condition.

Bearing in mind the relationships between still photography and cinema, this is unsurprising. André Bazin describes family photographs in the language of mortality and haunting:

> Those grey or sepia shadows, phantomlike and almost undecipherable, are no longer traditional family portraits but rather the disturbing presence of lives halted at a set moment in their duration, freed from their destiny … by the power of an impassive mechanical process: for photography … embalms time, rescuing it simply from its proper corruption.
>
> (1967: 14)

In *Le Cousin Pons* (1847), Honoré de Balzac sketched out a 'Theory of Spectres', according to which

> all physical bodies are made up entirely of layers of ghostlike images, an infinite number of leaflike skins laid one on top of the other. Since Balzac believed man was incapable of making something material from an apparition, … he concluded that every time someone had his photograph taken, one of the spectral layers was removed from the body and transferred to the photograph. Repeated exposures entailed the unavoidable loss of subsequent ghostly layers, that is, the very essence of life.
>
> (Nadar 1978: 9)

The commissioned portrait of the recently deceased was a staple of nineteenth-century commercial photography (see Krauss). Noël Burch describes Thomas Edison's ambition to connect 'to his phonograph an apparatus capable of recording and reproducing pictures' as a fantasy of 'triumphing over death through an ersatz of Life itself' (7), and argues that Muybridge's and Marey's experiments descended from 'the great Frankensteinian dream of … the recreation of life, the symbolic triumph over death' (12). Marey's assistant Georges Demeny insisted that the development of moving pictures would enable people 'for a moment [to] see again the living feature of someone who had passed away', and argued that the 'future will replace the still photograph, locked in its frame, with the moving portrait, which can be given life at the turn of a wheel! The expression of the physiognomy will be preserved as the voice is by the phonograph. The latter could even be added to the phonoscope to complete the illusion ... we shall bring [the face] to life again' (Doane 62). The only two newspapers to comment on the Lumières' Cinematographe première, Le Radical and La Poste, noted, respectively, that '[s]peech has already been collected and reproduced, now life is collected and reproduced [and now] it will be possible to see one's loved ones active long after they have passed away' and that 'when everyone can photograph their dear ones, no longer in a motionless form but in their movements, their activity, their familiar gestures, with words on their lips, death will have ceased to be absolute' (Burch 21).

The Asphyx (1973) reworks histories of posthumous portraiture, memorialisation and scientific and domestic photography so as to imagine a Victorian world in which it becomes possible to see into the invisible realm where the eponymous predator resides. In 1875, widower Sir Hugo Cunningham (Robert Stephens) and two other scientific photographers involved in psychical research notice a strange black smudge on photographs of people at the moment of death, which they hypothesise is an image of 'the soul at the moment it departs the body'. Hugo, who has also invented a moving picture camera, sets out to film two actualités on a cold autumn morning. In the first, his daughter, Christina (Jane Lapotaire), and adopted son, Giles (Robert Powell), who are in love with each other, punt across a river; but the second ends in disaster, with Hugo's fiancée, Anna (Fiona Walker), and his son, Clive (Ralph Arliss), drowning. When Hugo develops the footage – 'it's the only memento I have, I must see them again, I must see them now' – it reveals something that still photography could not: the dark smudge moves towards, rather than away from, Clive. Ostensibly testing the 'widely held belief that a dead man retains the indelible image of death', Hugo also photographs Clive's face – not an optogramme, but a belated deathbed portrait, which reveals nothing.

Some time later, Hugo films a public execution so as to expose 'the whole barbarous spectacle' and to try out his new electrochemical light booster.

The circle of light it casts on the wall behind the condemned man reveals the approaching Asphyx to the gathered crowd but also, unexpectedly, stalls its approach – it cannot escape the unusual beam of light. Although Hugo refuses to release his film for public consumption,[28] this sequence visually conflates recording with projection: Hugo films the image of the Asphyx captured in the beam that simultaneously appears to the crowd as a marvellous, technologically produced play of light and shadow.

Hugo designs a trap for the Asphyx, and begins to dream of immortality, rhapsodising about preserving – in the face of relentless change – what he perceives as benign feudal governance through personally 'govern[ing] the course of events perpetually'. Robbed of succession by Clive's death, he wishes to freeze time, while producing the illusion of change. He electrocutes himself, but captures his Asphyx in the instant before he should die. He insists that, if the sceptical Giles and Christina want to marry, they must join him in immortality. As if to mock the notions of reform and progress associated with Hugo, the means by which they are brought to the moment of death (the guillotine, gassing) were, like electrocution, intended to make executions more humane; and in both cases they prove fatal – Christina is decapitated and the remorseful Giles blows himself up. A century later, Hugo still wanders the Earth, a beggar hoping to expunge his guilt.

Minority Report also articulates this relationship between image technologies, memorialisation and emotional impasse, presenting the viewer with a hyperbolic visual field in which advanced screen technologies generate kaleidoscopic perception of 'delirium, kinesis, and immersion' (Bukatman 2003b: 114). These dizzying experiences are part of the attempt to conquer the sublime unknowability of the future. The pre-cognitive Pre-Crime technology – which utilises three 'precogs', children born to drug-abusing parents, who can predict murders – works to contain vast, unknowable possibilities, to give the illusion of control, while insisting contradictorily on both determinism and autonomy: these murders will happen and can be prevented. Similarly, individually tailored advertisements constantly situate and resituate individuals as consumer nodes in the relentlessly present moment of networked information: futures are reduced to consumer choices, collapsed backwards in time into one's past, even as the individual's past, reduced to his or her consumer record, is projected forward into the moment, the *now*.

Anderton himself is stuck in the eternal present of unresolved trauma over the abduction/murder of his son, Sean (Dominic Scott Kay), six years earlier, just before Pre-Crime was established.[29] He obsessively replays clips of his wife, Lara (Kathryn Morris), and son, in which the human figures holographically extend out from a flat wall screen. Constantly, tentatively on the verge of reaching out to touch the images as if they were the people themselves, he even joins in with the dialogue, anticipating or repeating his own recorded speech. Sean's murder mirrors that of the mother of one of the precogs by the designer of Pre-Crime, Lamar Burgess (Max von Sydow), because he needed her daughter to make the system work. It is only when Anderton presides over the death of his symbolic father, Lamar, that he is able – in a bizarre coda – to reunite with and impregnate the estranged Lara.

However, this conclusion is so overblown that it raises the possibility of reading it very differently. When Anderton is arrested, he is incarcerated in suspended animation, where 'they say you have visions, that your life flashes before your eyes, that all your dreams come true'. The film then cuts from the unconscious Anderton, lit only by the blue–white circlet attached to his head, to a final act in which Lara, realising Lamar framed Anderton, busts him out of containment so he can confront Lamar and bring down Pre-Crime. It is only after Anderton, unable to move on with his life, has his animation suspended that he can once more become animate, overcome his trauma, complete his stalled Oedipal trajectory and reproduce himself. Or none of these things happen, and he remains suspended, inanimate but dreaming of animation.

CONCLUSION

Returning to sf studies debates about cognition vs. spectacle and film theory debates about narrative vs. spectacle, this chapter sought to move beyond these false binaries. It argued that just as cinematic narrative and spectacle are inextricably interwoven, so too are cognition and spectacle, reason and affect. It situated sf in relation to the cinema of attractions that emerged with the expansion of capitalist modernity, and mapped out three kinds of sf spectacle (sublime, grotesque, camp) that hint at transformative utopian possibilities. It closed by considering the ways in which sf cinema frequently thinks about technologies of representation, especially cinema, through its own particular fascination with imagining the future of such technologies. The next chapter will return to questions about the politics of sf cinema, focusing on the ways in which it reproduces colonial ideology, negotiated the transition to contemporary forms of neo-colonialism and now articulates the structure and experience of neo-liberal globalisation.

3

SF, COLONIALISM AND GLOBALISATION

G.O.R.A. (2004) opens with a steadicam viewpoint prowling a spaceship's neon-bright corridors as Commander Logar (Cem Yilmaz) sweeps onto the bridge. A crewman announces: 'System is fucking activated, sir'. The crew busy themselves at their consoles, but their muted dialogue slips from procedural matters to ice-skating scores, URLs and cabin crew announcements, liberally interspersed with profanities. Kuna (Safak Sezer) approaches Logar and says: 'Komutan Logar. Ingilizce konuşuyorlar. Bir biştan hepsini Türkçe alabilir miyiz efendim? Baştan.' Logar swivels around in his throne-like chair to face the camera: 'Aliriz'. This exchange – 'Commander Logar, they're speaking English. Can we have it in Turkish from the start?', 'Sure thing!' – introduces G.O.R.A.'s concern with language and culture in the era of globalised media flows. Later, conman Arif Işik (Cem Yilmaz), abducted by these aliens, is disconcerted to find that all the aliens, robots and abductees speak Turkish rather than, as movies have led him to expect, English.

However, while the language of G.O.R.A. is predominantly Turkish, the story it tells derives from a tradition of Western European and American colonial fiction, extending from H. Rider Haggard's *She* (1887) to *Avatar* (2009). Villainous Commander Logar wishes to marry the unwilling Princess Ceku (Özge Özberk) so as to become king. He destroys the instruction manual for 'the sacred stones', Gora's planetary defence system, and arranges for a fireball to hit the planet, intending to step forward at the last moment with his newly invented 'hyperoptic vascular freezer' to avert fiery destruction. When the device fails, Arif intervenes, activating the sacred stones, thus saving Gora and winning Ceku's love. He knows how to do so because – like *G.O.R.A.*'s self-consciously plagiarising makers – he has seen *Le cinquième élément* (1997), a film that also embodies complex negotiations among national cinemas and colonial histories: between US blockbusters (a French film, shot on British soundstages, in English, starring Bruce Willis and Chris Tucker, and using New York effects and post-production houses), European pop culture (Moebius comics, Jean-Paul Gaultier designs, Donizetti's *Lucia di Lamermoor*), French multiculturalism (including North and West African elements but with problematic depictions of Afrodiasporic peoples), French colonial history (shooting in Mauritania, previously part of French West Africa) and white, patriarchal hierarchies. Such transnational cultural and economic exchanges might indicate that the US 'is no longer the puppeteer of a world system of images but ... only one node of a complex transnational construction of imaginary landscapes' (Appadurai: 31), but they also demonstrate the perpetuation of (colonial) asymmetries within the globalised media economy.

David Held and Anthony McGrew describe two broad tendencies within globalisation debates: the globalists, 'who consider that contemporary globalization is a real and significant historical development',[1] and the sceptics, 'who conceive it as a primarily ideological or mythical construction which has marginal explanatory value' (2). Fredric Jameson, who identifies four tendencies within globalisation debates (1998: 54), suggests that these issues are complicated by some theorists conceptualising globalisation as a communicational concept and others as an economic concept. The former emphasise the 'denser and more extensive communicational networks' girdling the world (55) – but, Jameson adds, when

> we attempt to think this new, still purely communicational concept, we
> begin to fill in the empty signifier with visions of financial transfers and

investment all over the world, and the new networks begin to swell with the commerce of some new and allegedly flexible capitalism.

(56)

That is, like a Möbius strip, the communicational concept flips over into the economic concept. Focusing on communicational aspects of global networks elicits 'a postmodern celebration of difference and differentiation' as 'a kind of immense cultural pluralism' produces new cultures, groups and identities (56–57); while focusing on the economic aspects reveals 'standardization on an unparalleled new scale', the 'rapid assimilation of hitherto autonomous national markets and productive zones into a single sphere, the disappearance of national subsistence [and] the forced integration of countries all over the globe into' the 'global division of labor' (57).

However, these two contrasting visions of globalisation are not 'logically incompatible' (57). For example, Arjun Appadurai outlines a process in which 'local political and cultural economies' absorb globally homogenising forces – including language, advertising, fashion and weapons – and transform them into 'elements of a heterogeneous local identity' that, as 'commodities of difference', re-enter homogenising global circuits (42). Ulrich Beck likewise points to the 'multiplicity of combinations' and 'motley collections' generated by global/local interactions, with the 'local self-differentiation industry ... becoming one of the (globally determined) hallmarks' of the contemporary world (54).

This chapter examines sf's reproduction of colonialist ideology, from the pre-First World War height of Western imperialism through the mid-century collapse of European empires and on into the twenty-first century. In light of the transition from colonialism to Empire (see Hardt and Negri),[2] it considers the 'post-imperial' melancholy of postwar British sf and Vietnam-era US sf's attempt to articulate anti-imperialism through the domestic politics of race. It concludes by exploring neo-liberalism's reconfigurations of time, space and labour as figured in sf since the 1980s.

SF, CINEMA AND THE COLONIAL IMAGINATION

Although European imperialism and colonialism can be traced back half a millennium, it reached it heights between 1870 and 1914,[3] concurrent with the emergence of cinema and of sf. Consequently, both are structured by and implicated in imperialist and colonialist practices and discourses, albeit often in complex, contradictory ways. As a technology, cinema contributed to the (profoundly ideological) narrative of Western civilisation and progress; and as a cultural practice, it reproduced and circulated such notions 'through biographical narratives about explorers, inventors, and scientists' and by charting 'a map of the world like the cartographer', chronicling 'events like the historian', unearthing 'the distant past like the archeologist' and anatomising 'the customs of "exotic" peoples like the anthropologist' (Shohat and Stam 92–93). Mediating between 'the Western spectator and … the cultures represented on the screen', cinema implied an objective perspective on the world (93); but, as Frantz Fanon observes, 'objectivity is always directed against' the native (1967: 61), normalising and reinforcing the power relationships of Western imperialism. Cinema not only reiterated racist structures of representation, but also played a role in the West's material domination of (and through) global communications infrastructures. It was central to the late-nineteenth-century commodity racism of mass-produced consumer spectacles, such as advertising, photography, department stores, museums and expositions (see McClintock), which enlarged 'the imaginative landscape of significant numbers in the imperial homeland, … instilling suppositions about the colonized's unwholesome nature and proclivities' while 'forming or confirming' the viewer's 'elevated self-image' (Parry 113). Cinema's contribution to the development of 'a national and imperial sense of belonging among many disparate people' extended to colonial elites, encouraging them to identify with the empire and 'against other colonized people' (Shohat and Stam 102–3).

Nineteenth-century fictions of empire were 'culturally constrained and ideologically inflected fabrications that were overwhelmingly received in the imperial homeland as authentic renderings of both distant geographical locations and social forms, and of the colonizer's deportment' (Parry 107). Sf emerged in 'precisely those [nations] that attempted to expand beyond their national borders in imperialist projects: Britain, France, Germany, Soviet Russia, Japan, and the US' (Csicsery-Ronay 2003: 231), where it 'articulate[d] the distribution of knowledge and power at a certain moment of colonialism's history' (Rieder: 3). Perhaps 10 per cent of all sf written before 1930 was lost-race fiction (35),[4] such as *She* (1887) and Pierre Benoît's *L'Atlantide* (1919), both of which have been filmed multiple times.[5]

Emulating the novel's nested narrative, *L'Atlantide/Queen of Atlantis* (1921) begins with a desert expedition, headed by Captain Aymard (Genico Missirio), in search of the lost expedition of Captain Morhange (Jean Angelo) and Lieutenant de Saint-Avit (Georges Melchior). Aymard finds Saint-Avit near death, and returns him to Timbuktu, where, delirious, he apparently confesses to murdering Morhange. Convalescing in Paris, Saint-Avit becomes nostalgic for 'magic horizons' and the 'mysterious attractions of wide open spaces'. He returns to the desert to take command of a remote outpost, where he recounts the story of the expedition to Lieutenant Ferrières (René Lorsay). He and Morhange were guided by Bou-Djema (Mohamed Ben Noui), who tells them about an earlier expedition, led by Lieutenant Massard (André Roanne), which was massacred by Tuargi nomads led by Cegheir ben Cheikh (Abd-ed-Kader Ben Ali). Morhange finds an inscription in a mountain cave, which is the furthest south that evidence of classical Greek civilisation has ever been located. They revive a Targui tribesman left to die by robbers, who tells Morhange of other similar inscriptions. However, the stranger is actually Cegheir ben Cheikh, who murders Bou-Djema and abducts Saint-Avit and Morhange to an ancient city hidden deep in the mountains. Ruled by Queen Antinea (Stacia Napierkowska), it is the last remnant of Atlantis (the Sahara, it transpires, is the seabed of the ocean that nine thousand years ago engulfed the continent and then receded).[6] Antinea has a taste for white male travellers, whom she seduces into an obsession with her, then spurns, driving them to suicide, after which she has their bodies galvanised in gold and preserved as statues. After

Massard's suicide, she turns her attention to Morhange, but sustained by his Catholic faith and homosocial loyalty to Saint-Avit, he refuses her advances. Saint-Avit, however, is driven mad by jealous desire. Antinea, unused to rejection, falls in love with Morhange. Enraged by her failure to prompt reciprocal feelings in him, she seduces Saint-Avit, drugs him and persuades him to kill his friend. Horrified by his crime, Saint-Avit escapes into the desert, aided by Antinea's maid, Tanit-Zerga (Marie-Louise Iribe), herself an abducted Mandinka princess. She dies before Aymard's expedition stumbles upon and saves Saint-Avit. Back in the present, Saint-Avit, haunted by the memory of Antinea and accompanied by the fatally intrigued Ferrières, sets out in search of Atlantis, 'intoxicated with the sacred attraction of mystery, in a state of ecstasy that the certainty of not coming back made sharper and greater'.

L'Atlantide projects repressed sexual desires and anxieties about racial degeneration onto Africa, casting European characters adrift in a vast landscape apparently devoid of life and meaning, dwarfing them beneath an equally overpowering sky that mirrors and extends this emptiness. The camera's proprietorial gaze can find nothing to fasten upon, other than human figures diminished by the sheer fact of the desert's borderless and objectless scale.[7] Imperialist narratives – dreading a 'catastrophic boundary loss … associated with fears of impotence and infantilization' but in thrall to 'boundary order and fantasies of unlimited power' (McClintock: 26) – typically compensate for this sense of void by feminising the landscape. *L'Atlantide* does this in various ways. It depicts military outposts as homosocial enclaves fortified against the feminine desert's uncertain drift and perilous flow. In Paris, whether seated near the Eiffel Tower or crossing a busy intersection, Saint-Avit's thoughts return incessantly to the colonised space, figured in terms of peace and solitude; but in a nightclub, surrounded by indecorous women who are as intoxicated by a black jazz drummer's frenzied playing as by the alcohol they guzzle, his thoughts turn to an exotic woman commanding a harem-like setting, whose heavily veiled figure suggests a restraint lacking in Parisiennes, but also promises, when unveiled, the erotic paroxysms betokened by the drummer.[8] Saint-Avit's terror of infantilisation and impotence is mapped onto his desire for Antinea and his sexual jealousy of Morhange, his superior in rank and restraint, setting the scene for oedipal catastrophe. The framing narrative suspends Saint-Avit and Ferrières for much of the film, emasculated before the intoxicating allure of empty spaces to be penetrated and veiled female interiors to be exposed. When they finally embrace their fate as Antinea's playthings, knowing that Ferrières will replace Saint-Avit, thus ensuring a fresh iteration of this seemingly eternal cycle, her face is superimposed onto the sky above the desert.

L'Atlantide also reproduces the ideological association of French imperialism with a 'scientific' mission to map, catalogue and understand, as well as civilise, the world. Morhange not only finds the inscription and recognises its significance, but presses on, exploring further, hoping to find further evidence that will 'justify' a European presence in Africa. Antinea's comparison of herself to Cleopatra and her possession of the only complete copy of Plato's *Critias* reproduce 'the popular fantasy of Haggard's time that the Egyptian civilization, the cradle of humanity, was not truly African' (McClintock: 244), bringing the distant 'territory' into the legitimate space of empire while transforming violent imperial conquest 'into a much longer, slower process, obviously more acceptable to the European sensibility ... than the shattering experience' would have been to those who suffered it (Said: 38).

Colonialism typically 'distorts, disfigures and destroys' the 'past of the oppressed people' (Fanon 1967: 169). Locating Atlantis deep in the Sahara helps to construe human history as Eurocentric – as if other 'regions of the world have no life, history, or culture to speak of, no independence or integrity worth representing without the West' (Said: xxi) – and temporally extends it beyond classical Rome and Greece while remaining unequivocally not Arab, African or Asian. By proposing an even more ancient white Atlantis, a fragment of which survived an unparalleled catastrophe, *L'Atlantide* maintains this Eurocentric prejudice even as it reworks the conflict between barbarism and civilisation as a gendered conflict between female monarch and representatives of republican colonialism (although she triumphs over certain individual, male colonisers, they are depicted as reverting from a higher pinnacle of civilisation). Decorating Antinea's palace with Classical and post-Renaissance artefacts, while admitting only unauthored traces of African styles, further implies that Arabs and Africans 'are just there', lacking any 'accumulating art or history that is sedimented in works' (232). Consequently, *L'Atlantide* reproduces a racial hierarchy that, conflated with the notion of historical progress culminating in white Europe, treats non-European spaces and peoples as being mired in a primitive past from which they can only be raised by European colonialism.[9]

L'Atlantide makes its hierarchisation of cultures explicit by evoking comparisons with the Islamic Songhai Empire, which controlled much of West Africa in the fifteenth and sixteenth centuries.[10] When Tanit-Zerga speaks of her origins and status among the Mandinka people, there is nothing to suggest the extent of the Songhai Empire.[11] Although she was born in the 'tallest' house in Gao, her flashback is to life in the ruins of an ancient city, where a sorcerer prophesies that 'one distant day' she will 'see Gao shining ... the splendid Gao of the past, with the mosque with the five cupolas'; later, fleeing through the desert, she hallucinates such a vision in the moments before her death. Thus African civilisation is consigned to the past, and any dream of its independent recovery reduced to a mirage, as *L'Atlantide* sutures African history into a narrative of world history whose purpose and goal is Western civilisation. The contrast between marginal, derelict Gao and Timbuktu, partially restored and modernised by the French, reinforces the notion that 'the better part of history in colonial territories was a function of the imperial intervention', while Saint-Avit's *aberrant* flight back to the desert reflects the 'equally obstinate assumption that colonial undertakings were marginal and perhaps even eccentric to the central activities of the great metropolitan cultures' (Said: 40). This imaginary relationship between the colonising power and the colonised people and land occludes the violent realities of empire.

Saint-Avit's adventures rework colonialist fiction's depiction of 'the journey into the interior ... as a journey forward in space but backward in time': 'as the men progress, they enter the dangerous zones of racial degeneration' (McClintock: 242). Such treks combine two opposed notions – 'the progress forward of humanity from slouching deprivation to erect, enlightened reason' and 'regression backward … from white male adulthood to primordial, black degeneracy usually incarnated in women' (9–10) – that are still evident in contemporary sf, such as *Predator* (1987), *Lost in Space* (1998), *District 9* (2009) and *Pandorum* (2009). The next section will focus on the ways in which this contradiction was played out as twentieth-century anti-colonial revolutions brought Western empires to an end.

SF'S COLONIAL IMAGINARY

Fanon wrote that '[i]t has been said that the Negro is the link between monkey and man – meaning, of course, white man' (1986: 30). Such an exclusion from humanity props up white, male identity by reducing peoples of colour to a buffer zone between (white, male) humanity and animals; but this buffer also connects (white, male) humanity to animals and pre-human ancestors *and* surrounds (white, male) humanity with terrifying, abject, interstitial monsters that too closely resemble, while being different from, (white, male) humanity (see Berenstein: 160–97). Imperialism also tended to conflate race with gender and class, treating peoples of colour, women and the working class as degenerate, as children or primitives lagging behind mature, civilised, middle-class white men, and subjecting them 'to increasingly vigilant and violent policing' (McClintock: 44).

In *Himmelskibet*, Avanti Planetaros (Gunnar Tolnæs), who sees himself as a new Columbus, captains the first interplanetary expedition, an endeavour closely associated with modern, internationalist science. These colonial adventurers discover a Martian utopia that combines elements familiar from nineteenth-century lost-race fiction: pseudo-classical architecture, costume and customs; divine ancient wisdom; telepathy; social, psychological and physiological engineering; a scattering of superscience technologies; and a beautiful, natural environment. The emphasis, however, is not on socio-economic structures but on the chaste spirituality of the stately, graceful Martians. Marya (Lilly Jacobson), the daughter of the Martian Wise Man (Philip Bech), falls in love with Avanti, and returns with him to Earth so as to propagate her father's 'message of enlightenment'. Avanti's father welcomes her with the words: 'In you I greet the new generation – the flower of a superior civilization, the seed of which shall be replanted in our earth, so that the ideals of love may grow strong and rich', asserting patriarchal hierarchy by reducing this 'superior' woman to a literal and symbolic womb.

Just Imagine combines a vision of a magnificent future metropolis with a colonial expedition to Mars.[12] In its version of 1980, Prohibition is still in effect and the state arranges marriages. To prove himself more worthy than MT-3 (Kenneth Thompson) of marrying LN-18 (Maureen O'Sullivan), J-21 (John Garrick) undertakes the hazardous journey to Mars, where – in a colonialist fantasy of plenty and simplicity – the population, divided between good and evil twins, primarily consists of scantily clad chorus girls, promising a libidinous fulfilment denied by the rational, terrestrial city. The expedition returns to Earth in time to persuade the judge presiding over J-21's appeal to decide in his favour but, while he and LN-18 are in love, they are far too staid to betoken the introduction of utopian libidinal excess into this priggish dystopia. However, Single O (El Brendel), has brought back the evil Martian Boko (Ivan Linow), who he controls by squeezing his earlobe. The very queerness of this relationship disrupts the social stabilisation of desire figured by heterosexual marriage.

20,000 Leagues under the Sea (1916), which incorporates elements from Verne's 1870 novel and its sequel, *The Mysterious Island* (1875), introduces an intriguing boundary figure in the dark but innocent Child of Nature (Jane Gail). She is discovered by Union soldiers who are marooned on a remote island after escaping in a balloon from a Confederate prison. Coalescing around her are contradictory colonialist discourses in which nature, depicted as both 'virginal and libidinal', mirrors 'the madonna/whore dichotomy' (Shohat and Stam: 143), in which the land is imagined as a 'female to be saved from her environ/mental disorder' and women as being in need of salvation 'from dark men' who would rape them (156), and in which women, along with animals and colonised people, must be rescued from 'their putatively "natural" yet, ironically, "unreasonable" state of "savagery"', to be domesticated and inducted 'into a hierarchical relationship to white men' (McClintock: 35). The Child of Nature is introduced – in a state of nature, but clothed – innocently frolicking among the tropical flora and fauna. A tail dangles behind her, momentarily blurring her status (human or animal?), but it is only part of the animal skin she wears. Cyrus Harding (Howard Crampton) persuades her to exchange this costume for Western clothes. She demonstrates a 'natural' modesty about removing her clothes, confirming the rightness of her elevation to child of civilisation; but this transformation is simultaneously troubled by her masculine costume and by the belt that hangs behind her like a tail. One of the soldiers attempts to rape her: being white and male, he presumes a right to possess and ravage the dark female; but he is, simultaneously, a dark, subhuman proletarian, his bestial nature aroused by her natural purity.

Captain Nemo (Allen Holubar), whose submarine has been disrupting imperial commerce, eventually reveals that he used to be Daaker, an Indian prince, governing his kingdom with the consent of Western imperial powers. Charles Denver, a white trader who coveted Daaker's wife, took advantage of native discontent to accuse the Prince of inciting rebellion. The Prince's imprisonment triggered an uprising, resulting in a bloody massacre of natives and colonial forces. Amid the chaos, the drunken Denver attempted to rape and accidentally killed the Princess, and abducted the only witness, the Prince's young daughter. As his 'native land' turns into 'a place of death and destruction', Daaker fled and, transformed into Nemo, avenges himself on the colonial powers' shipping while seeking any trace of his lost daughter – who is, of course, the Child of Nature. This royal heritage from a 'high civilisation' paradoxically reinforces her 'natural' aristocracy, while diffusing anxieties about the potential romance between her and a white officer. Significantly, he does not belong to the Western powers occupying her birthplace, but serves in a war purportedly concerned with ending

American slavery, thus occluding the imperialist role of US forces.[13] This chaste romance suggests a rough equivalence between the elites of an ancient monarchy and a democratic republic, an apparent egalitarianism that merely reinforces race, class and gender hierarchies as a white male officer 'civilises' a dark woman.

In *She* (1925), Leo Vincey (Carlyle Blackwell) sets out in search of the ancient African city where, family legend says, his ancestor Kallikrates was murdered 2,000 years ago by Queen Ayesha (Betty Blythe), whose love he spurned. The seemingly immortal Ayesha recognises Vincey as a reincarnation of Kallikrates. He refuses to renounce his beautiful native wife, Ustane (Mary Odette, in blackface),[14] and although Ayesha's ire ostensibly results from her millennia-long wait for Kallikrates's return, it is tinged with outraged disbelief at Vincey choosing loyalty to an African wife over marriage to a white queen. However, Ayesha soon seduces him. Her irresistible allure is figured through a series of titillating veilings/unveilings. When Vincey's companion, Holly (Heinrich George), asks to see her unveiled, she turns to him to raise her veil, revealing to the viewer her naked back, which he will barely glimpse as she steps through a curtained exit. Later, seeking her help, he parts the curtains to the chamber in which she, in a transparent blouse, watches over Kallikrates's preserved corpse. Finally, in order to entice Vincey into the flame that will make him immortal, she drops her gown, covering her naked torso with her long, unbound hair. Throughout, the presentation of Ayesha recalls the tradition of veiled women in orientalist art who tend to 'expose more flesh than they conceal', a denuding that allegorises 'the availability of Eastern land for Western penetrating knowledge and possession' (Shohat and Stam: 149).

She (1935), made under the Production Code that specifically forbade representations of 'miscegenation', relocates the lost kingdom to a temperate Arctic valley, reinforcing the insistent whiteness of imperious Ayesha (Helen Gahagan). Ustane is replaced with Tanya Dugmore (Helen Mack) – plucky, self-effacing, convent-raised and white – so as to keep Vincey (Randolph Scott) from any racially undesirable contact. Consequently, the eroticism essential to the narrative diffuses into the mise-en-scène, overwhelming these denials of miscegenation with sensuous excess. In both versions, Vincey is unable to resist the exotic, interstitial, white/not-white queen, and he is only saved from regression into primitive degeneracy by the fatal error to which her sexual desires drive her.

The doubling of female characters – chaste white/erotically dark – was played out more overtly in US sf before the Production Code was enforced. In *Island of Lost Souls*, Edward Parker finds himself the subject of an experiment by Dr Moreau, an autocratic, queer sadist who wishes to discover whether one of his surgically transformed beast-people can breed with a human. Parker is almost seduced by the childlike, light-skinned-but-dark panther woman, Lota, but is repulsed by her claw-like fingernails; later, Moreau decides to mate Parker's fiancée, Ruth Thomas, with one of his more bestial creations instead. In *The Mask of Fu Manchu* (1932), Fah Lo See (Myrna Loy) yelps with sexual arousal at the flogging of Terence Granville (Charles Starret). Subsequently drugged into zombie-like submission, he is only saved from sexual enslavement when his fiancée, Sheila Barton (Karen Morley), breaks through his mental haze by reminding him of their love for each other. Fu Manchu (Boris Karloff), wielding relics recovered from Genghis Khan's tomb in an attempt to incite a pan-Asian uprising against the 'accursed white race', displays Sheila to his followers, saying: 'Would you all have maidens like this for your wives? Then conquer and breed. Kill the white man and take his women'. Even under the Production Code, this doubling continued to operate, giving access to and denying libidinal energies, and reinforcing racial divisions that simultaneously tended to break down. In *Flash Gordon* (1936), Princess Aura (Priscilla Lawson), the dark-haired daughter of the orientalised Ming the Merciless (Charles Middleton), desires Flash (Larry 'Buster' Crabbe) on sight, attempts to seduce him and to despatch his true love, the pale, blonde Dale Arden (Jean Rogers). The overtly sexual(ised) Aura's petulance, impulsiveness, and childish cruelty seems to unlock the wholesome Dale's more 'primitive' sexual nature: her costumes soon become skimpier, and she becomes prone to bouts of sexually-charged asphyxiation. Moreover, the threats of violent torment Dale faces undermine her white purity by emphasising her sexuality.

As the age of empires drew to a close, sf became 'driven by a desire for the imaginary transformation of imperialism into Empire', into 'a technological regime that affects and ensures the global control system of de-nationalized communication' (Csicsery-Ronay 2003: 232). In *Things to Come*, war between rival European empires breaks out: tanks race across battlefields, vast aerial fleets bomb cities flat, poison gas fills the air. After 15 years, the elaborate technologies of ultramodern warfare have broken down; ragtag bands of poorly armed men in tattered clothing scurry between trenches. After 25 years of relentless attrition, a plague sweeps the globe. Humanity, scrabbling among the ruins, apparently has no future. But from Basra, Wings Over the World – an organisation of engineers and mechanics, a 'brotherhood of efficiency', a 'freemasonry of science', the 'last trustees of civilisation' – govern the Mediterranean and aim to bring 'common sense', 'law and sanity' and 'order and trade' to a unified world. John Cabal (Raymond Massey) outlines the plan for 'a new world' without 'independent sovereign nations', 'flags' or 'folly': 'we set ourselves to an active and aggressive peace, … we direct our energies to tear out the wealth of this planet and exploit all these giant possibilities of science that have been squandered hitherto on war and senseless competition'. This vision fulfils the characteristics of Empire described by Michael Hardt and Antonio Negri – it 'effectively encompasses the spatial totality' of the world; it 'presents itself not as a historical regime originating in conquest, but … as an order that effectively suspends history and thereby fixes the existing state of affairs for eternity'; it 'operates on all registers of the social order extending down to the depths of the social world'; and 'is continually bathed in blood' but 'is always dedicated to peace – a perpetual and universal peace outside of history' (xiv–xv). Simultaneously, the film's mise-en-scène of monumental architecture and uniformed ranks embodies a desire for rational planning and totalitarian governance that, with the disappearance of the working class and peoples of colour, leaves the future to seemingly universal, white, middle-class prigs.

Faced with a global wave of anti-colonial revolutions in the mid-twentieth century, colonialist ideology was reworked into 'development theory'. Deeply influenced by and implicated in Cold War politics, it argued that that all nations developed along the same basic pattern, albeit at different paces, thus enabling the US to represent itself as the 'most developed' state upon which 'less developed' states should model themselves. The USSR did much the same thing, as can be seen in *Der schweigende Stern*'s hierarchical representations of multiracial and multinational institutions. An East German/Polish co-production, it pointedly includes numerous African and Asian characters, but continues to privilege white Europeans. The World Federation of Space Research's Venus expedition consists of a Japanese doctor, a Polish engineer, a Soviet astronaut, an Indian mathematician, a German pilot, a Chinese linguist, an African technician and, against his government's wishes, an American physicist. This cosmopolitanism – albeit limited by ethnic stereotyping and gender bias – is contrasted with American nationalism, which is later equated with Venusian aggression and reckless nuclear proliferation.

Development theory's colonialist ideology is also evident in *Independence Day*. For example, the climactic montage of destroyed alien spaceships around the globe, which cuts from bushmen at the base of Mount Kilimanjiro to Arabs at the Egyptian pyramids to the Sydney Opera House, reproduces racial hierarchy: 'primitive' Africans, who apparently have never achieved anything of note and thus can only be shown alongside an iconic natural feature; structures built by a pre-European high civilisation, the descendants of which seem to have achieved nothing since; and an iconic image of post-war modernism in a white settler culture. Only the US, it seems, is capable of overcoming advanced alien technology and uniting humanity.

Furthermore, despite depicting the African-American fighter pilot Steven Hiller (Will Smith) and Jewish-American computer genius David Levinson (Jeff Goldblum) saving the world, *Independence Day* negatively stereotypes black men and women, homosexual men and successful women, while reinforcing compulsory heterosexuality and white patriarchy. Hiller is repeatedly reduced to a shirtless, spectacular black body, while his girlfriend, Jasmine Dubrow (Vivica A. Fox), is a black single mother and 'exotic dancer'. Levinson was 'abandoned' by his wife, Constance Spano (Margaret Collins), when he would not support her career. Heroic white President Thomas Whitmore (Bill Pullman), a Gulf War veteran, lovingly cares for his young daughter; his dutiful wife, Patricia (Mary McDonnell), loyally performs the public role of the First Lady, before suffering, with self-effacing, silent dignity, a prolonged death from internal injuries with no visible physical trauma. Much of the film is set near the Mexican border, and Whitmore only organises global resistance after he has a terrifying vision of the aliens as migrant labour: 'They're like locusts. They're moving from planet to planet … After they've consumed every natural resource they move on. And we're next. … Let's nuke the bastards'.

Independence Day's colonialist discourse comes to the fore during Whitmore's rallying cry, staged in imitation of the St Crispin's day speech in the propagandist *Henry V* (1944), before the final assault on the alien ships:

> Mankind – that word should have new meaning for all of us today. We can't be consumed by our petty differences any more. We will be united in our common interest. Perhaps it is fate that today is the Fourth of July and you will once again be fighting for our freedom. Not from tyranny, oppression or persecution, but from annihilation. We're fighting for our right to live and to exist and should we win the day, the Fourth of July will no longer be known as an American holiday, but as the day the world declared in one voice: we will not go quietly into that night, we will not vanish without a fight, we're going to live on, we're going to survive. Today we celebrate Independence Day!

The film's vision of triumphant airpower seeks to assimilate the entire world into an American narrative, in which America is the pinnacle of accomplishment and 'natural' leader – the thing all others should desire and seek to become. It also resonates with the form of multiculturalism that Slavoj Žižek describes as the cultural logic of multinational capital.

Treating 'each local culture the way the colonizer treats colonized people – as "natives" whose mores are to be carefully studied and "respected"', this multiculturalism is

> a disavowed, inverted, self-referential form of racism, a 'racism with a distance' – it 'respects' the Other's identity, conceiving the Other as a self-enclosed 'authentic' community towards which he, the multi-culturalist, maintains a distance rendered possible by his privileged universal position. Multiculturalism is a racism which empties its own position of all positive content (the multiculturalist is not a direct racist, he doesn't oppose to the Other the *particular values* of his own culture), but nonetheless retains this position as the privileged *empty point of universality* from which one is able to appreciate (and depreciate) properly other particular cultures – the multiculturalist respect for the Other's specificity is the very form of asserting one's own superiority.
>
> (1997: 13–14)

The evacuation of identity's meaningfulness that accompanies this kind of multiculturalism can be seen in *Muppets from Space* (1999). Gonzo's recurring nightmare of being turned away from Noah's ark – he is one of a kind and thus cannot enter two by two – prompts him to explore his origins. He is variously figured as Jewish, homosexual, mad, an immigrant and – when his fellow aliens finally descend in a Parliament-Funkadelic-style mothership that matches the film's soul/funk soundtrack – African American; but simultaneously, all such specificities dissolve into the film's equivalisation of any and all identities, as if they are singular, interchangeable and free from history. An even more explicit example occurs in *Banlieue 13–Ultimatum/District 13–Ultimatum* (2009). Cleaner-than-clean cop Damien Tomasso (Cyril Raffaelli) must, with the aid of ethnically ambiguous Leïto (David Belle), persuade rival gangs to join forces against the Harriburton corporation and the Department of Internal State Security, who together plan to destroy the walled-off, multi-ethnic, impoverished banlieue and build a profitable middle-class suburb in its place. While each gang leader espouses the value of family and community in resisting capitalist and state power, standing alongside the East Asian, African-Caribbean and Arab/North-African gangs are seedy French mafiosa and neo-Nazi skinheads, as if all identities are merely personal choices with no material history. Moreover, this unlikely alliance serves to situate Tomasso, a self-proclaimed upholder of the constitution, and the white president (Philippe Torreton), to whom they all ultimately defer, outside of this multicultural field, as if the state itself was a neutral framework under which all identities are, and have always been, equal.

Many discussions of capitalism as a global system attribute a significant role to the US, with Hardt and Negri, for example, treating it as Empire's military enforcer, 'the only power able to manage international justice, *not as a function of its own national motives but in the name of global right*' (180). This apparent contradiction between exterritorial system and territorial base can be explained by world-system theory, according to which nation-states attempt to achieve dominance in two ways: either turn the world-system into a world empire, as Charles V attempted in the 1500s, Napoleon in the 1800s and Hitler in the 1900s, or achieve hegemony within the world-system, as the Netherlands did in the 1600s, Britain in the 1800s and the US in the 1900s. Each nation was, for a time, 'able to establish the rules of the game in the interstate system, to dominate the world-economy (in production, commerce, and finance), to get their way politically with a minimal use of military force (which however they had in goodly strength), and to formulate the cultural language with which one discussed the world' (Wallerstein: 58). Postwar American 'imperialism-without-colonies' largely achieved this through the 'power of … finance capital and huge multinational corporations to command the flows of capital, research, consumer goods and media information', coercively perpetuating and extending international political and economic imbalances (McClintock: 13). While a world empire's 'political structure' would 'stifle capitalism' by overriding the prioritisation of endless capital accumulation, a hegemonic power would eventually have to 'divert itself into a political and military role' and deploy '"imperial" force' even though it 'undermines the hegemonic power economically and politically' (Wallerstein: 58–59).

In part, the militarisation of US blockbuster sf through and after the final throes of the Cold War can be understood as part of the symbolic turn to imperial force – which includes real, media-saturated military actions in Latin America, Africa, the Balkans, Asia and the Middle East – in order to reassert (an increasingly in-crisis) US hegemony, with the 'spectacularity – the versatility, harshness and promptness – of punitive operations matter[ing] more than their effectiveness' (Bauman 1998: 119). Since 9/11, with successive US governments pursuing 'a program centered around unilateral assertions ... of military strength' (Wallerstein: 87), the sabre-rattling jingoism that *Starship Troopers* satirised returned as a straight-faced norm. For example, the *Transformers* trilogy refracts what Said would describe as a 'justificatory regime of self-aggrandizing, self-originating authority interposed between the victim of imperialism and its perpetrator' (82). *War of the Worlds* (2005), *Cloverfield* (2008), *Skyline* (2010) and *Battle: Los Angeles* (2011), which cast the US as the innocent victim of massive, inexplicable attacks by alien others, rework two familiar colonial narratives: the passage through hostile territory as a purposeful expedition that therefore overrides the priorities, rights or needs of those encountered en route; and the attack on an isolated outpost that operates as a far-flung bastion of civilisation and thus serves to make indigenous people 'appear intruders on their own land' (Shohat and Stam: 119).[15]

Battle: Los Angeles maps the 'war on terror' onto anxieties about immigration, treating the Latinisation of California as a threat to be met with massive military force before it can turn Los Angeles into Mogadishu or Fallujah. An isolated, multi-ethnic platoon led by the inexperienced 2nd Lieutenant William Martinez (Ramon Rodriguez), and including Nigerian Corpsman Jibril Adukwu (Adetokumboh M'Cormack) who signed up so as to speed his application for American citizenship, must learn to respect the superior knowledge, skill and commitment of veteran white Sergeant Michael Nantz (Aaron Eckhart). Weary of the military, to which he has sacrificed life outside of the service, and traumatised by his experiences, he nonetheless continues to give his all. He wins the admiration of white civilian Michele (Bridget Moynhan) and Latina airforce Technical Sergeant Elena Santos (Michelle Rodriguez); he becomes a surrogate father to Chicano Hector Rincon (Bryce Cass), whose father, Joe (Michael Peña), inspired by Nantz, died saving the platoon; and he earns the platoon's respect, with Lance-Corporal Peter Kerns (Jim Parrack) taking on the last duty of sacrificial white masculinity in his place – the young soldier dies, allowing the white patriarch to live on.

POST-IMPERIAL MELANCHOLY IN BRITISH SF

If the melancholy aura surrounding Sergeant Nantz expresses a wavering sense of US hegemony as it deploys imperial force, a similar mood can be discerned throughout postwar British sf as the UK struggled to come to terms with the loss of empire. Paul Gilroy suggests that Britain's 'continued', 'neurotic' evocations of the Second World War, a war against 'foes who [were] simply, tidily, and uncomplicatedly evil', reveals 'a desire to find a way back to the point where the national culture – operating on a more manageable scale of community and social life – was, irrespective of the suffering involved in the conflict, both comprehensible and habitable' (97). The obsessively repeated 'themes' of 'invasion, war, contamination, loss of identity' that Gilroy associates with the 'anxious, melancholic mood' found behind 'the nation-defining ramparts of the white cliffs of Dover' (15) are shared by postwar British sf, from the *Quatermass* (1955–67) trilogy to *Moon* (2009), *Monsters* (2010) and *Attack the Block* (2011).

Gilroy argues that the longing for 'lost … moral and cultural bearings' manifests in fantasies of an organic Englishness, which marginalises other British identities, is antipathetic to immigrants and often terrified by 'the perceived dangers of pluralism and … the irreversible fact of multiculture' (97). For example, *The Man in the White Suit* (1951) imagines this national community in terms of the postwar settlement between capital and labour moderating a 'natural' hierarchy of power, which is unsettled by technoscientific innovation; but the new, apparently indestructible and dazzlingly white artificial fabric around which the story is centred turns out to be completely unstable and crumbles to shreds. Later films, such as *Village of the Damned* (1960), *The Damned* (1963), *Lord of the Flies* (1963), *Children of the Damned* (1964), *Privilege* (1967) and *A Clockwork Orange* (1971), depict postwar children as avatars of a future unbearably alien to organic Englishness, while the absurdist *The Bed Sitting Room* (1969), in which a handful of survivors subsist in the post-apocalyptic ruins and wastelands of Britain, ends with the declaration of a national emergency even though 'there is nothing of the nation left beyond that very emergency' (Williams 2011: 67).

In psychoanalytic theory, melancholy derives from the loss of a narcissistic fantasy of omnipotence, and is characterised by an 'inability to surrender the lost object, by a brooding refusal of the new' (Baucom: 184). The sense of bereavement comes 'not from the death of the desired object, but from its degradation, from the subject's reevaluation of it as diminished or tarnished' (184). For example, *The Day the Earth Caught Fire* (1961) depicts Britain as absolutely powerless in the face of rising temperatures as, thanks to US and Soviet H-bomb tests, the Earth begins to spiral in towards the Sun. This displacement by global superpowers leaves the prime minister with little to do but make reassuring noises and jokes about Britons coping with the weather. While newspapers evoke the Blitz and ration books are issued, the entire population is left suspended, with no way of influencing their fate. Indeed, the film ends in suspense, with two newspaper front pages ready to go to press, one declaring the success and the other the failure of the superpowers' last-ditch effort to restore the Earth to its orbit. This refusal of closure suggests that a world in which Britain is so far removed from global power might not be worth preserving, especially if the loss of empire means becoming a colony of a new imperial power. Throughout the 1950s, the casting of minor and fading American stars in British sf so as to obtain co-production financing from US distributors[16] served as a constant reminder of British cinema's, and hence Britain's, global position – a point reiterated more recently by *Shaun of the Dead*'s pub being named after the American rifle rather than the British town of Winchester. Indeed, *28 Weeks Later* (2007) prefers to depict the failure to reclaim London from a zombie plague rather than Britain becoming a US colony.

According to Ian Baucom, the melancholic subject turns 'longingly to the past' only to see 'the portrait of lost perfection', and 'resentfully to the present', finding only 'diminishment' (185), a process illustrated by *The Perfect Woman* (1949). Dotty Professor Belmon (Miles Malleson) builds a robot called Olga (Pamela Devis), modelled on his sheltered niece, Penelope (Patricia Roc). Roger Cavendish (Nigel Patrick), a penniless man about town, and his valet, Ramshead (Stanley Holloway), are hired to field test Olga by taking her out in society, not realising that Penelope has swapped places with the robot. Despite vague hints that a war has happened in the recent past, there is no glimpse of London's still very evident wartime devastation and no hint of postwar austerity to upset the film's conventional West-End-farce upper-class milieu. Indeed, much of its humour derives from proliferations and profligacies, from racy *doubles entendres* and other systems of doubling. For example, when Belmon hires Olga's escorts, he talks at length about a woman he has 'made' without revealing that he means a robot. Bubbling below the surface is a sense of impropriety, of everything Belmon says in innocence being taken to mean something else, culminating in a series of puns on 'working women' and 'scrubbers'. Such polysemic wordplay and gags about pronunciation, meaning and repetition with variation extend the fantasy of plenitude (rationing had intensified in the late 1940s and did not end until 1954). Ordering dinner, Ramshead asks for 'something light. Say some soup, fish, chicken, joint, sweet, cheese, dessert, coffee, anything else that occurs to you ... A bottle of Scotch, two dozen bottles of beer, another bottle of Scotch, a small fizzy lemonade and a bottle of Scotch'. At the prospect of food, Penelope licks her lips in lascivious close-up. Later, a carefully constructed shot makes much of her fabulous underwear, offering up the female body as a sensuous object, part of a 'natural' plenitude, while her lingerie's luxurious 'femininity' contrasts with Olga's rather more fetishistic underclothing, proletarian build and look. Unsurprisingly, Roger and Penelope fall in love, while the robot – a modern, labouring woman – self-destructs.

A similar dynamic drives *Devil Girl from Mars* (1954) in which diverse Britons – a journalist, a professor, a fashion model fleeing a failed romance, a wrongly imprisoned convict on the run – gather at an inn in the Scottish highlands, run by an elderly Scots couple whose young nephew is visiting, a crippled handyman and a barmaid who is really the convict's lover, relocated to the highlands to be near the prison where he is serving his sentence. When a Martian spaceship en route to London sets down for repairs, this exemplary social microcosm, far from the seat of national government, pulls together, reiterating the fantasy of wartime national unity and, through the remote rural location, of a pre-capitalist and supposedly organic system of class and nation. The Martian Nyah (Patricia Laffan) – an autocratic woman in black fetishistic garb, accompanied by a towering robot – sneers at their attempted resistance. She haughtily compares Earth to a period several hundred years in Mars's past, before a final gender war assured female emancipation while driving the male population into impotent decline. With the birth rate falling, she is searching for human breeding stock. However, any hint of masculine British potency connected with a technological future is undermined by the not-exactly-robust men from whom Nyah must choose, and the fact that their role in repopulating Mars is merely a stop-gap measure until reproductive technologies are developed. Ultimately, all that the men can do is compete with each other to be the one who boards Nyah's spaceship in order, suicidally, to destroy it.

Zeta One (1969) more overtly mocks fantasies of British potency. Department 5's clumsy and rather dim secret agent James Word (Robin Hawdon) finds himself embroiled in an attempt by villainous Major Bourdon (James Robertson Justice) to locate and conquer Angvia. This anagrammatic, women-only colony, hidden in a fold of space-time, is ruled by the alien Zeta (Dawn Addams), who abducts and converts terrestrial women into sexually liberated feminists. This confusion of the sexual revolution with the women's movement produces a peculiarly proleptic vision of consumerist post-feminism, with the Angvians wearing mini dresses, kinky boots and other, more revealing costumes; but the film does also attack the corrupt remnants of feudal hierarchies and ridicules the masculinist state. Bourdon is depicted as a brutal country gentlemen, given to torturing Angvians, hunting them with hounds and threatening them with rape, and he and his henchmen are thoroughly trounced by mighty, if scantily clad, Angvian warriors. The pratfalling Word is continually distracted by women, who are all obviously smarter than him, and never quite realises what is going on. He is ultimately abducted and put out to stud in the Angvian Insemination Room. Although the final scene seems to show him living a life of luxury, with countless sexual partners, nearly naked servants and his own personal topless go-go dancer, a certain weariness is already evident – as if even he is beginning to realise that this is not about his pleasure or sexual prowess, but merely his reproductive capacity.

The sex-role reversals of *Queen Kong* (1976) offer a similarly contradictory version of the sexual and gender politics of 1960s and 1970s Britain. Autocratic filmmaker Luce Habit (Rula Lenska) and her crew of hot-pants-wearing feminists kidnap the naïve, pot-smoking petty criminal Ray Fay (Robin Askwith) to star in their next film. In Africa, the eponymous 60-foot ape falls in love with Ray. Captured and brought in chains to London, she escapes after the local council insists that she must wear a bra before being put on public display and goes on the rampage, accidentally destroying a 'thousand years of English history'. Reunited with Queenie, who has torn off her chains and her bra, Ray realises that he loves her, too. His impassioned plea for her safety argues that she is being persecuted not because she is a giant ape but because she is a woman – prompting a feminist uprising, in which housewives, secretaries, students, bunny girls and prostitutes march to her defence. The film concludes with the interspecies lovers returning to Africa to live together, simultaneously envisioning, albeit in exaggerated and confused form, a pluralist future *and* ejecting its avatars from the nation.

British sf's inns and pubs usually offer a fantasy image of white 'organic community', reinforcing 'natural' class and gender hierarchies while resisting assaults by monstrous Others and thus articulating anxieties about postwar immigration, the increasing visibility of peoples of colour and Britain's *de facto* multiculture. The many country houses in British sf (e.g., *Village of the Damned* (1960), *Island of Terror* (1966), *The Asphyx* (1973), *Prey* (1978), Hammer's *Frankenstein* series (1957–73)) fulfil a similar function while also evoking, usually unintentionally, 'those distant, all but invisible, spaces of empire to which' they, both as locations and as settings, are 'connected through a perpetual passing of bodies, capital, and commodities' (Baucom: 166). While country houses evoke nostalgia for the 'ordered and disciplinary England' of Britain's imperial ascendancy (172), they also serve as a reminder of loss (not least in their role as a production economy for an ailing national cinema). In *28 Days Later* (2002), for example, the Duke of Beaufort's Badminton House, standing in for an unnamed country house northeast of Manchester, houses a platoon of desperate soldiers under the command of Major West (Christopher Eccleston). Increasingly power crazed and deranged, he condenses brutal colonial history by chaining up an infected black soldier to see how long it takes for the zombies to starve to death, and by attempting to force British-Jamaican Selena (Naomie Harris) into sexual servitude. Although the film ends with the formation of an interracial couple and surrogate family, it can do so only by eradicating Britain as we know it.

RACE AND ANTI-IMPERIALISM IN US COUNTERCULTURAL SF

Japanese post-imperial melancholy is evident in, among many other films, *Gojira* (2002), *Sengoku jieitai/G.I. Samurai* (1979) and *Bekushiru: 2077 Nihon sakoku/Vexille* (2007), with the Korean nationalist *2009: Lost Memories* (2002) criticising Japanese imperialism. A similar mood inflects the dismay about neo-liberal capitalism's devastating effects on post-Soviet society in

Chetyre/4 (2005), *Pervye na Lune/First on the Moon* (2005), *Pyl/Dust* (2005) and *977* (2006). However, since the US was born in a colonial revolution, it has not typically perceived itself as an imperial power, despite being built on the violent displacement and genocide of Native Americans and the seizure of their land, on overseas military interventions and, especially in Latin America, on an 'imperialism-without-colonies' policy of providing economic and military aid to often-dictatorial regimes that favour US regional aims and business interests. Moreover, with the US on the ascendant as an economic, political and military power throughout the twentieth century, it was only with the drawn-out defeat in Vietnam that US sf began to express a variety of post-imperial melancholy. For example, anxieties about changing values and power structures mark *Planet of the Apes* (1968) and *The Omega Man* (1971), both of which cast Charlton Heston as the patriarchal individualist and violent white saviour of humanity from racially coded Others; and yet they also struggle to express something of the countercultural values complexly shaping 1960s and 1970s sf.

While 1960s British films tend to be ambivalent in their depictions of children and young people, US films, such as *Wild in the Streets* (1968), *Gas-s-s-s! or It Became Necessary to Destroy the World in Order to Save It* (1970), *Glen and Randa* (1971) and *Dark Star* (1974), are rather more sympathetic to countercultural youth. Anti-nuclear and antiwar films, such as *Dai-sanji sekai taisen: Yonju-ichi jikan no kyofu/The Final War* (1960), *Sekai Daisenso/The Last War* (1962), *Dr Strangelove or: How I Learned to Stop Worrying and Love the Bomb* (1964), *The War Game* (1965), *Konec srpna v Hotelu Ozon/The End of August at the Hotel Ozone* (1967) and *Gladiatorerna/Peace Game* (1969), found American counterparts in *Five* (1951), *On the Beach* (1959), *Panic in Year Zero!* (1962), *Fail-Safe* (1964) and *The Bedford Incident* (1965). Environmental concerns, including overpopulation, resource depletion, pollution, habitat destruction and species extinction were articulated in *Gojira tai Hedorâ/Godzilla vs. the Smog Monster* (1971), *Z.P.G.* (1972), *Doomwatch* (1972) and in such US films as *No Blade of Grass* (1970), *Silent Running* (1972), *Soylent Green* (1973), *Chosen Survivors* (1974), *It's Alive* (1974), *Phase IV* (1974), *Dogs* (1976), *Day of the Animals* (1977),

The Swarm (1978) and *Alligator* (1980). The dehumanising consequences of urban life, consumerism and the faceless power of corporations, the media and other institutions, illustrated in *Alphaville* (1965), *Fahrenheit 451* (1966), *Tanin no kao/The Face of Another* (1966), *Rollerball* (1975), *The Man Who Fell to Earth* (1976) and *La Mort en Direct/Death Watch* (1980), were also explored in such US films as *Invasion of the Body Snatchers* (1956), *Seconds* (1966), *THX 1138* (1971), *The Terminal Man* (1974), *The Stepford Wives* (1975), *Death Race 2000* (1975), *Logan's Run* (1976), *Capricorn One* (1978), *Coma* (1978), *Invasion of the Body Snatchers* (1978) and *The China Syndrome* (1979). However, overtly anti-imperialist sf is rare[17] and, during this period, the major example by an American – *Mr Freedom* (1969) – was not made in the US and the major example made in the US – *Punishment Park* (1971) – was not by an American.

The former's eponymous superhero – a none-too-bright, loudmouthed, bigoted bully – is sent to Paris by Freedom, Inc., an organisation head-quartered in the same building as Texaco, Shell, Aramco, General Motors, Standard Oil, United Fruit and Unilever. The evil Red Chinaman, having murdered Captain Formidable (Yves Montand), is infiltrating communist forces into France and, as Dr Freedom (Donald Pleasence) explains to his crass, swaggering protégé: 'The French are the White Man's Burden'. After Marie-Madeline (Delphine Seyrig) gives Mr Freedom (John Abbey) a tour of the Parisian organisation, which runs a prosti-tution ring to fund the cause of freedom, he delivers a stirring speech about the Land of Freedom, accompanied by a film full of images of consumer goods, support for the Vietnam War, black urban poverty and sex shops. During a visit to the American Embassy, which is a super-market, the US ambassador explains that France could be a great nation if only it understood democracy properly, but some of the French have even been calling for free elections. Eventually Mr Freedom blows up half the country to prove to Red Chinaman that aggression does not pay.

In contrast to William Klein's raucous superhero burlesque, Peter Watkins's *Punishment Park* is a pseudo-documentary, ostensibly shot by a BBC team invited to observe the system introduced to address political dissent in the US. Under the terms of the 1950 McCarran Internal

Security Act, the president has declared a 'state of insurrection' and an 'internal security emergency', enabling the arrest and detention of people considered likely to conduct subversive acts and sabotage, and the creation of the Punishment Parks as a 'punitive deterrent'. Corrective Group 638 appear before a tribunal to be sentenced – for writing anti-establishment songs, draft dodging and organising movements against poverty, racism and the Vietnam War – either to lengthy prison terms or a three-day period in southern California's Bear Mountain Punishment Park. Corrective Group 637, who have already opted for the latter, must make their way, without water or supplies, across 53 miles of desert, where day/night temperatures vary between 110° and 65° Fahrenheit, while being pursued by trainee National Guardsmen, riot police and federal marshals. If they are captured or fail to complete the course, they will serve their prison sentences. When some of the group break away, killing a policeman and stealing his weapons, the pursuers turn murderously violent. Others of the group eventually reach the American flag marking the course's end, but the assembled police and soldiers, disregarding the rules, brutally assault them. Throughout, the film insists that military aggression overseas and domestic repression of dissent are inextricably linked, parts of the same American tradition of violence that includes slavery and genocide.

The Crazies (1973), *Piranha* (1978) and *Night of the Living Dead* (1968) likewise subject US citizens to the kinds of violence suffered by many Southeast Asians in this period. In *The Crazies*, a biological weapon is spilled near a rural small town, and soldiers are sent to kill everyone within the quarantined zone, regardless of whether or not they are infected. *Piranha*'s genetically engineered killer fish, accidentally released in the US, were developed as part of a project to 'destroy the river systems of the North Vietnamese' by developing 'a strain ... that could survive in cold water and then breed at an accelerated rate'. A secretive military is more concerned with deniability than saving lives, and business interests conspire to keep a new lakeside leisure park open even though 'the piranhas ... are eating the guests'. *Night of the Living Dead* reworks the colonialist narrative of an isolated outpost relentlessly assaulted by subhuman Others. When African-American protagonist Ben (Duane Jones) emerges into daylight, the sole survivor, he is gunned down by local police and state-sanctioned vigilantes. If the resonances with the white supremacist violence of Jim Crow and Civil Rights era America were not sufficiently clear, the film underscores the point with a closing montage of stills that recall newspaper images of lynchings. The audience's sympathies are also positioned with allegorical African Americans in *Conquest of the Planet of the Apes* (1972). Caesar (Roddy McDowell) – the son of Cornelius (Roddy McDowell) and Zira (Kim Hunter), the sympathetic chimpanzees from the preceding three *Apes* films who time travelled back to the present to escape a global apocalypse – leads a revolution to free the apes humans have enslaved. Indeed, the anti-imperialist currents within US culture find their most sustained treatment in sf concerned with the politics of race.[18]

In *Change of Mind* (1969), a successful white district attorney with terminal cancer undergoes experimental surgery to transplant his brain into the body of an African-American man. In this rather earnest melodrama, David Rowe (Raymond St. Jacques) struggles to integrate back into a white society that had always accepted him, while prosecuting a bigoted white sheriff for the murder of an African-American woman. Although *The Thing with Two Heads* (1972) plays interracial brain transplants for laughs, its story of a white sense of entitlement to own and exploit black bodies cannot help but acknowledge slavery and the systematic underdevelopment of black America.[19] Wealthy, white, elderly, diseased bigot and surgical innovator Maxwell Kirshner (Ray Milland) plans to survive death, but when he slips into a final coma, the only body available to receive his transplanted head belongs to Jack Moss ('Rosey' Grier), a wrongly convicted African-American on death row. Faced with the electric chair, Moss agrees to what he thinks is posthumous organ donation to buy some more time to prove his innocence. When Kirshner and Moss regain consciousness after surgery, they are horrified (for different reasons) to find Kirshner's head grafted alongside Moss's head – when full control of Moss's body passes to Kirshner, Moss's head will be amputated, fulfilling his death sentence.

Other films are rather more militant. In *The Watermelon Man* (1970), racist white insurance man Jeffrey Gerber (Godfrey Cambridge) wakes up to discover that he has turned black overnight.[20] Gerber's social position immediately changes: his wife's liberalism wavers and her sexual interest in him wanes, while his Nordic secretary suddenly finds him very attractive; when he is out jogging, police assume he is fleeing a crime; and neighbours, fearing property values will drop, band together to buy his house. Finally, he moves to a black neighbourhood, learns Black Pride and joins other working-class African Americans covertly practicing martial arts in preparation for self-defence and revolution. In *The Spook who Sat by the Door* (1973), the CIA recruits Dan Freeman (Lawrence Cook) and other African Americans to train as field operatives in order to 'prove' that the agency is not racist, while stacking the decks so as to ensure their failure. Freeman, however, passes the course and becomes the CIA's token black. Five years later, he resigns and returns to Chicago, where he becomes prominent in social services – and secretly recruits and trains gang members into a revolutionary army. The film ends as black insurgency spreads to other cities.

Space is the Place (1974) is less optimistic about the possibility of revolution or genuine social transformation. Sun Ra (himself) wanders in the alien garden in which he intends to establish a black colony in order to see what can be achieved without white people around. After challenging the Overseer (Ray Johnson), who appears as a well-dressed black pimp, to a game of 'the end of the world', Ra flies to Oakland in a spaceship powered by his Intergalactic Solar Arkestra, where he recruits the 'black youth of planet Earth' to his cause, which is visually associated with such African-American revolutionaries as Angela Davis, Malcolm X, Huey Newton and George Jackson. When the Overseer is defeated, he is punished by his underlings, white and black alike, suddenly seeing him – and treating him – as just a 'nigger'. Ra's followers, taken up in his spaceship, fly away to a new, more homely world, effectively reversing the Middle Passage; and Ra destroys the Earth behind them, just to be on the safe side.

Dr Black, Mr Hyde (1976) is similarly ambivalent. Successful African American Dr Henry Pride (Bernie Casey) spends his spare time either working in a free clinic in Watts or conducting research into restoring damaged livers to health. The latter endeavour is inspired by his own alcoholic mother's death. A maid in an up-market brothel, she died of liver failure as the child Henry tried, and failed, to get any of the prostitutes to come to her aid.[21] Henry, unable to test his new serum on humans, injects it into himself, prompting his intermittent transformation into a bestial, prostitute-murdering brute, with a loping gait. However, in a striking inversion of the imagery found in earlier adaptations of Stevenson's novel, his subhuman nature is associated not with ape-like negritude but with whiteness, and his whiteness is depicted as a revolting, corpse-like pallor. By becoming even more white, the upwardly mobile African-American becomes an etiolated, cadaverous predator on the impoverished black community from which he came. Significantly, just a decade after the Watts Riots and anticipating the use of the World Trade Center in the same year's *King Kong* remake, Henry is brought down by an excessive display of police force – helicopters, dogs, countless guns – as he attempts to climb the Watts Towers.

Born in Flames (1983), set ten years after the Social Democratic War of Liberation, captures something of the demise – and transformation – of countercultural struggles around race, class and gender. The Social Labour Party government, which espouse an anti-communist American socialism of moral and ethical humanism, has left many pre-revolutionary structures and institutions intact and, confronted by economic crisis, becomes increasingly reactionary. To protect themselves against growing sexism, heterosexism and racism, groups of women begin to take matters into their own hands. As this grassroots radicalism spreads, forces of repression intensify. Adelaide Norris (Jean Satterfield), a leader in the Women's Army and an advocate of armed struggle, is arrested on her return from training with female revolutionaries in the Western Sahara and dies in custody. Charging the state with her murder, some women are driven to desperate, spectacular action, blowing up the transmitters on the World Trade Center.

Made over five years, *Born in Flames* documents the transition from white, middle-class Second Wave Feminism to a Third Wave Feminism shaped by and expressing the experience of working-class women and women of colour. This is played out most pointedly in the contrast between the Women's Army's radical black leaders and the white editors of the Social Labour Party's *Socialist Youth Review*. Initially the editorial trio adhere to the Party line, defend the Party from criticism and fail to recognise the (relative) class and ethnic privilege they enjoy. Indeed, they even consider the Women's Army – mostly working-class women of colour – guilty of interpreting everything in terms of gender and ignoring other factors, such as class and race. But after Adelaide's death, they acknowledge the Party's patriarchal condescension, quit the paper and join the revolutionary struggle. Through this break with the Party, the film also reworks many women's dissatisfaction with and disaffiliation from the masculinist discourse and practice of many New Left and radical black groups of the period.[22] Furthermore, Adelaide's North African trip links fictional feminist revolution to the real-world struggle of women who fought in anti-colonial wars only to find themselves returned to the home and patriarchal subordination once Western powers were evicted.

NEO-LIBERALISM AND THE SF OF DEINDUSTRIALISATION

The years 1978–80 constitute a 'turning-point in the world's social and economic history', with the elections of Margaret Thatcher and Ronald Reagan in the UK and US and Deng Xiaoping's economic reforms in China inaugurating the neo-liberal turn (Harvey 2005: 1). Neoliberalism is an economic doctrine that claims that 'human well-being can best be advanced by liberating individual entrepreneurial freedoms and skills within an institutional framework characterized by strong private property rights, free markets, and free trade' and by restricting the role of the state to the creation and preservation of this framework (2). The neo-liberal agenda includes privatising and commodifying public assets, deregulating and financialising the global economy, managing and manipulating crises, giving corporations subsidies and tax breaks, and imposing regressive tax regimes that redistribute wealth to those who already have plenty (160–65). Neoliberalism has 'not been very effective in revitalizing global capital accumulation', but it has restored and increased 'the power of an economic elite' (19). While the overall 'slowdown in the world economy has not really affected' multinational corporations, whose 'share of [rising] world GDP' has more than doubled, societies 'are in rather poorer shape', with widespread impoverishment of working age populations, increased unemployment and job insecurity (Boltanski and Chiapello xxxvii–ix).

One consequence – or goal – of neoliberalism is the 'wrenching of the decision-making centres, together with the calculations which ground the decisions such centres make, free from territorial constraints' (Bauman 1998: 8). This dislocation exacerbates the asymmetry between 'the now unanchored power, able to move at short notice without warning' to escape the consequences and costs of its actions, and the populations it 'is free to exploit and abandon' (9). In earlier times, capital – because of 'the massiveness of the factory buildings, the heaviness of the machinery' and the slower pace of innovation – was no more 'eager, or able, to move' than labour (Bauman 2000: 116), but neoliberal deregulation offered mobile, financial capital significant advantages over the fixed, industrial capital, and better enabled capital to relocate to sites that lowered costs (cheaper labour, weaker and poorly enforced regulations concerning pollution and worker well-being) and increased profitability for shareholders. Early glimpses of neo-liberalism's 'decrepit landscape of deindustrialization and post-industrial decay' (Harvey 1989: 310) can be seen in *A Clockwork Orange* (1971), *Una gota de sangre para morir amando/Murder in a Blue World* (1973), *Soylent Green* (1973), *Eraserhead* (1977) and *Mad Max* (1979), and it becomes ubiquitous from the early 1980s in films such as *Escape from New York* (1981), *Blade Runner* (1982), *Café Flesh* (1982), *Turkey Shoot* (1982), *Videodrome* (1983), *The Brother from Another Planet* (1984), *Forbrydelsens element/The Element of Crime*

(1984), *Repo Man* (1984), *The Terminator* (1984), *Darkman* (1990), *Hardware* (1990), *Delicatessen* (1991), *Acción Mutante* (1993) and *Fire in the Sky* (1993).

RoboCop (1987) is set in Detroit, the prime US example of deindustrialisation. As technological innovations reduced the labour force and factories relocated in pursuit of lower costs, standards of living and tax revenues slumped, exacerbating – and exacerbated by – the desertion of Detroit by half its population in half a century, leaving a third of the remaining population below the poverty line. Extrapolating from this unfolding real-world situation, *RoboCop* sees multinational Omni Consumer Products take over the Detroit police force, because in the words of the Old Man (Dan O'Herlihy), 'shifts in the tax structure have created an economy ideal for corporate growth' but detrimental to 'community services'. However, just as OCP has profited from hospitals and prisons, so it intends to profit from investing in the police. The Old Man plans to demolish old Detroit, replacing it with Delta City – a project typical of 'spectacular urban' renewal schemes intended 'to attract capital and people (of the right sort) in a period ... of intensified inter-urban competition and urban entrepreneurialism' (Harvey 1989: 92) – but it is necessary to cut out the 'cancer' of crime before bringing in two million construction workers. Dick Jones (Ronny Cox), the Old Man's heir apparent, introduces the ED209, a 'self-sufficient law enforcement robot' – a '24-hour-a-day ... cop who doesn't need to eat or sleep' and possesses 'superior firepower'. Detroit police, it seems, are destined to be automated out of their jobs, while the new policing will be more concerned with 'urban pacification' and militarised control of the population than with crime prevention or investigation. OCP's approach to policing also serves Jones's intention not to root out such profitable criminal endeavours as drugs, gambling and prostitution but to take them over. In addition to ensuring optimal conditions for Delta City's construction and Jones's criminal ambitions, the ED209 is destined, following 'a successful tour of duty in old Detroit', to 'become the hot military product for the next decade', with 'a guaranteed military sale ... Renovation program, spare parts for 25 years'. When the ED209 goes disastrously wrong, OCP's back-up plan suggests neo-liberalism's divorce of decision making from the people it directly affects and its exploitation for profit of the workforce's constraints of locality. Officer Alex Murphy (Peter Weller), identified without his knowledge or consent as a potential subject for the RoboCop project, is reassigned from the comparatively safe Metro South precinct to Metro West, where he is far more likely to be killed in the line of duty, enabling OCP to harvest his brain as a component with law-enforcement experience for its heavily armoured cyborg.

They Live (1988) is equally jaundiced about deindustrialisation's profiteers. George Nada (Roddy Piper) drifts into Los Angeles from Denver, where he was laid off after ten years, and finds construction work alongside Frank Armitage (Keith David), who was laid off from a Detroit steel mill. They squat in Justiceville, a shantytown in the midst of plenty, which is soon demolished by police, its population assaulted and driven away,[23] because several residents have uncovered a secret: Earth has been covertly taken over by alien 'free-enterprisers', for whom it 'is just another developing planet, their Third World', to be 'deplete[d]' before 'mov[ing] on to another'. The rebels are not the first to discover this, but most people 'sell out right away' in exchange for promotions, bigger bank accounts, new houses and cars. Nada and Frank even witness humans teleporting to other worlds, pursuing wealth as they escape a planet doomed to immiseration and ecological devastation. The dispersed people of Justiceville have no such freedom of movement or possibility of escape.

In *Dead-End Drive In* (1986), Crabs (Ned Manning) and Carmen (Natalie McCurry), on a date at an out-of-town drive-in, have their wheels stolen by police. There is no telephone, and it is illegal to walk on the only road out of there, and so they must join the permanent population of car-dwelling, unemployed youths who see no point in escaping from what is actually a state-run concentration camp since there is no future for them outside. Their racist ire when police start shipping in groups of Asian Australians is rooted in their realisation that the state has as little regard for them as it does for peoples of colour. 'Deposited in a territory without denomination', their exclusion seems permanent, with 'all the roads leading back to meaningful places and to the spots where socially legible meanings can be and are forged daily ... blocked for good' (Bauman 2007: 42).

Tetsuo: The Iron Man (1989) offers the most striking vision of neo-liberal post-industrialism. A metal fetishist (Tsukamoto Shinya) inserts a ridged metal pipe into his thigh so as to become a better athlete, but his body promptly rejects it and maggots infest the wound. Limping away, he is run over by a sarariman (Taguchi Tomorowo) and his girlfriend (Fujiwara Kei). They dump the body and, aroused by it all, have sex while the dead metal fetishist watches, his viewpoint presented as a flickering video image. As the sarariman begins to cyborg, he is pursued by a female commuter (Kanaoka Nobu) who, possessed by the metal fetishist, develops a mechanically enhanced arm. When the sarariman kills her, she seems to have transformed into the metal fetishist. In a dream, the sarariman is sodomised by his girlfriend, who wears a snake-like, machinic strap-on dildo; when he wakes, his penis becomes a massive drill, which kills her. The metal fetishist returns, corroding. His salvation lies with the sarariman, who was infected by stainless steel rather than iron. They battle, then, declaring their love, merge into a single creature, prefiguring a homoerotic, cyborg apocalypse.

While director Tsukamoto Shinya is particularly adept at capturing the unhomeliness of anonymous central business districts, characterless mall spaces and the concrete wasteland of urban apartment blocks,[24] in *Tetsuo* he constructs a mise-en-scène that is post-industrial – not in the sense of invisible, global computer networks 'made of sunshine', 'all light and clean because they are nothing but signals, electromagnetic waves, a section of the spectrum' (Haraway 1991a: 153), but in the sense of abandoned factories and rusting industrial equipment; of leaking fluids and rot; of textures and material; of detritus and dereliction; and of in-between spaces, of tunnels, ducts, shafts, pipes, telephone wires, plumbing, railway stations, subway lines, commuter trains, service corridors, minor roads and alleyways. Even the metal fetishist's mysteriously uploaded posthumous existence is imagined in these terms, as he squats and rages in a hollowed-out space bounded by wires, mesh and sharp-edged protrusions, which threaten his flesh with abrasion and penetration. *Tetsuo* insists on the material basis of a global technological interconnectedness, and the film's emphasis on rusting and wetness, on iron rather than electronic 'men', is a reminder of the labour that neo-liberal capital seeks to escape. This materialist sensibility extends to the film's distinctive visual style, with several frenetic sequences, shot at a low frame-rate and then projected at the standard speed, precipitating characters through space at breakneck pace. However, each of these accumulations of (effectively) jump-cutted frames are experienced as a judderingly discontinuous continuum, with the handheld camera exacerbating the disorientating feeling of being made to see every single frame. Such sequences, which flicker between photogram and flow, produce, like the film's stop-motion sequences, a filmic stutter that insists that both the film and the world are analogue, rather than digital, and are weighted down by history and materiality.

SF FIGURATIONS OF NEOLIBERAL SPACES

Because neoliberalism claims that 'the social good will be maximized by maximizing the reach and frequency of market transactions', the development and use of information technologies – able to 'accumulate, store, transfer, analyse, and use massive databases to guide decision in the global marketplace' – has been central to cementing neoliberal hegemony (Harvey 2005: 3). Capitalist global information networks are intent on

> deepening the capitalist logic of profit-seeking in capital-labor relation-ships; enhancing the productivity of labor and capital; globalizing production, circulation, and markets, seizing the opportunity of the most advantageous conditions for profit-making everywhere; and marshaling the state's support for productivity gains and competitive-ness of national economies, often to the detriment of social protection and public interest regulations.
>
> (Castells 2000a: 19)

Within this framework, the state orients itself not towards the interests of its people but towards a particular kind of economic development, while redefining economic development as the principal interest of its people:

> In the cabaret of globalization, the state goes through a striptease and by the end of the performance it is left with the bare necessities only: its powers of repression. With its material basis destroyed, its sovereignty and independence annulled, its political class effaced, the nation-state becomes a simple security service for the mega-companies ... The new masters of the world have no need to govern directly. National governments are charged with the task of administering affairs on their behalf.
>
> (Subcommandante Marcos in Bauman 1998: 66)

Alongside the development of global information networks, the implementation of 'deregulation and liberalization policies' by neo-liberal states and international organisations (WTO, IMF, World Bank, OECD and UN, among others) enabled capital to become 'truly global' (Castells 2000a: 101) and 'core production networks' and 'an elite specialty labor force' to become 'increasingly globalized' (131). The 'bulk of labor', however, 'is local' (131) and 'highly constrained ... for the foreseeable future, by institutions, culture, borders, police, and xenophobia' (247). Consequently, 'capital and labor increasingly tend to exist in different spaces and different times: the space of flows and the space of places, instant time of computerized networks versus clock time of everyday life' (506). The vast majority of people find themselves struggling to conform to the demands of a network logic that breaks down 'the rhythms, either biological or social, associated with the notion of a life-cycle' (476).

The challenge for globalised specialty labour is to reconcile embodied self to the pace and demands of capital flows, since the '[p]eople who move and act faster, who come nearest to the momentariness of movement, are now the people who rule' (Bauman 2000:119). Modern citizenship privileged settlement, property and a fixed abode, and marginalised the rootless and nomadic; but the information age privileges business-class nomadism over settlement, while forcing locatedness on impoverished populations. This shift has produced new architectures and spaces. Marc Augé, for example, points to a proliferation of 'non-places', such as airports, motorways, trains, planes and supermarkets, which 'discourage the thought of "settling in"' (Bauman 2000: 102) and 'subject the individual consciousness to entirely new experiences and ordeals of solitude', replacing any sense of organic community with 'the shared identity of passengers, customers or Sunday drivers' (Augé: 75, 83). Non-places are marked by their use of 'words and texts' and 'codified ideograms', whether 'prescriptive', 'prohibitive' or 'informative', to instruct us in their proper use and our relationship to the institutions that own, control and police them (77–78). Augé describes the non-place as 'the opposite of Utopia' inasmuch as 'it exists' and, like the rational dystopias of *Just Imagine*, *Things to Come*, *The Creation of the Humanoids*, *Alphaville*, *Fahrenheit 451*, *THX 1138*, *Le couple témoin*, *The Satisfiers of Alpha Blue* and *Equilibrium*, 'does not contain any organic society' (90).

Several sf films are set in non-places, the 'installations needed for the accelerated circulation of passengers and goods' (28). *Demonlover* (2002) transits between the Tokyo and Paris of the international business class, taking place almost entirely in aeroplanes, airports, cars, squash courts, hotels, restaurants, nightclubs, limousines, taxis, subterranean parking lots and apartments whose décor is so minimalist and devoid of personal touches that the offices seem more homely. Such non-spaces are frequently depicted through glass, from the outside looking in, emphasising their exclusivity while also rendering them as washed out, enervated spaces, in which disoriented, jet-lagged passengers experience the disjunction between material embodiment and the instantaneous circulation of capital. *Code 46* (2003) ranges from Shanghai to the Persian Gulf, with protagonist William Geld (Tim Robbins) seeming more like a visitor in his Seattle home than a resident. This near future – in which everyone speaks a global English containing elements of Spanish, French, Italian, Arabic, Farsi and Mandarin – is divided between walled cities and barren landscapes. Elaborate security protocols separate those inside from those condemned to life outside. In order to travel, it is necessary to obtain insurance from The Sphinx Corporation, although the real purpose of 'cover' is regulating population and movement. In Shanghai, Geld has an affair with Maria Gonzalez (Samantha Morton), which is illegal since they share 50 per cent of their genetic material (their mothers came from the same batch of *in vitro* births). When they are caught, Geld's memories of the affair are wiped without his consent but with his wife's collusion, while Maria, her citizenship revoked, is exiled into the wilderness.

Cypher is set in the non-places of lesser US cities, with a washed-out visual style and a restricted palette of blacks, whites and pastel browns emphasising the interchangeability of airport hotels in San José, Buffalo, Omaha, Boise, Wichita, Redmond, Provo and Nantucket. Human identity seems equally devoid of qualities, and thus malleable. Morgan Sullivan (Jeremy Northam), posing as Jack Thursby, goes undercover for Digicorp Technologies, visiting national sales conferences for shaving foam and processed cheese. The presentations, it transpires, are actually brainwashing sessions organised by Digicorp to convince Sullivan that he really is Thursby, so that a rival corporation, Sunways Systems, will recruit him; which they do, knowing full well he is Sullivan. In order to extricate himself from these complex entanglements, Sullivan seeks out legendary industrial spy Sebastian Rooks, only to discover that he himself is Rooks. He erased his own identity in order to become Sullivan and set in train the series of events in which he has been mired so that he could remove from an isolated data bank information about his lover, Rita Foster (Lucy Liu), with whom the unwitting Sullivan fell in love during his adventures. Rooks and Rita sail off on his yacht, finally extracted – and liberated by Rooks's wealth – from worldly entanglement.

X (Willem Dafoe), the protagonist of *New Rose Hotel* (1998), is less fortunate. He and Fox (Christopher Walken), partners in corporate espionage, recruit Sandii (Asia Argento), an Italian prostitute in Tokyo, to lure scientific genius, Hiroshi (Yoshitaka Amano), away from Maas corporation and into working for rival corporation Hosaka. Things start to go wrong when X falls in love with Sandii. While X and Fox celebrate the apparently successful corporate defection, Sandii disappears and a virus kills Hiroshi and Hosaka's leading scientists, who have gathered in his new laboratory. Maas knew about the plan and used it to put Hosaka out of business by wiping out their R&D capability. With Fox murdered by Maas assassins and the $100 million fee missing from their account, X hides out in a coffin hotel, trying to work out when exactly Sandii betrayed them. For the concluding 22 minutes of screen time, X lies in a small, dark room, examining and re-examining a handful of Sandii's possessions and replaying events in his mind. Close-ups of his face intercut with surveillance footage and flashbacks that are out of chronological order, and contain alternative takes, dialogue variations and new footage. While the viewer does witness what appears to be Sandii deciding to betray her partners, it is only an illusion of closure. Since her back was to X, her change of expression might merely be his fantasy; and even if he has identified the right moment, it actually explains nothing. The film ends with X spiralling deeper and deeper into constrained locality, from globetrotting criminal to solipsistic fugitive trapped in a cycle of memory and speculation that he can neither resolve nor escape.

Neoliberal globalisation has also transformed cities into zones of 'spatial segregation, separation and exclusion' (Bauman 1998: 3). Public spaces have been replaced, often at public expense, with privatised civil spaces, where 'everything within sight inspires awe yet discourages staying', or which are dedicated to the mass but 'utterly, irredeemably individual pastime' of consumption (Bauman 2000: 96, 97). Zygmunt Bauman describes various interdictory spaces, which combine to exclude certain potential users, and thus enforce the separation between territorialised local and exterritorialised global populations (1998: 20–21), and emic spaces and phagic spaces, which eject or assimilate difference (2000: 101–2), and which often combine to produce 'diversity without tension' by offering a reductive, stylised version of otherness (Barber: 209). Stephen Graham and Simon Marvin describe the instruments and architectures of bypass, 'parallel infrastructure network[s]' that connect 'valued users and places' with each other and 'global circuits of infra-structural exchange', while simultaneously 'bypassing non-valued users and places within a city' (167). Such bypasses 'allow the global city enclaves, the cyber districts, the manufacturing space, the "techno-poles", the back office zones and the logistics enclaves to remove themselves from the surrounding social world of the city' (377), while 'electronic tagging' and 'biometric scanning devices' enable the devel-opment and use of 'city-wide, national, even international systems of intimate monitoring and control' to classify 'individuals into the spaces and times where they are deemed to "belong"' (243).

In 'the world of the globally mobile, … space has lost its constraining quality and is easily traversed in both its "real" and "virtual" renditions', but for 'the world of the "locally tied", of those barred from moving and thus bound to bear passively whatever change may be visited' upon their locality, 'the real space is fast closing up' (Bauman 1998: 88). These two worlds do however mirror each other in one respect. The first, rather than engaging with the consequences (for the second) of its drive to obtain 'as much leeway and freedom of manoeuvre' (69), instead fortresses the locations in which, however briefly, its population settles, building walled and gated communities, employing surveillance technologies and private security forces, criminalising more and more of the second's activities, incarcerating its population, removing them from view. Similarly, the inhabitants of the second – in their ghettoes, estates, projects, banlieues and favelas (e.g., *Shopping* (1994), *Welcome II the Terrordome* (1995), *Banlieue 13/District 13* (2004), *Gusha no bindume/Hellevator* (2004), *La horde/The Horde* (2009), *Attack the Block* (2011)), in their transit camps, refugee camps, interment camps and prisons (e.g., *Le temps du loup/The Time of the Wolf* (2003), *Children of Men* (2006), *28 Weeks Later* (2007), *District 9* (2009), *Gamer* (2009)) – 'try to install on the borders of their … home ground "no trespassing" signs of their own making', but these 'attempts to make their territorial claims audible and legible' tend to be criminalised and aggressively suppressed (22).

The dialectics of mobility and confinement, of exclusion and excludedness, are played out in numerous recent sf films. *Doomsday*

(2008), which repeatedly alludes to Thatcher's neoliberal regime, focuses on barriers separating populations. A rebuilt, militarised Hadrian's Wall keeps out Scots infected by a zombie plague; and the zombie which finally infects Prime Minister John Hatcher (Alexander Siddig) must first pass through the succession of 'impenetrable' barriers that separate him from the people he governs. *Eden Log's* (2007) eponymous corporation promises to reward immigrants labouring in their factory with citizenship, while concealing from citizens that the plant actually feeds on the workers. Eden Log publicly espouse 'a new social order' built upon the 'integration' of non-citizens into 'our civilisation', and believe that, when the truth emerges, 'our citizens will accept what our needs impose on these populations'. In *Cube* (1997), seven strangers, all named after prisons, wake up in a structure composed of 17,576 14-foot cubes, some of them lethally booby trapped, which move around within the larger cube. To navigate this shifting maze, they must work out the relationships among each cube's code number, Cartesian coordinates, prime numbers, factored primes and primes of primes. Worth (David Hewlett), who just 'work[s] in an office building doing office building stuff', realises that he designed the cube's outer shell but, like the rest of the dispersed labour force subcontracted to construct it, has no useful knowledge of the total project. Ironically, after murderous conflicts, they find themselves back where they started, just as the cube shifts to the exit position − despite their relentless movement through space, they merely repeatedly escaped from one space of confinement to another, without affecting their overall condition of confinement. In *Death Race* (2008), a corporation that runs prisons expands the exploitation of inmate labour, following to-the-death cage fights with death races. Warden Hennessey (Joan Allen) covers up the demise of extremely popular masked champion Frankenstein (voiced by David Carradine) and sets in motion a plan to place another driver behind the mask in this lethal, but very profitable, sport. She frames Jensen Ames (Jason Statham), a disgraced former racing driver and newly unemployed steelworker, for the murder of his wife, and coerces him into adopting Frankenstein's identity. The bulk of the film is then taken up with images of confinement and of heavily armed and armoured vehicles speeding around a sprawling, but contained, circuit. In *Jigureul jikyeora!/ Save the Green Planet* (2003) the tables are turned as Kang Man-Shik (Yun-Shik Baek), the latest corporate executive to be abducted by Lee Byeong-gu (Ha-kyun Shin), is confined in a now-derelict mining installation, strapped into a chair and tortured until he confesses to being an evil alien.

REPRESENTATIONS OF LABOUR IN CONTEMPORARY SF

In conclusion, this chapter will consider three films that illustrate the relationship between global, networked, neo-liberal capitalism and the varieties of labour upon which it is built: *Transformers* (2007), *Africa Paradis* (2006) and *Sleep Dealer* (2008). *Transformers* opens with Blackout, an evil, shapeshifting, alien Decepticon, attacking a US base in Qatar. Captain Lennox (Josh Duhamel) escapes with his ethnically integrated but racially hierarchised platoon: his second-in-command is African American Tech Sergeant Epps (Tyrese Gibson), and they all mock Puerto Rican Private Figuero (Amaury Nolasco) for occasionally speaking Spanish. Pursued by the Decepticon Scorponok, they take a stand at a desert village of semi-modern Arab herdsmen, but Lennox's urgent cell phone call to the Pentagon requesting an airstrike is delayed by an Indian telephone operator (Ravi Patel) trying to sell him the 'premium plus world service gold package'. This sequence – an imbroglio of geopolitics, cutting-edge military technologies, consumer communication technologies, military command networks, electronic commercial flows – demonstrates the combined and uneven development of the global economy while contrasting different kinds of labour force in a racialised, developmentalist narrative.

The herdsmen represent the remnants of subsistence agriculture, a pre-capitalist form that the logic of capital demands must be destroyed so as to transform the population into labour power, thus enabling both mass consumption and wage-suppression (there are always other workers available); this process, as the commodities dotting the mise-en-scène suggest, is well underway. The call centre represents offshored labour, relocated from a core to a semiperipheral nation where labour, land and construction are cheaper, so as to enable mobile finance capital to become fixed capital (buildings, facilities) for a shorter amortisation period and thus more rapidly available to move on in search of further profit. The military personnel, who move across continents and timezones, improvising temporary solutions to the Decepticon threat, are neither quite Castells's 'elite specialty labor force' nor the 'patriots of wealth' who 'cease to be citizens of their own country and become nomads belonging to, and owing allegiance to, a superterrestrial topography of money' (Seabrook: 211). Within the dialectics of mobility and confinement, they can go apparently anywhere but only on command. In many ways, they exemplify the kind of labour force demanded by 'the new spirit of capitalism': like a Transformer, the worker must be '*adaptable* and *flexible*, able to switch from one situation to a very different one, and adjust to it; and *versatile*, capable of changing activity or tools, depending on the nature of the relationship entered into with others or with objects' (Boltanski and Chiapello: 112).

At the film's climax, Lennox deliberately leads the Decepticons into downtown Mission City for a confrontation with the good, shapeshifting alien Autobots. The choice of location for this 'hot demolition'[25] of fixed capital resonates with the heavily criticised practice of contracting US-based corporations to rebuild infrastructure destroyed by the US military (see Klein) and with the Pentagon's perception that cities will be the distinctive, twenty-first-century battlespace. For example, USAF Captain Troy Thomas recommends training troops in their 'own blighted cities', where 'massive housing projects have become uninhabitable and industrial plants unusable' but are 'nearly ideal for combat-in-cities training' (online). It is significant, then, that one of the real-world locations from which Mission City is cobbled together is Detroit's Michigan Central Station, probably the iconic image of American deindustrialisation. Glimpses of it unconsciously register the fact that US cities are more commonly devastated not by WMDs or evil space-robots but by the neoliberal deregulation that increased the mobility of finance capital so as to leave amortised fixed capital behind to rot, along with former workers. Consequently, while *Transformers* (2007) champions imperial force deployed to maintain global hegemony, it also sometimes accidentally speaks 'the truth of globalization' (Jameson 2005: 381).

Africa Paradis (2006) is set in 2033, after the European Union, reduced to 'an underdeveloped continent', has collapsed into a chaos of epidemics, famines and wars: Turks have taken over Germany, Switzerland is a fundamentalist kingdom, Monaco a Democratic Republic, England a colony of Guatemala and the Vatican a protestant dictatorship. Europe is in the process of becoming one of '*the black holes of informational capitalism*', those 'regions of society from which, statistically speaking, there is no escape from the pain and destruction inflicted on the human condition' (Castells 2000b: 167). Meanwhile, united, democratic pan-Africa is a technologically advanced economic powerhouse faced with the problem of European illegal immigrants. In France, where unemployment is at 65 per cent, computer engineer Olivier (Stéphane Roux) and school-teacher Pauline (Charlotte Vermeil) reject legal immigration when they realise that they will only be offered menial work as garbage collectors or domestic servants. Instead, human traffickers smuggle them into Africa, where they are immediately captured and detained for deportation. Olivier escapes, adopts the identity of a worker killed in a hit and run and settles in White City, the immigrant ghetto. Pauline finds work as a maid in the household of Modibu Kodossou (Sylvestre Amoussou) and as a tutor for his nephew and niece. Believing Olivier dead, she falls in love with Kodossou, genial President of the Liberal African Party. He introduces a bill to give immigrants citizenship rights after five years of labour, but it is opposed in the Chamber of Deputies by the 'Africa for Africans' Patriotic Party, whose leader, Yokossi (Emile Abossolo M'bo), believes that there are fundamental differences between blacks and lazy whites. Yokossi and the Chief of Police M'Doula (Eriq Ebouaney) set out to discredit white immigrants, permitting the Union for White Integration to march in support of the bill, but also hiring a sniper to shoot a policeman so as to justify violent repression of the 'riot'.

Taiwo Adetunji Osinubi criticises *Africa Paradis* for offering 'no glimpse of how Africans resolved all their differences and achieved continental unity' (272), but the film is uninterested in extrapolation as traditionally understood in sf criticism. Instead, it juxtaposes and recombines 'heterogeneous or contradictory elements of the empirical real world' into 'piquant montages' (Jameson 2005: 276), presenting an absurd future Europe so as to cover over the problem of representing the transition to Utopia, while incidentally demonstrating the oft-noted inability to envision the end of capitalism. While it is relatively easy to imagine the European Union fragmenting and being consumed by recession, a booming Pan-Africa seems impossible. At the annual IMF/ World Bank meeting in 2004, Gordon Brown 'observed that the UN's Millennium Development Goals for Africa, originally projected to be achieved by 2015, would not be attained for generations: "Sub-Saharan Africa will not achieve universal primary education until 2013, a 50 percent reduction in poverty in 2150 and the elimination of avoidable infant deaths until 2165"' (Davis: 18–19). However, even though most African nations would benefit from alternative models of development that involve 'partial delinking' of their economies 'from global networks of capital accumulation, given the consequences of the current asymmetrical linkages', they are unable to do so because 'the interests and values of the majority of Africa's political elites and their networks of patronage' benefit from structural asymmetries, 'historically produced' and 'structurally maintained by the European/American powers', which underdevelop Africa and impoverish Africans (Castells 2000b: 129).

Sleep Dealer (2008) is set south of the US/Mexico border fence, that potent symbol of the contradictions between the nation-state's territorial logic and capital's processual logic, between fixed capital and hypermobile finance capital (Harvey 2010: 204–6). It starts in the dry, dusty, disconnected village of Santa Ana del Rio, in Oaxaca, Mexico. Memo Cruz (Luis Fernando Peña) unintentionally intercepts transmission from a paramilitary security drone operated from El Rio Water Inc's San Diego HQ. El Rio destroyed milpa subsistence agriculture by damming the local river and piping the water to the US. Memo's father must now pass through a security fence guarded by cameras and remote-operated machine guns to purchase water. He argues that the pipeline that denies them water cuts them off from the land and thus their future. This 'accumulation by dispossession' (Harvey 2010: 249) – turning a common, shared resource into a commodity – is part of a neoliberal capitalism that, through 'the ever-accelerating extension of *credit*' monetises and thus appropriates and accumulates 'the future itself' and 'thereby *uses it up*' (Shaviro 2010a: 32). The distinction between national military and corporate paramilitary having more or less completely eroded, El Rio defines any opposition as 'terrorism' and defends its property with lethal force. Memo's accidental intercept is traced, and a drone, operated by Chicano Rudy Ramirez (Jacob Vargas), blows up his home, killing his 'terrorist' father. It is Rudy's first mission, broadcast on *Drones!*, a reality show featuring '[g]raphic violence against evildoers – if you have children, you will not want them to miss it'.

Searching for work to support his bereaved family, Memo heads to Tijuana – 'The biggest border town in the world. It pulls in people like a magnet. Even today, long after the border has been closed. Wandering souls keep coming, carrying nothing but their dreams'. There, fitted with cybernetic nodes, he works exhausting, dangerous twelve-hour shifts in a sleep dealer, a *maquiladora* in which Mexican labourers remote-operate robots in the US. The foreman explains: 'This is the American Dream. We give the United States what they've always wanted … all the work – without the workers'.[26] The sleep dealers even maintain the gendering of Chicano/a labour: Maria's robot is a nanny in Washington, José's an Iowa slaughterhouse worker and Memo works high steel. 'Finally', Memo says of his nodes, 'I could connect my nervous system to the other system, the global economy' – at which point the film cuts to the precarious *favela* in which he lives.

Student loan defaulter Luz Martínez (Leonor Varela) tries to make a living through freelance reportage on the conditions in, and her experience of, Mexico. Through her nodes, she sells her memories/reports online. When the remorseful Rudy, googling Santa Ana del Rio, finds her piece on Memo, he commissions further memories of Memo in an attempt to find out the consequences of his mission. As Memo and Luz spend more time together, they fall in love; but the nodes do not permit her to edit her memories, and Memo is outraged when he discovers she is selling her memories of him.

Memo works on the cusp between 'material labour' and 'immaterial labour', manipulating information through somatic movement, but with an actual physical product, while Rudy's labour is immaterial since his manipulation of information merely pilots the drone, producing nothing. Luz's labour is immaterial, too, combining 'creative and intelligent manipulation' of information with 'routine symbolic tasks'; but it is also 'affective labour', geared towards 'the creation and manipulation of affect' (Hardt and Negri: 293) in her subscribers. Affective labour involves 'what feminist analyses of "women's work" have called "labor in the bodily mode"' (Hardt and Negri: 293) – something *Africa Paradis*'s Pauline, a teacher hired as a maid and tutor, who feels affection for her charges, would recognise. Luz is drawn, against her wishes, into labour in the bodily mode because node technology, which is also often used for pornography and prostitution, prevents her from concealing her affective involvement in the memories she records. She wants her reportage to be affective, but she cannot conceal or suppress her own affect, her love for Memo. Between them, these three characters demonstrate the move from the 'formal' to the 'real subsumption' of labour under capital, as distinctions between the production and circulation of commodities disappear:

> There is no longer any way to distinguish between work and leisure, or between economic activities and other aspects of human life. … Affective labor, under the regime of real subsumption, conflates production and circulation. … circulation is no longer external to production … The very performance of affective or immaterial labor is already an exchange in which value is, all at once, produced, realized, and consumed. … passion is indistinguishable from economic calculation, and our inner lives are as thoroughly monetized and commodified as our outward possessions. Libidinal flows are coextensive with financial ones.
>
> (Shaviro 2010a: 48–49)

At the end of *Sleep Dealer*, Rudy leaves the US behind, heading further south, while Memo and Luz reconcile. Although Memo knows he cannot delink from that other system, the global economy, he plants and tends his own *milpa* and sets himself the problem of how to fashion a future with a past.

CONCLUSION

Noting the more-or-less simultaneous emergence of both cinema and sf during the height of European imperialism and colonialism, this chapter outlined the ways in which sf cinema reproduced – and continues to reproduce – colonial ideology, from early narratives of exotic lands and alien worlds through to the contemporary militaristic blockbuster. However, as extended examples from postwar British sf and US counter-cultural sf demonstrate, this does not mean that either the medium or the genre is incapable of reflecting upon dominant ideology – or of trying to articulate alternate visions of the world. Indeed, in the period in which the capitalist world market consolidated its grasp, sf cinema frequently offered accounts of the world being produced by neoliberal globalisation and of its consequences for people and environments. While many such films could be seen as merely confirming the idea, variously ascribed to Fredric Jameson or Slavoj Žižek, that it is easier to imagine the end of the world than the end of capitalism, they nonetheless speak truths about the world and indicate the possibility of and desire for a different world.

These three chapters – these three tours through the streets of the sf city – can only offer partial views of the genre. Taken together, they can only offer a prismatic view of aspects of the genre. There are many more chapters to be written, streets to be wandered, sights to be seen, pasts to be unearthed, alternative traditions to be encountered and futures to unfold. There is no totalising, rationalised model of sf to be attained or imposed; but there remain countless intertwined, unrecognised poems below the threshold of visibility to be sought out and relished, and guidebooks to be composed.

NOTES

INTRODUCTION

1 On film genre theory, see Altman; Moine.

1 THE SCIENCE IN SCIENCE FICTION

1 http://www.scienceandentertainmentexchange.org/about (accessed on 8 February 2012).

2 On the representation of scientists in literature, film and other media, see Haynes; Frayling. On the role of scientific advisers on films, see David Kirby.

3 Suvin admits that, despite some overlaps, the genre he has chosen to call sf is not the same as 'the twentieth-century SF from which the name was taken' (13). On Suvin, see Parrinder; Bould and Miéville.

4 In 1954, about a hundred fishing vessels and several of the Marshall Islands were exposed to radioactive fallout from a US H-bomb test on the Bikini Atoll. The blast was more powerful than anticipated and wind patterns changed unexpectedly. The *Daigo Fukuryū Maru*'s crew all suffered from radiation sickness and the radio operator died six months later. Contaminated catches had to be destroyed. The US initially denied everything, but fearing

that the growing anti-nuclear movement would push Japanese politics in an anti-US direction, eventually paid $2 million in compensation. It is unsurprising, then, that Susan Sontag, for example, considered 'the super-destructive monster … an obvious metaphor for the Bomb' (1994a: 218). However, Gojira is far more symbolically rich than this. His abrupt attack from the south, reducing Tokyo to flaming ruins, recalls the massive US firebombing of this and other cities. The path of his rampage also suggests the returning souls of the Japanese soldiers who died in the Pacific War (see Inuhiko), a reading explicitly stated and expanded upon in *Gojira, Mosura, Kingu Gidorā: Daikaijū sôkôgeki/Godzilla, Mothra and King Ghidorah: Giant Monsters All-Out Attack* (2001). Gojira's association with the Odo islanders suggests the traditional culture mourned by many Japanese in the face of modernisation/Westernisation. Simultaneously, being radioactive and destroying both traditional and modernised sites, he symbolises an even greater and irresistible modernity *and* resistance to it (see Anderson). He is both nature *and* technology; he is feudal/patriarchal power demanding a return to a masculinised executive politics contemptuous of the masses *and* associated with female emancipation and the other democratising forms introduced by the US-authored constitution; he is the local responding to the national, and the national responding to the global. See also Brophy; Igarashi; Napier; Noriega.

5 The 'only way to transmute heavy elements [are] radioactive decay and nuclear fission, both of which must begin with radioactive elements and must end with elements of a lower number; thus, proposing to convert a heavy element with no radioactive isotopes into an element with a higher atomic number [makes] no sense' (Westfahl 1999: 53).

6 Although elsewhere he does discuss *This Island Earth* in relation to race, gender and the expansion of television in the postwar period (see Westfahl 2000).

7 For a refutation of the notion that there is a single, correct way to interpret an sf text, see Vint and Bould.

8 For an introduction to science studies, see Biagioli and, in relation to sf, Vint. On boundary work in science, see Gieryn 1999; Hess; Luckhurst; Milburn; Willis. On contemporary scientific cultures of knowledge production, see Knorr Cetina; Traweek.

9 They describe such benefits in terms of 'contribut[ing] more exactly, and exactingly, to improving present and future societal arrangements, stimulating wealth creation, informing social values, enhancing life-styles and individual choices, and helping to develop more sustainable relationships with the natural environment (while halting processes leading to its degradation)' (56).

10 Merton lists various unacceptable criteria of exclusion, but appears blind to his own assumption that scientists are male (on the systematic exclusion of women from science, see Harding 1986; Rossiter 1984, 1995). J.D. Bernal notes the pressures, especially on working-class scientists, to be conformist and to conform to middle-class values (388). Warren Hagstrom demonstrates the extent to which scientific careers are built around competitive individualism, and Sharon Traweek highlights the significance of personality traits in career advancement. Such competition is partly a consequence of the increasing proletarianisation of scientists, disempowered by industrial divisions of labour that concentrate information (and wealth) in managers and owners rather than distributing it among scientific workers (Harding 1986: 73–76).

11 Significantly, '"autonomy of science" rhetoric … reached its heyday in the United States' in the post-war period, when 'leaders of the scientific establishment [were attempting] to protect science from the kind of public scrutiny and accountability which such huge federal expenditures … and the vastly increased investment in scientific research and development signalled by the Manhattan Project would seem to demand' (Harding 2008: 91).

12 There were German, French and English language versions with different stars but much of the same footage.

13 Professor Planetaros (Nicolai Neiiendam) is a stable bourgeois patriarch, his observatory uncluttered, his spacious home well-appointed with solid-looking furniture. His rival, the vain Professor Dubius (Frederik Jacobsen), lives alone; his study, strewn with books and papers, is presided over by a stuffed owl, symbolising his more arcane pursuits.

14 The watchtower can be seen in relation to the creation of European identity in opposition to the northward and westward advance of Islamic cultures in medieval and early modern times, and to the suppression of this Orientalised other's scientific advances upon which much of 'Western science' is

built (see Harding 1998; Hobson). Buildings evoking former modes of production and privileged seclusion as sites of scientific experimentation remain common in sf, such as the castles, plantations, country houses, lodges, walled gardens and greenhouses of *This Island Earth* (1955), *The Fly* (1958), *Island of Terror* (1966), *Flash Gordon* (1980), *Tajemství hradu v Karpatech/ The Mysterious Castle in the Carpathians* (1983), *Minority Report* (2002), *Patalghar* (2003) and *Subject Two* (2006). In the post-industrial *Tetsuo: The Iron Man* (1989), *Tetsuo II: Bodyhammer* (1992), *La cité des enfants perdus/The City of Lost Children* (1995) and *Splice* (2009), derelict factories, oil rigs and smallholdings become sites for experimentation.

15 Shapin outlines the gentleman scientist's struggle to resolve the contradiction between needing privacy in which to conduct experiments and the social expectation that, as a gentleman, he is always ready to receive visitors in the public rooms of his private house, the frustrations of which are suggested by Frankenstein's 'Of all the times for anybody to come!' and his whinging that their intrusion will 'ruin everything'.

16 Louis A. Sass's description of schizoids emphasising the disjunction between inner and public self through 'a radical contrariness, in which one declares one's freedom from social constraint through the unconventionality of one's behavior; or a blatant inauthenticity, in which one flaunts the falseness of one's behavior' (103) captures something of Colin Clive's performance of Frankenstein.

17 Shapin notes that the most common form in which working-class figures appear in accounts of experimental work is as obstacles whose inattention and errors wreck experiments. Fritz, of course, procures for the creature not the required exemplary brain but a degenerate one.

18 Such miscegenation anxieties are common in mad science films. For example, Fredric March's Mr Hyde is depicted as a brutish, black ape who rapes and murders working-class Ivy and is narrowly prevented from a similar assault on upper-class Muriel. In *Island of Lost Souls* (1932), Dr Moreau (Charles Laughton) abandons plans to mate the shipwrecked Edward Parker (Richard Arlen) with dark-skinned Lota (Kathleen Burke), a panther surgically transformed into human form, in favour of one of his even darker beast-men raping Parker's fiancée, Ruth Thomas (Leila Hyams).

19 The fantasy of returning to the mother–child dyad that pre-existed the infant's recognition of itself as a distinct entity, separate from the maternal body, continues to be associated with the horrific engulfment of the subject, consumed by the (feminised) nature (masculinised) science attempts to objectify and hold at a distance. In *Star Trek: First Contact* (1996), the specific aural quality of Alice Krige's delivery of the Borg Queen's dialogue 'envelops and absorb[s] the listener', emphasising through this 'maternal and all-engulfing' voice the threat she poses to 'individual agency' (Cornea 159–60). In *Altered States* (1980), Eddie Jessup (William Hurt), who moans about the 'clatter and clutter' of marriage, children and departmental politics, combines powerful hallucinogens with sensory deprivation in order to achieve a transcendence that is also a regression through human genetic heritage to the origins of the life. However, the abyss that confronts him when he tries to merge with the 'first thought' of the universe takes the form of recurring vaginal images, a reminder of the maternal body and sexual difference. The film ends as his wife, Emily (Blair Brown), rescues him once more from this desire for disembodiment that threatens to shatter and consume subjectivity. *Contact* (1997) conflates alienation from the maternal body with the female scientist's 'unnatural' pursuit of empirical knowledge, and the sudden loss of a nurturing father with atheism. The film begins in near-Earth orbit with a cacophony of broadcasts being emitted into space at the speed of light. As the viewpoint accelerates away from the planet, these broadcasts thin out as, travelling faster than the speed of light, it overtakes past transmissions (albeit too quickly) and heads into the depths of interstellar space. Silence reigns. The viewpoint continues to accelerate into intergalactic space, completing the sense of being expelled from the maternal body, becoming isolated and alone. This is emphasised by the way the blazing screen of light morphs into a reflection in the eye of nine-year-old Ellie Arroway (Jena Malone), a ham radio novice who quizzes her gentle, nurturing father about the range of the radio – not just whether it would be possible to talk to Alaska, China, the moon, Jupiter or Saturn but to her mother, who died giving birth to her. When he dies soon afterwards, she sits alone in her room, trying to raise him on the radio. Years later, the adult Ellie (Jodie Foster), a SETI radio astronomer, detects an alien transmission containing blueprints for the

machine that will ultimately project her through a wormhole to a distant world. The tunnel of light into which she is plunged signals a return to the maternal body, here conflated with a reassurance that neither she – the alien who summoned her adopts the appearance of her father – nor humanity are alone. This encounter ideologically disciplines her into tempering empirical reason with faith, freeing her finally to pursue a romantic relationship with spiritually inclined Palmer Joss (Matthew McConaughey).

20 Alongside his rejection of embodiment and social and affective entanglements, the film hints at suppressed racial differences. The drug that deranges him comes 'from a flower that's grown in India', where it is used as a bleach, simultaneously evoking suppressed Eastern science and opium addiction, another solitary, degenerate vice. There are implications of racial passing (and the possibility of miscegenation) when a radio broadcast breaks the news of a 'mysterious disease' that 'takes the form of a delusion that an invisible man is living among' the villagers affected by it, and when a variety of mob violence is sanctioned as the police recruit thousands of volunteers to track down Griffin.

21 Sandra Harding argues that industrialised science inevitably produces discrepancies between scientists' ambitions and the 'assembly-line' work they are actually likely to spend an entire career doing on projects designed by people and institutions whose 'research priorities may differ from' their own (1986: 79). Consequently, a 'tension is increasingly obvious between the ethic that draws young people into the arduous training necessary for a career in science and the realities produced by the actual projects for which they are recruited'; after all, she aks, who would actually 'choose a career goal of building bombs, torturing animals, or manufacturing machines that will put one's sisters and brothers out of work?' (79).

22 As *Alraune* (1918), *Alraune, die Henkerstochter, genannt die rote Hanne/Sacrifice* (1918), *Alraune/A Daughter of Destiny* (1928), *Alraune/Daughter of Evil* (1930) and *Alraune/Unnatural* (1952). Similar material preoccupies *Embryo* (1976), the *Species* franchise (1995–2007) and *Splice*. On *Species*, see Stacey 2010: 66–92; on *Splice*, see Shaviro 2010b.

23 *Demon Seed* (1977) demonstrates the extent to which such films are underpinned by rape fantasies. Proteus IV, an organic artificial intelligence

developed by the unemotional Alex Harris (Fritz Weaver), imprisons, terrorises, rapes and impregnates its creator's estranged wife, Susan (Julie Christie), and forces her to carry its offspring to term. When Alex eventually comes to the rescue, he is too fascinated by Proteus's cyborg progeny to let Susan destroy it.

2 SF, SPECTACLE AND SELF-REFLEXIVITY

1 On Méliès' special effects techniques, see Ezra: 24–34.

2 See Mulvey; Bukatman 2006.

3 This ability to see texture partially explains the strong preference before the mid-1990s, evident in *Tron* and *The Last Starfighter* (1984), of deploying CGI in pursuit of 'a hyperreal electronic aesthetic that took the cinematographic as a possible point of departure' rather than a 'realist aesthetic that took the cinematographic image as an absolute point of reference' (Pierson: 87).

4 This spectatorial dual consciousness, which surrenders to *and* scrutinises the spectacle, was cultivated among audiences of pre-cinematic spectacles and stage magic shows that both deployed and demonstrated the technical apparatus of illusions (Pierson: 11–51; North: 24–65). Stage-magician-turned-filmmaker Méliès bridged between these entertainment forms, remediating and expanding upon stage illusions as he explored cinema technologies.

5 The latter recall Frederick Edwin Church's luminist landscapes, in which Scott Bukatman (2003a) sees Douglas Trumbull's special effects sequences prefigured. Such paintings were a precinematic spectacular entertainment: when Church unveiled his *The Heart of the Andes* (1859), over five feet high and ten feet wide, it was to viewers equipped with opera glasses and seated in a darkened room with a spotlight on the canvas, which was framed by drawn curtains.

6 Sequences that flatten, blur and distend the action displace the uncanny onto Skull Island's natives, amplifying the film's racism. The white Driscoll is replaced by the black Hayes (Evan Parke) as first mate but not as Ann's lover. The stageshow in which Kong is revealed to a Broadway audience

reworks elements of the original's 'bride of Kong' sequence and Ann's sacrifice to the giant ape, chiding the original's racism without recognising its own offensive depiction of the islanders. Furthermore, removing the erotic element of Kong's interest in Ann – to avoid casting the ape as a black rapist of white women – problematically introduces another long-standing, derogatory view of black men as infantile.

7 This is not an exhaustive list of sf's spectacular pleasures. For example, recent years have seen a number of sf films with a high level of narrative complexity, including *eXistenZ* (1999), *Possible Worlds* (2000), *Primer, Southland Tales, Los cronocrímenes/Timecrimes* (2007), the *20-seiki shônen* trilogy (2008–09), *Mr Nobody* (2009), *Fisshu sutôrî* (2009), *Inception* (2010) and even the *Matrix* (1999–2003) and *Star Wars* prequel (1999–2005) trilogies. Jason Mittel argues that a similar phenomenon in television drama over the last 20 years offers not merely the pleasure of being 'swept away in a realistic narrative world' but also of 'watch[ing] the gears at work, marveling at the craft required to pull off such narrative pyrotechnics' (35). Narratively complex texts 'offer another mode of attractions: the narrative special effect. These moments [call] attention to the constructed nature of the narration and [ask] us to marvel at how the writers pulled it off; often these instances forgo realism in exchange for a formally aware baroque quality in which we watch the process of narration as a machine rather than engaging in its diegesis' (35). For example, *Fisshu sutôrî*, which interweaves stories of groups of characters in different postwar periods, ends with a brief sequence in chronological order that makes explicit the connections between these stories to finally explain how an obscure Japanese punk rock record could save the world. At the opposite end of the spectrum is *Star Wars: Episode One – The Phantom Menace* (1999) 'a film that is all plot and no narrative' (Pierson: 150). Michelle Pierson speculates that the 'sharp contrast' between its 'thin story world' and 'its dense layering of plot' might be a consequence of how 'it was actually written' (151). With George Lucas 'treating the arranging and rearranging of the elements of a story world as a potentially endless process', perhaps only 'the weakest form of narrative causality, that is, the temporal succession and spatial locatedness of events' is possible: 'As the film moves from one locale to another, often between parallel lines of

action, viewers have no choice but to make identifying where rather than why events are taking place their primary means of orienting themselves to the action' (Pierson: 150–51). Pierson also relates *Phantom Menace*'s peculiar complexities and bagginess to the 'move from a production to a post-production-based medium' (151), which accentuates the atomisation of the filmmaking process. In contrast, the 'compositional logic of *Southland Tales* is paratactic and additive', 'it overlays, juxtaposes, and restlessly moves between multiple images and sound sources' replacing conventional 'hierarchical organization' with 'an affective constellation' of 'correspondences and con-nections': 'Nothing in the film makes sense in terms of linear causality, or in terms of action grounded in character, or even in terms of dialectical contrast. The onward flow of the film, as it zigzags towards catastrophe, is rather a matter of juxtaposition, dreamlike free association, and the pro-liferation of self-referential feedback loops' (Shaviro 2010a: 70–74). On database narratives, see Kinder; Manovich: 218–43; Shaviro 2010a: 64–92. On temporal displacement narratives, see Booth. On modular narratives, see Cameron.

8 On microcinematography as both scientific research method *and* popular entertainment, see Landecker; cf. Cartwright.

9 See Csicsery-Ronay 2008: 162–75.

10 Organ transplant sf, such as *Repo! The Genetic Opera* (2008) and *Repo Men* (2010), foregrounds this tension between enclosure/containment and leaky openness.

11 On the monstrous womb in sf and horror, see Creed.

12 On faeces and sewage as boundary markers in the construction of subjectivity, see Laporte.

13 In *The Fly* (1986), Seth Brundle (Jeff Goldblum), in order to bring to an end 'all concepts of transport, of border and frontiers, of time and space', must teach the teleportation technology he is developing to appreciate the poetry and erotics of fleshly existence. Accidentally gene-spliced with a housefly during a test transmission, he misattributes his newfound strength and agility to being purified by going 'beyond the veil of the flesh', by being broken down into information and reconstituted as a material being. How-ever, this sublime aspiration soon collapses as his body begins to transform,

changes spreading like 'a bizarre form of cancer': he grows bristling hairs, secretes fluid from his fingertips, loses nails and teeth and ears, becomes unable to digest solids but develops the ability to vomit an acid enzyme that liquefies food. His lumpy, lesion-covered body eventually rips apart, but there is no starchild transcendence, just a brutal, resolutely other materiality, associated with disease and effluence. A similar fleshly excess marks the end of *Akira* (1988). After Tetsuo's psionic powers are awoken, he becomes monstrous. He replaces his severed arm with a mechanical replica that swells and grows. This organic riot escapes his control, growing tentacles and toes and countless extrusions, ballooning, engulfing him. A massive, grotesque parody of his face looms into the air, its eyes sealed and its gaping mouth spewing a bilious tongue; hills of flesh spill over each other, briefly revealing Tetsuo's swamped eye. Suddenly Akira – the product of a military experiment to harness massive destructive powers – appears in a blaze of white light that expands, pushing Tetsuo back and destroying parts of Neo-Tokyo before shrinking to a tiny sphere. It is the birth of a new universe, somewhere in *and* adjacent to our own.

14 Tinkcom's examples – musical numbers in Vincente Minnelli's early musicals; 'the playful corporeality' of 'all the eating and fondling' in Andy Warhol's or John Waters's films (28) – find sf equivalents in, for example, the musical numbers in *The Rocky Horror Picture Show* (1975) and the prolonged necrophilic frotteurism and inner organ fondling in which Frankenstein (Udo Keir) indulges in the Warhol-produced *Flesh for Frankenstein* (1973).

15 For example, when Susan Sontag described *Rodan*, *The Mysterians* and *The H-Man* as camp 'because, in their relative unpretentiousness and vulgarity, they are more extreme and irresponsible – and therefore touching and quite enjoyable' (1994b: 285), she was not referring to *Sora no daikaijû Radon* (1956), *Chikyû Bôeigun* (1957) or *Bijo to Ekitainingen* (1958) but to versions of these films adapted for US consumption. This industrial practice built on the success of Terry Morse's *Godzilla, King of the Monsters* (1956), which re-edited Ishiro Honda's *Gojira*, replacing its anti-nuclear stance, political criticisms and sombre mood with a more juvenile adventure story told from the viewpoint of an American reporter, courtesy of newly shot footage and voiceover narration. Morse's reworking proved successful in Japan and, faced with

increasingly costly miniature effects, the Japanese productions thus became increasingly oriented towards both children and the US market. This is not to say that the Japanese productions do not possess camp qualities, but to indicate the degree of disavowal that is often involved when the notion of camp is evoked in relation to what are perceived as shoddy or incompetent films. The denigration of *kaiju eiga* frequently casts them as the product of a foreign other failing in its attempts to imitate American productions (and their presumed universal norms), rather than recognising that they worked within culturally specific popular traditions and circulated globally, that they were increasingly made for children rather than adults, and that some of their exaggerated qualities were self-orientalising postures based on what was deemed to appeal to US audiences by (or in negotiation with) Western producers and distributors.

16 The mechanical musicians – clockwork automata who do not really play the instruments but move in time to pre-recorded music, they are clearly extras dressed and masked to play machines but not the music – also function as an extravagant metaphor for labour-as-production constraining work-as-play. This extravagance is emphasised by their complete superfluity to the narrative despite appearing prominently in the opening sequence, a part of narrative film normally devoted to the economical, unambiguous introduction of plot and character.

17 Undercranked footage had already been used to science-fictional effect in such films as *How to Make Time Fly* (1906), *La ceinture électrique/The Wonderful Electric Belt* (1907), *Liquid Electricity* (1907), *Energizer* (1908) and *A Marvellous Invention* (1911).

18 On such 'affective turn' claims about cultural theory's shortcomings, see Hemmings.

19 Early cinema was fascinated with animating inanimate objects – paintings, portraits and clothes-bedecked hat stands come to life in *The Artist's Dilemma* (1901), *L'auberge du bon repos/The Inn Where No Man Rests* (1903), *Rêve d'artiste/The Artist's Dream* (1903), *Animated Painting* (1904) and *The Artist's Dilemma* (1904) – and by robots, as in *Gugusse et l'automaton/Gugusse and the Automaton* (1897), *Coppélia: la poupée animée/Coppélia, the Animated Doll* (1900), *L'Omnibus des toques blancs et noirs/Off to Bedlam* (1901), *The Doll Maker's Daughter* (1906), *The Mechanical Statue*

and the *Ingenious Servant* (1907), *Work Made Easy* (1907), *An Animated Doll* (1908), *The Rubber Man* (1909), *L'Automat du Dr Smith/Dr Smith's Automaton* (1910), *The Mechanical Husband* (1910), *The Automatic Motorist* (1911), *The Inventor's Secret* (1911), *The Automatic House* (1915), *Die Große Wette/The Great Bet* (1915), *Hoffmanns Erzählungen/Tales of Hoffman* (1915), *The Mechanical Man* (1915), *A Clever Dummy* (1917), *Die Puppe* (1919), *The Master Mystery* (1920) and *L'uomo meccanico/The Mechanical Man* (1921).

20 *Der schweigende Stern* is perhaps the period's only sf film to refer explicitly to these shadow images, connecting the traces of a Venusian apocalypse to the Hiroshima bomb. In *Kairo/Pulse* (2001), similar shadows play a vital role in a rather diffuse apocalypse.

21 There is a similar moment of recoil in *Test Pilota Pirx*. Commander Pirx (Sergei Desnitsky) is recruited for a mission to Saturn, the real purpose of which is to test the ability of humanoid robots to serve alongside – and perhaps replace – humans in space. Pirx, whose prejudice against androids ironically makes him ideal for the job, is given a mixed crew of humans and androids but is not permitted to know which is which. Brown (Vladimir Ivashov) presents Pirx with tenuous evidence that Otis (Bolesaw Abart) is not human – Brown's claim that when Otis is 'sitting or standing, he's absolutely motionless' is accompanied by a cut to slow-motion footage of Otis walking through the ship, including a momentary freeze frame as he turns, in close-up, to look at the camera; this is followed by a slow-motion zoom, which stutters in and out of freeze frame, up from a lower deck as Otis again turns to face the camera – a series of peristaltic convulsions that accompany Brown's voice-over observation that at meal times Otis eats everything, as if he has no personal preferences at all. Later, Weber (Tõnu Saar) 'proves' Brown is not human, while Calder (Zbigniew Lesien), who ultimately turns out to be a murderously megalomaniacal android, refuses to offer any information, and the doctor, Nowak (Aleksandr Kaidanovsky), confides that he is an android (although the truthfulness of this claim is opened to doubt). Pirx asks whether Nowak has ever observed reactions of 'surprise, fear or disgust' when others realised he was not human. Nowak narrates a flashback of a nurse unaware of his status accidentally cutting open the back of his hand when passing a scalpel during surgery. Eyes wide

in terror and revulsion at the sight of his inner workings, she tears off her surgical mask, screaming 'No! No! No!', and backs away from the pallid, unthreatening – and rather bemused – Nowak. While revealing the absurdity of such prejudice, this sequence also demonstrates one of the shortcomings of sf's means of exploring alterity: because Nowak is a white male authority figure – a surgeon and an officer – in a social system dominated by white men, the ability of androids to stand in for actual victims of oppression, and of the film thus to say something meaningful about the operations of power, is curtailed.

22 Similar effects are created in Craig Baldwin's found-footage sf films, *RocketKitKongoKit* (1986), *Tribulation 99: Alien Anomalies Under America* (1992) and *Spectres of the Spectrum* (1999), Lev Manovich's installation film *Mission to Earth* (2003–04) and Guy Maddin's 'docufantasia' *My Winnipeg* (2007).

23 *Deja vu* (2006) and *Source Code* (2011) extend such fantasies, imagining technologies that can transform the past into a navigable landscape and thus exploring determinism, autonomy and identity. This is typical of time-travel, time-loop and parallel-world narratives, such as *Je t'aime, je t'aime* (1968), *Sengoku jieitai/G.I. Samurai* (1979), *Happy Accidents* (2000), *Possible Worlds* (2000), *Donnie Darko* (2001), *Feedback* (2002), *2009: Lost Memories* (2002), *Primer* (2004), *Los cronocrímenes* (2007), *Mr Nobody* (2009), *Triangle* (2009), *Action Replayy* (2010) and *The Terminator* (1984–) and *Back to the Future* (1985–90) franchises.

24 *Horror Express* (1973) features a variant on the optogramme. Professor Saxton (Christopher Lee) and Dr Wells (Peter Cushing) discover that a two-million-year-old fossilised prehuman discovered in Manchuria is host to an energy-based alien lifeform capable of transmitting itself via the eyes into new host bodies. Examining fluid extracted from the eyeball of the reanimated – and then killed – mummy, they find it contains not only the image of its killer but also of sights only the alien could have seen: a brontosaurus, a pterodactyl, and the Earth from space.

25 This reduction of the subject to labour power is evident in *Buck Rogers*, when Buck (Larry 'Buster' Crabbe) is turned into a robot-like slave by a mind-control helmet; in such brainwashing films as *The Manchurian Candidate* (1962, 2004); and in such alien body-snatcher films as *Invaders from Mars* (1953, 1986),

It *Came from Outer Space* (1953), *Invasion of the Body Snatchers* (1956, 1978), *Body Snatchers* (1993) and *The Invasion* (2007). *The Stepford Wives* (1975) recognises the extent to which capital depends upon excluding from its calculations certain costs involved in reproducing labour power. As the women become increasingly aware of the domestic tasks they perform – housework, parenting, supporting their husbands – as forms of labour, an emerging feminist consciousness threatens the patriarchal, suburban idyll of Stepford's menfolk, who replace their wives with robots. In *S1mØne* (2002), actor-hating filmmaker Viktor Taransky (Al Pacino) produces computer-generated synthespian Simone (Rachel Roberts) from a database of thousands of actresses' performances and characteristics – their labour – but pretends she actually exists. The same dynamic of subjectivity and labour power is addressed in films featuring artificial lifeforms who wish to 'become human', or at least have their subjectivities acknowledged by humans, such as *Android* (1982), *Short Circuit* (1986), *Making Mr Right* (1987), *Star Trek: First Contact* (1996), *Bicentennial Man* (1999), *I, Robot* (2004) and *Endhiran* (2010).

26 Althusser immediately adds that ideological hailing or interpellation is a far more complex process than this, a point his critics typically neglect.

27 Sf's non-human and less-than-fully human lifeforms open up films in which subjects fail to match ideological interpellation or properly to perform associated social roles for queer readings. Examples include the aggressively misogynist homosociality, awkwardnesses around women, failures to impregnate wives and preferences for male company in *I Married a Monster from Outer Space* (1958) (see Ostherr: 111–18), and the secretive, closeted lifestyle and bodily self-monitoring of Vincent (Ethan Hawke) and Jerome (Jude Law) in *Gattaca* (1997) (see Stacey 2010: 113–36).

28 See Doane on early cinema's 'particularly popular subgenre of the execution film' (145).

29 Sf often depicts a strong interrelationship between trauma/loss/grief and visual technologies. In *Static* (1985), Ernie Blick (Keith Gordon) builds a television that can tune into a live image of heaven – 'it's a lot like life, but different … better'. However, when he unveils it, other people can only see static. It subsequently emerges that he is still struggling to deal with his

parents' deaths a couple of years earlier. In *Strange Days* (1995), Lenny has never come to terms with his girlfriend, Faith (Juliette Lewis), leaving him, and thus cannot properly perceive or respond to the feelings Mace (Angela Bassett) has for him; in *Eternal Sunshine of the Spotless Mind* (2004), a similar sense of loss prompts Joel (Jim Carrey) and Clementine (Kate Winslet) to have each other edited out of their memories.

3 SF, COLONIALISM AND GLOBALISATION

1 Globalists also differentiate between kinds or elements of globalisation. For example, Ulrich Beck distinguishes between informational globalisation, ecological globalisation, economic globalisation, globalised labour cooperation and cultural globalisation (17–19), while Arjun Appadurai identifies five interrelated 'dimensions of global cultural flows' – ethnoscapes, mediascapes, technoscapes, financescapes and ideoscapes (33).

2 This transformation can also be understood in terms of the transition from monopoly capitalism to late capitalism, from Fordism to post-Fordism and from Keynesianism to neo-liberalism (see, respectively, Mandel; Harvey 1989: 119–97; Harvey 2005).

3 The percentage of the world's landmass under European control increased from 35 per cent in 1800 to 67 per cent in 1878 and 85 per cent in 1914 (Said: 6).

4 The typical elements of lost-race fiction are 'the map or document that initiates the expedition, the perilous journey to a nearly inaccessible destination, and a strictly circumscribed set of locations for the lost land itself (the under-ground world, the polar paradise, the isolated island, plateau, or valley)', 'a beautiful princess, a corrupt priesthood, an architecturally impressive pagan idol, and a treasure or a fabulously rich mine', 'the return of an important native in the company of the explorers, the instigation and resolution of a civil war, and of course romantic involvements between the explorers and the princesses' (Rieder: 22). The 'fundamental "mythic" power' of such fiction derives 'from the way it negotiates the basic problem of ownership by simultaneously reveling in the discovery of uncharted territory and

representing the journey as a return to a lost legacy, a place where the travellers find a fragment of their own history lodged in the midst of a native population that usually has forgotten the connection' (40).

5 Adaptations of Haggard's novel include *She* (1908, 1911, 1916, 1917, 1925, 1935, 1965, 2001), *The Vengeance of She* (1968) and, nominally, *She* (1982). Adaptations of Benoît's novel include *L'Atlantide* (1921, 1961, 1972, 1992), G.W. Pabst's 1932 film (shot in German, French and English versions known, respectively, as *Die Herrin von Atlantis*, *L'Atlantide* and *The Mistress of Atlantis*) and *Siren of Atlantis* (1949); *Ercole alla conquista di Atlantide/Hercules and the Captive Women* (1961) merely borrows the name of Benoît's Queen of Atlantis.

6 The 'concept of Atlantis in the Sahara is not original to' Benoît, 'but is one of the lesser traditional theories' (Bleiler with Bleiler: 55).

7 In contrast, *The Mistress of Atlantis* shows little of the sky, instead emphasising oppressive mountain heights that dwarf the human characters; and in one of its most effective sequences, Saint-Avit (John Stuart) finds himself in the disorientating, irrational maze of an ancient Casbah, built above the labyrinth that will ultimately lead him to Antinea. *Siren of Atlantis* reuses much of *Mistress*'s desert/mountain footage to similar effect, but situates a more noirish account of the psychological disintegration of St. Avit (Jean-Pierre Aumont) within a Hollywood-expressionist Atlantis.

8 This duality echoes the whore/Madonna dichotomy found in the colonial fiction of Haggard and others, which reflects not some 'universal archetype' but 'the class structure of the [upper middle-class, Victorian] household' (McClintock: 87), in which the mother remained aloof and frequently absent while the child was effectively raised by the physically proximate nurse – a source of comfort and discipline whose role was framed by her position as waged labour. Intriguingly, *Mistress* suggests that Antinea (Brigitte Helm) is either the daughter of cancan star Clementine (Odette Florelle), who married a Tuareg prince; or her illegitimate daughter; or Clementine herself, somehow transformed. This irresolvable mystery extends the film's association of female identity with mazes. This elusiveness contrasts with Antinea's relentless defeat of Saint-Avit at chess, checking his king 12 consecutive times before reaching checkmate, but the effect of both her slipperiness and her implacability is to unman Saint-Avit.

9 This logic is perhaps most evident in the notion – found in such unorthodox histories as Erich von Däniken's *Chariots of the Gods* (1968) and Graham Hancok's *Fingerprints of the Gods* (1995), and in films such as *Atlantis, the Lost Continent* (1961), *Stargate* (1994), *Le cinquième élément* (1997), *AVP: Alien vs. Predator* (2004), *Indiana Jones and the Kingdom of the Crystal Skull* (2008) and *Transformers: Revenge of the Fallen* (2009) – that ancient civilisations were insufficiently technologically advanced to build the pyramids in Egypt, Asia and Latin America without the aid of extraterrestrials or a forgotten (white) civilisation. *2001: A Space Odyssey* goes further, suggesting that humanity could not have evolved from African hominids without alien intervention.

10 The Songhai state, eventually centred around Gao, originated in the eighth century and was a vassal kingdom of the Mali Empire, which lasted from the thirteenth to the fifteenth century.

11 Tanit-Zerga's role is reduced in each of the subsequent adaptations, but the contrast between her and Antinea reproduces the long-standing distinction between 'good' and 'bad' natives in, for example, Daniel Defoe's *Robinson Crusoe* (1719), James Fenimore Cooper's *Last of the Mohicans* (1826), Rudyard Kipling's 'Gunga Din' (1892), various versions of *Flash Gordon*, *Star Wars'* Jawas and Tusken Raiders, the Newcomers Sam Francisco (Mandy Patinkin) and William Harcourt (Terence Stamp) in *Alien Nation* (1988), and so on.

12 It also combines these forms of sf narrative with ethnic comedian comedy and a light, romantic musical. In the 1930s, the musical was, like sf, a genre of modernity – see, for example, James Cagney's manic embodiment of capitalist urban modernity in *Footlight Parade* (1933) – and both are spectacular genres. The starring role given to El Brendel, a Philadelphia-born comedian who developed a 'simple Swede' vaudeville persona, must be understood in terms of the importance to early 1930s Hollywood of 'ethnic' stars such as Cagney, Edward G. Robinson and Paul Muni (see Munby: 39–65).

13 In the 50 years after the end of the Civil War, US forces were deployed in Abyssinia, Argentina, Brazil, Chile, China, Colombia, Cuba, the Dominican Republic, Egypt, Formosa, Haiti, Hawai'i, Honduras, Korea, Mexico, Morocco, Nicaragua, Panama, the Philippines, Samoa, Syria, Turkey and Uruguay, sometimes more than once.

14 Unlike Haggard's novel, the film does not insist that Ustane is a dark-skinned white.

15 These narratives, common in westerns and desert and jungle adventures, can be found in numerous sf films, including *Rocketship X-M* (1950), *The Day of the Triffids* (1962), *Planeta Bur* (1962), *Terrore nello spazio* (1965), *Fantastic Voyage* (1966), *Week End* (1967), *Night of the Living Dead* (1968), *No Blade of Grass* (1970), *Punishment Park* (1971), *The Crazies* (1973), *The Cars That Ate Paris* (1974), *A Boy and His Dog* (1975), *Damnation Alley* (1977), *Long Weekend* (1978), *Escape from New York* (1981), *Mad Max 2* (1981), *Spacehunter: Adventures in the Forbidden Zone* (1983), *Aliens* (1986), *Predator* (1987), *Tremors* (1990), *The Postman* (1997), *Starship Troopers* (1997), *Pitch Black* (2000), *Red Planet* (2000), *Ever Since the World Ended* (2001), *28 Days Later* (2002), *Shaun of the Dead* (2004), *The Mist* (2007), *Avatar* (2009), *Pandorum* (2009), *The Road* (2009) and *Predators* (2010).

16 For example, Brian Donlevy in *The Quatermass Xperiment* (1955) and *Quatermass 2* (1957), Dean Jagger in *X: The Unknown* (1956) and Forrest Tucker in *The Abominable Snowman* (1957), *The Strange World of Planet X* (1958) and *The Trollenberg Terror* (1958).

17 See *Week End* (1967), *O Bandido da Luz Vermelha/The Red Light Bandit* (1968), *Brasil Ano 2000/Brazil Year 2000* (1969), *Gladiatorerna* (1969), *RocketKitKongoKit* (1986) and *Tribulation 99: Alien Anomalies Under America* (1992).

18 On related popular fiction, see Bould; Tal.

19 See Marable. This history is also evoked in *The Brother from Another Planet* (1984), *Sankofa* (1993), *Cosmic Slop* (1994), *White Man's Burden* (1995) and *C.S.A.: The Confederate States of America* (2004).

20 Director Melvin van Peebles is reputed to have fought with the studio to have a black actor in whiteface makeup for the opening scenes, rather than a white actor in blackface for the majority of the film, and to have changed the script, which ended with a white Gerber waking up from what had merely been a nightmare.

21 The limited life options for African-American woman are repeatedly cast in these terms: when Henry tries to persuade Linda Monte (Marie O'Henry), a free clinic patient, to quit prostitution, she insists that it is better than being a maid for white people; when another prostitute, Cissy (Elizabeth Robinson), points out to a regular client who wants her to live with him that his wife

might object, he suggests they describe her as a live-in maid. There are also several African-American female nurses and one doctor, Billie Worth (Rosalind Cash), but she is clearly subordinated to Henry as his assistant and largely disregarded lover.

22 On masculinism in civil rights, black nationalist and black power discourse and practice, see Estes.

23 Justiceville was constructed on 'a marginal zone west of Harbor Freeway', 'cleared by speculative developers in the late seventies and early eighties to make way for more of the luxury towers contemplated by Nada and Frank as they gaze across the freeway in the distance' (Lethem: 12). *They Live* was filmed in the months before and released shortly after resistance to New York's gentrification policies resulted in the Tompkins Square Park police riot (18–19).

24 See *Tetsuo II: Body Hammer* (1992), *Tokyo Fist* (1995) and *Rokugatsu no hebi/A Snake of June* (2002).

25 The term originally described landlord arson of slums, so as to clear them for more profitable use (Davis: 127).

26 *A Day Without A Mexican* (2004) imagines the disastrous social and economic consequences for California if all Chicano/a workers were suddenly to disappear. Describing an earlier era, Anne McClintock identifies 'those whom industrial imperialism rejects but cannot do without: slaves, prostitutes, the colonized, domestic workers, the insane, the unemployed' as 'abject peoples', noting their confinement to 'certain threshold … abject zones [that] are policed with vigor: the Arab Casbah, the Jewish ghetto, the Irish slum, the Victorian garret and kitchen, the squatter camp, the mental asylum, the red light district, and the bedroom' (72). Those abjected by modernity return to 'haunt' it 'as its constitutive, inner repudiation: the rejected from which ones does not part' (72). *Monsters* (2010) ambivalently reimagines the region south of the US/Mexico border – the principle site of *maquiladoras* and consequently of high levels of pollution and precarious labour – as an abject zone, the infected spawning ground of mysterious, monstrous aliens.

BIBLIOGRAPHY

Adorno, Theodor W. and Ernst Bloch 1988 [1975]. 'Something's Missing: A Discussion between Ernst Bloch and Theodor W. Adorno on the Contradictions of Utopian Longing', trans. Jack Zipes and Frank Mecklenburg, in Ernst Bloch, ed., *The Utopian Function of Art and Literature: Selected Essays*. Cambridge, MA: The MIT Press. 1–17.

Ahmed, Sara 2004. *The Cultural Politics of Emotion*. Edinburgh: Edinburgh University Press.

Althusser, Louis 1971 [1970]. 'Ideology and Ideological State Apparatuses (Notes Towards an Investigation)', trans. Ben Brewster, in *Lenin and Philosophy and Other Essays*. London: New Left Books. 121–73.

Altman, Rick 1999. *Film/Genre*. London: BFI.

Anderson, Mark 2006. 'Mobilizing *Gojira*: Mourning Modernity as Monstrosity', in William M. Tsutsui and Michiko Ito, eds, *In Godzilla's Footsteps: Japanese Pop Culture Icons on the Global Stage*. Basingstoke: Palgrave Macmillan. 21–40.

Appadurai, Arjun 1996. *Modernity at Large: Cultural Dimensions of Globalization*. Minneapolis: University of Minnesota Press.

Arendt, Hannah 1958. *The Human Condition*. Chicago: The University of Chicago Press.

Augé, Marc 2008 [1992]. *Non-Places: An Introduction to Supermodernity*, second edition, trans. John Howe. London: Verso.

Baillie, John 1996 [1747]. 'An Essay on the Sublime', in Andrew Ashfield and Peter de Bolla, eds, *The Sublime: A Reader in British Eighteenth-Century Aesthetic Theory*. Cambridge: Cambridge University Press. 87–100.

Bakhtin, Mikhail 1984. *Rabelais and His World*, trans. Hélène Iswolsky. Bloomington: Indiana University Press.

Barber, Benjamin R. 2001. 'Malled, Mauled, and Overhauled: Arresting Suburban Sprawl by Transforming Suburban Malls into Usable Civic Space', in Marcel Hénaff and Tracy B. Strong, eds, *Public Space and Democracy*. Minneapolis: University of Minnesota Press. 201–20.

Baucom, Ian 1999. *Out of Place: Englishness, Empire, and the Locations of Identity*. Princeton, NJ: Princeton University Press.

Bauman, Zygmunt 1998. *Globalization: The Human Consequences*. Cambridge: Polity.

——. 2000. *Liquid Modernity*. Cambridge: Polity.

——. 2007. *Liquid Times: Living in an Age of Uncertainty*. Cambridge: Polity.

Bazin, André 1967 [1945]. 'The Ontology of the Photographic Image', in Hugh Gray, trans. and ed., *What is Cinema?, volume I*. Berkeley: University of California Press. 9–16.

——2000 [1947]. 'Science Film: Accidental Beauty', trans. Jeanine Herman, in Andy Masaki Bellows, Marina McDougall and Brigitte Berg, eds, *Science is Fiction: The Films of Jean Painlevé*. Cambridge, MA: MIT Press. 144–47.

Beck, Ulrich 2000 [1997]. *What Is Globalization?*, trans. Patrick Camiller. Cambridge: Polity.

Benjamin, Walter 1999. *The Arcades Project*, trans. Howard Eiland and Kevin McLaughlin. Cambridge, MA: The Belknap Press of Harvard University Press.

Berenstein, Rhona J. 1996. *Attack of the Leading Ladies: Gender, Sexuality, and Spectatorship in Classic Horror Cinema*. New York: Columbia University Press.

Bernal, J.D. 1940 [1939]. *The Social Function of Science*. London: George Routledge & Sons.

Biagioli, Mario, ed. 1999. *The Science Studies Reader*. London: Routledge.

Bleiler, Everett F. with Richard J. Bleiler 1990. *Science-Fiction: The Early Years*. Kent, OH: The Kent State University Press.

Boltanski, Luc and Eve Chiapello 2006. *The New Spirit of Capitalism*, trans. Gregory Elliott. London: Verso.

Booth, Paul 2010. 'Memories, Temporalities, Fictions: Temporal Displacement in Contemporary Television', *Television & New Media* 12.4: 370–88.

Bould, Mark 2007. 'Come Alive By Saying No: An Introduction to Black Power Sf', *Science Fiction Studies* 102: 220–40.

Bould, Mark and China Miéville, eds, 2009. *Red Planets: Marxism and Science Fiction*. London: Pluto.

Britton, Piers D. 2009. 'Design for Screen SF', in Mark Bould, Andrew M. Butler, Adam Roberts and Sherryl Vint, eds, *The Routledge Companion to Science Fiction*. London: Routledge. 341–49.

Brophy, Philip 2006 [2000]. 'Monster Island: Godzilla and Japanese Sci-Fi/Horror/Fantasy', in Dimitris Eleftheriotis and Gary Needham, eds, *Asian Cinemas: A Reader and Guide*. Edinburgh: Edinburgh University Press. 56–60.

Bukatman, Scott 2003a. 'The Artificial Infinite: On Special Effects and the Sublime', in *Matters of Gravity: Special Effects and Supermen in the 20th Century*. Durham, NC: Duke University Press. 81–110.

——. 2003b. 'The Ultimate Trip: Special Effects and Kaleidoscopic Perception', in *Matters of Gravity: Special Effects and Supermen in the 20th Century*. Durham, NC: Duke University Press. 111–30.

——. 2006. 'Spectacle, Attractions and Visual Pleasure', in Wanda Strauven, ed., *The Cinema of Attractions Reloaded*. Amsterdam: Amsterdam University Press. 71–82.

Burch, Noël 1990. *Life to those Shadows*, trans. and ed. Ben Brewster. London: BFI.

Burke, Edmund 1990. *A Philosophical Enquiry into the Origin of Our Ideas of the Sublime and the Beautiful*. Oxford: Oxford University Press.

Cameron, Allan 2006. 'Contingency, Order, and the Modular Narrative: 21 *Grams* and *Irreversible*', *The Velvet Light Trap* 58: 66–78.

Cartwright, Lisa 1995. *Screening the Body: Tracing Medicine's Visual Culture*. Minneapolis: University of Minnesota Press.

Castells, Manuel 2000a. *The Information Age: Economy, Society and Culture, Volume I: The Rise of the Network Society*, second edition. Oxford: Blackwell.

——2000b. *The Information Age: Economy, Society and Culture, Volume III: End of the Millennium*, second edition. Oxford: Blackwell.

Chion, Michel 2001. *Kubrick's Cinema Odyssey*, trans. Claudia Gorbman. London: BFI.

Cleto, Fabio 1999. 'Introduction: Queering the Camp', in Fabio Cleto, ed., *Camp: Queer Aesthetics and the Performing Subject – A Reader*. Edinburgh: Edinburgh University Press. 1–42.

Cohan, Steven 1997. *Masked Men: Masculinity and Movies in the Fifties*. Bloomington: Indiana University Press.

Cornea, Christine 2007. *Science Fiction Cinema: Between Fantasy and Reality*. Edinburgh: Edinburgh University Press.

Creed, Barbara 1993. *The Monstrous-Feminine: Film, Feminism, Psychoanalysis*. London: Routledge.

Csicsery-Ronay, Jr, Istvan 2003. 'Science Fiction and Empire', *Science Fiction Studies* 90: 231–45.

——2008. *The Seven Beauties of Science Fiction*. Middletown, CT: Wesleyan University Press.

Cubitt, Sean 2004. *The Cinema Effect*. Cambridge: The MIT Press.

Davis, Mike 2006. *Planet of Slums*. London: Verso.

Debord, Guy 1983 [1967, rev. 1977]. *Society of the Spectacle*. Detroit: Black & Red.

——. 1998 [1988]. *Comments on the Society of the Spectacle*, trans. Malcolm Imrie. London: Verso.

De Certeau, Michel 1984 [1974]. *The Practice of Everyday Life*, trans. Steven Rendall. Berkeley: University of California Press.

Derrida, Jacques 1984. 'NO APOCALYPSE, NOT NOW (Full Speed Ahead, Seven Missiles, Seven Missives)', *Diacritics* 14.2: 20–31.

Doane, Mary Ann 2002. *The Emergence of Cinematic Time: Modernity, Contingency, the Archive*. Cambridge, MA: Harvard University Press.

Douglas, Mary 1996 [1966]. *Purity and Danger: An Analysis of the Concepts of Pollution and Taboo*. London: Routledge.

Dowling, David 1987. *Fictions of Nuclear Disaster*. London: Macmillan.

Dyer, Richard 1992 [1977]. 'Entertainment and Utopia', *Only Entertainment*. London: Routledge. 17–34.

——1997. *White*. London: Routledge.

Estes, Steve 2005. *I Am a Man! Race, Manhood, and the Civil Rights Movement*. Chapel Hill: University of North Carolina Press.

Ezra, Elizabeth 2000. *Georges Méliès*. Manchester: Manchester University Press.

Fanon, Frantz 1967 [1961]. *The Wretched of the Earth*, trans. Constance Farrington. Harmondsworth: Penguin.

——1986 [1952]. *Black Skin, White Masks*, trans. Charles Lam Markmann. London: Pluto.

Foucault, Michel 1991 [1975]. *Discipline and Punish: The Birth of the Prison*, trans. Alan Sheridan. London: Penguin.

Franklin, H. Bruce 1982. 'America as Science Fiction: 1939', *Science-Fiction Studies* 26: 38–50.

Frayling, Christopher 2005. *Mad, Bad and Dangerous? The Scientist and Cinema*. London: Reaktion.

Freedman, Carl 1998. 'Kubrick's 2001 and the Possibility of a Science-Fiction Cinema', *Science-Fiction Studies* 75: 300–318.

——2000. *Critical Theory and Science Fiction*. Middleton, CT: Wesleyan University Press.

Gieryn, Thomas 1983. 'Boundary-Work and the Demarcation of Science from Non-Science: Strains and Interests in Professional Ideologies of Scientists', *American Sociological Review* 48: 781–95.

——1999. *Cultural Boundaries of Science: Credibility on the Line*. Chicago: The University of Chicago Press.

Gilroy, Paul 2004. *After Empire: Melancholia or Convivial Culture?* London: Routledge.

Glassy, Mark C. 2001. *The Biology of Science Fiction Cinema*. Jefferson, NC: McFarland.

Goldberg, David 2010. 'To the Writers and Director of "Hot Tub Time Machine," From A Physics Professor', http://io9.com/5504813/to-the-writers-and-director-of-hot-tub-time-machine-from-a-physics-professor (accessed on 15 February 2012).

Graham, Stephen and Simon Marvin 2001. *Splintering Urbanism: Networked Infra-structures, Technological Mobilities and the Urban Condition*. London: Routledge.

Grosz, Elizabeth 1992. 'Julia Kristeva', in Elizabeth Wright, ed., *Feminism and Psychoanalysis: A Critical Dictionary*. Oxford: Blackwell. 194–200.

——1994. *Volatile Bodies: Toward a Corporeal Feminism*. Bloomington: Indiana University Press.

Gunning, Tom 1990 [1986]. 'The Cinema of Attractions: Early Film, Its Spectator and the Avant-Garde', in Thomas Elsaesser, ed., *Early Cinema: Space, Frame Narrative*. London: BFI. 56–62.

——1995. 'Tracing the Individual Body: Photography, Detectives, and Early Cinema', in Leo Charney and Vanessa R. Schwartz, eds, *Cinema and the Invention of Modern Life*. Berkeley: University of California Press. 15–45.

——2006. 'Attractions: How They Came into the World', in Wanda Strauven, ed., *The Cinema of Attractions Reloaded*. Amsterdam: Amsterdam University Press. 31–39.

Hagstrom, Warren 1965. *The Scientific Community*. New York: Basic Books.

Haldane, J.B.S. 1924. *Daedalus, or Science and the Future*. London: Kegan Paul, Trench, Trubner & Co.

Haraway, Donna J. 1991a. 'A Cyborg Manifesto: Science, Technology, and Socialist-Feminism in the Late Twentieth Century', in *Simians, Cyborgs and Women: The Reinvention of Nature*. London: Free Association. 149–81.

——1991b. 'Situated Knowledges: The Science Question in Feminism and the Privilege of Partial Perspective', in *Simians, Cyborgs, and Women: The Reinvention of Nature*. London: Free Association. 183–201.

Harding, Sandra 1986. *The Science Question in Feminism*. Milton Keynes: Open University Press.

——1998. *Is Science Multicultural: Postcolonialisms, Feminisms, and Epistemologies*. Bloomington: Indiana University Press.

——2008. *Sciences from Below: Feminisms, Postcolonialities, and Modernities*. Durham, NC: Duke University Press

Hardt, Michael and Antonio Negri 2000. *Empire*. Cambridge, MA: Harvard University Press.

Harpham, Geoffrey Galt 1982. *On the Grotesque: Strategies of Contradiction in Art and Literature*. Princeton, NJ: Princeton University Press.

Harvey, David 1989. *The Condition of Postmodernity: An Enquiry into the Origins of Cultural Change*. Oxford: Basil Blackwell.

——2005. *A Brief History of Neoliberalism*. New York: Oxford University Press.

——2010. *The Enigma of Capital and the Crises of Capitalism*. London: Profile.

Haynes, Roslynn D. 1994. *From Faust to Strangelove: Representations of the Scientist in Western Literature*. Baltimore, MD: The Johns Hopkins University Press.

Held, David and Anthony McGrew 2000. 'The Great Globalization Debate: An Introduction', in David Held and Anthony McGrew, eds, *The Global Transformations Reader: An Introduction to the Globalization Debate*. London: Polity. 1–45.

Hemmings, Clare 2005. 'Invoking Affect: Cultural Theory and the Ontological Turn', *Cultural Studies* 19.5: 548–67.

Hess, David J. 1993. *Science in the New Age: The Paranormal, Its Defenders and Debunkers, and American Culture.* Madison: The University of Wisconsin Press.

Hobson, John M. 2004. *The Eastern Origins of Western Civilisation.* Cambridge: Cambridge University Press.

Humphries, Reynold 2006. *The Hollywood Horror Film, 1931–1941: Madness in a Social Landscape.* Lanham, MD: Scarecrow.

Igarashi, Yoshikuni 2000. *Bodies of Memory: Narratives of War in Postwar Japanese Culture, 1945–1970.* Princeton, NJ: Princeton University Press.

Inuhiko, Yomota 2007. 'The Menace from the South Seas: Honda Ishirō's *Godzilla* (1954)', trans. Sachiko Shikoda, in Alastair Phillips and Julian Stringer, eds, *Japanese Cinema: Texts and Contexts.* London: Routledge. 102–11.

Jameson, Fredric 1998. 'Notes on Globalization as a Philosophical Issue', in Fredric Jameson and Masao Miyoshi, eds, *The Cultures of Globalization.* Durham, NC: Duke University Press. 54–77.

——2005. *Archaeologies of the Future: The Desire Called Utopia and Other Science Fictions.* London: Verso.

Jones, Gwyneth 1999 [1987]. 'Getting Rid of the Brand Names', *Deconstructing the Starships: Science, Fiction and Reality.* Liverpool: Liverpool University Press. 9–21.

Kael, Pauline 1986. *Taking It All In.* London: Marion Boyars.

Kant, Immanuel 1987 [1790]. *Critique of Judgment*, trans. Werner S. Pluhar. Cambridge: Hackett.

Karp, Jonathan 2005. '"Minority Report" Inspires Technology Aimed at Military'. *The Wall Street Journal* (12 April): B1.

Keller, Evelyn Fox 1999. 'The Gender/Science System or, Is Sex to Gender as Nature Is to Science', in Mario Biagioli, ed., *The Science Studies Reader.* London: Routledge. 234–42.

Kinder, Marsha 2002. 'Hot Spots, Avatars, and Narrative Fields Forever – Buñuel's Legacy for New Digital Media and Interactive Database Narrative', *Film Quarterly* 55.4: 2–15.

King, Geoff 2000. *Spectacular Narratives: Hollywood in the Age of the Blockbuster.* London: I.B. Tauris.

King, Geoff and Tanya Krzywinska 2000. *Science Fiction Cinema: From Outerspace to Cyberspace*. London: Wallflower.

Kirby, David A. 2011. *Lab Coats in Hollywood: Science, Scientists, and Cinema*. Cambridge, MA: The MIT Press.

Kirby, Lynne 1997. *Parallel Tracks: The Railroad and Silent Cinema*. Exeter: Exeter University Press.

Klein, Naomi 2007. *Shock Doctrine: The Rise of Disaster Capitalism*. London: Allen Lane.

Knorr Cetina, Karin 1999. *Epistemic Cultures: How the Sciences Make Knowledge*. Cambridge, MA: Harvard University Press.

Kramnick, Isaac 1977. *The Rage of Edmund Burke: Portrait of an Ambivalent Conservative*. New York: Basic Books.

Krauss, Rosalind 1978. 'Tracing Nadar', *October* 5: 29–47.

Kretschmer, Ernst 1925. *Physique and Character: An Investigation of the Nature of the Constitution and of the Theory of Temperament*. London: Kegan, Paul, Trench & Trubner.

Kristeva, Julia 1982 [1980]. *Powers of Horror: An Essay on Abjection*, trans. Leon S. Roudiez. New York: Columbia University Press.

Kuznick, Peter J. 1987. *Beyond the Laboratory: Scientists as Political Activists in 1930s America*. Chicago: The University of Chicago Press.

Landecker, Hannah 2005. 'Cellular Features: Microcinematography and Film Theory', *Critical Inquiry* 31.4: 903–37.

Landon, Brooks 1992. *The Aesthetics of Ambivalence: Rethinking Science Fiction Film in the Age of Electronic (Re)Production*. Westport, CT: Greenwood.

Laporte, Dominique 2002 [1978]. *History of Shit*, trans. Nadia Benabid and Rodolphe el-Khoury. Cambridge, MA: The MIT Press.

Lasch, Christopher 1985. *The Minimal Self: Psychic Survial in Troubled Times*. London: Picador.

Latour, Bruno 1993 [1991]. *We Have Never Been Modern*, trans. Catherine Porter. Cambridge, MA: Harvard University Press.

Lebowitz, Michael A. 2003. *Beyond Capital: Marx's Political Economy of the Working Class*, second edition. Basingstoke: Palgrave.

Lethem, Jonathan 2010. *They Live*. Berkeley: Soft Skull.

Luckhurst, Roger 2002. *The Invention of Telepathy*. Oxford: Oxford University Press.

Mandel, Ernest 1998 [1975] *Late Capitalism*. London: Verso.

Manovich, Lev 2001. *The Language of New Media*. Cambridge, MA: The MIT Press.

Marable, Manning 2000 [1983]. *How Capitalism Underdeveloped Black America: Problems in Race, Political Economy, and Society, updated edition*. London: Pluto.

Marcuse, Herbert 1955. *Eros and Civilization: A Philosophical Inquiry into Freud*. Boston, MA: Beacon.

——1970. *Five Lectures: Psychoanalysis, Politics, and Utopia*, trans. Jeremy J. Shapiro and Shierry M. Weber. Boston, MA: Beacon.

Marks, Laura U. 2000. *The Skin of the Film: Intercultural Cinema, Embodiment, and the Senses*. Durham, NC: Duke University Press.

Massumi, Brian 2002. *Parables for the Virtual: Movement, Affect, Sensation*. Durham, NC: Duke University Press.

McClintock, Anne 1995. *Imperial Leather: Race, Gender and Sexuality in the Colonial Contest*. London: Routledge.

Merck, Mandy 1996. 'Figuring Out Andy Warhol', in Jennifer Doyle, Jonathan Flatley and José Esteban Muñoz, eds, *Pop Out: Queer Warhol*. Durham, NC: Duke University Press. 224–37.

Merton, Robert K. 1973a [1938]. 'Changing Foci of Interests in the Sciences and Technology', in Norman W. Storer, ed., *The Sociology of Science: Theoretical and Empirical Investigations*. Chicago: The University of Chicago Press. 191–203.

——1973b [1935]. 'Interactions of Science and Military Technique', in Norman W. Storer, ed., *The Sociology of Science: Theoretical and Empirical Investigations*. Chicago: The University of Chicago Press. 204–9.

——1973c [1942]. 'The Normative Structure of Science', in Norman W. Storer, ed., *The Sociology of Science: Theoretical and Empirical Investigations*. Chicago: The University of Chicago Press. 267–78.

——1973d [1938]. 'Science and the Social Order', in Norman W. Storer, ed. *The Sociology of Science: Theoretical and Empirical Investigations*. Chicago: The University of Chicago Press. 254–66.

Meyer, Moe 1994. 'Introduction: Reclaiming the Discourse of Camp', in Moe Meyer, ed., *The Politics and Poetics of Camp*. London: Routledge. 1–22.

Michelson, Annette 1979. 'Dr. Crase and Mr. Clair', *October* 11: 30–53.

Milburn, Colin 2008. *Nanovision: Engineering the Future*. Durham, NC: Duke University Press.

Miller, Toby and Robert Stam 2000. 'Introduction to Part III', in Robert Stam and Toby Miller, eds, *Film and Theory: An Anthology*. Oxford: Blackwell. 85–101.

Moine, Raphäelle 2008 [2002]. *Cinema Genre*, trans. Alistair Fox and Hilary Radner. Oxford: Blackwell.

Morris, Nigel 2007. *The Cinema of Steven Spielberg: Empire of Light*. London: Wallflower.

Mulvey, Laura 1989 [1975]. 'Visual Pleasure and Narrative Cinema', *Visual and Other Pleasures*. Basingstoke: Macmillan. 14–26.

Munby, Jonathan 1999. *Public Enemies, Public Heroes: Screening the Gangster from Little Caesar to Touch of Evil*. Chicago: University of Chicago Press.

Muñoz, José Esteban 2009. *Cruising Utopia: The Then and There of Queer Futurity*. New York: New York University Press.

Musser, Charles 2006 [1994]. 'Rethinking Early Cinema: Cinema of Attractions and Narrativity', in Wanda Strauven, ed., *The Cinema of Attractions Reloaded*. Amsterdam: Amsterdam University Press. 389–416.

Nadar [Gaspard Felix Tournachon] 1978. 'My Life as a Photographer', trans. Thomas Repensek, *October* 5: 6–28.

Napier, Susan 1993. 'Panic Sites: The Japanese Imagination of Disaster from *Godzilla* to *Akira*', *Journal of Japanese Studies* 19.2: 327–51.

Neale, Stephen 1980. *Genre*. London: BFI.

Noriega, Chon 2006 [1987]. '*Godzilla* and the Japanese Nightmare: When *Them!* is U.S.', in Dimitris Eleftheriotis and Gary Needham, eds, *Asian Cinemas: A Reader and Guide*. Edinburgh: Edinburgh University Press. 41–55.

North, Dan 2008. *Performing Illusions: Cinema, Special Effects and the Virtual Actor*. London: Wallflower.

Nowotny, Helga, Peter Scott and Michael Gibbons 2001. *Re-Thinking Science: Knowledge and the Public in an Age of Uncertainty*. Cambridge: Polity.

Nye, David E. 1994. *The American Technological Sublime*. Cambridge, MA: MIT Press.

Osinubi, Taiwo Adetunji 2009. 'Cognition's Warp: African Films on Near-Future Risk', *African Identities* 7.2: 255–74.

Ostherr, Kirsten 2005. *Cinematic Prophylaxis: Globalization and Contagion in the Discourse of World Health*. Durham, NC: Duke University Press.

Paci, Viva 2006. 'The Attraction of the Intelligent Eye: Obsessions with the Vision Machine in Early Film Theories', in Wanda Strauven, ed., *The Cinema of Attractions Reloaded*. Amsterdam: Amsterdam University Press. 121–37.

Parrinder, Patrick, ed., 2001. *Learning from Other Worlds: Estrangement, Cognition, and the Politics of Science Fiction and Utopia*. Durham, NC: Duke University Press.

Parry, Benita 2004. *Postcolonial Studies: A Materialist Critique*. London: Routledge.

Perkowitz, Sidney 2007. *Hollywood Science: Movies, Science, and the End of the World*. New York: Columbia University Press.

Pierson, Michele 2002. *Special Effects: Still in Search of Wonder*. New York: Columbia University Press.

Prince, Stephen 1996. 'True Lies: Perceptual Realism, Digital Images and Film Theory', *Film Quarterly* 49.3: 27–37.

Reynolds, Frances 1996 [1785]. 'From *An Enquiry Concerning the Principles of Taste*', in Andrew Ashfield and Peter de Bolla, eds, *The Sublime: A Reader in British Eighteenth-Century Aesthetic Theory*. Cambridge: Cambridge University Press. 124–26.

Rieder, John 2008. *Colonialism and the Emergence of Science Fiction*. Middletown, CT: Wesleyan University Press.

Røssaak, Elvind 2006. 'Figures of Sensation: Between Still and Moving Images', in Wanda Strauven, ed., *The Cinema of Attractions Reloaded*. Amsterdam: Amsterdam University Press. 321–36.

Rossiter, Margaret W. 1984. *Women Scientists in America: Struggles and Strategies to 1940*. Baltimore, MD: The Johns Hopkins University Press.

——1995. *Women Scientists in America: Before Affirmative Action, 1940–1972*. Baltimore, MD: The Johns Hopkins University Press.

Russell, Bertrand 1924. *Icarus, or the Future of Science*. London: Kegan Paul, Trench, Trubner & Co.

Russo, Mary 1995. *The Female Grotesque: Risk, Excess and Modernity*. London: Routledge.

Said, Edward W. 1993. *Culture and Imperialism*. London: Chatto & Windus.

Sample, Ian 2010 'Drive to make Hollywood obey the laws of science', *Guardian* (21 February), http://www.guardian.co.uk/film/2010/feb/21/hollywood-films-obey-laws-science (accessed on 15 February 2012).

Sass, Louis A. 1992. *Madness and Modernism: Insanity in the Light of Modern Art, Literature, and Thought*. New York: Basic Books.

Sawchuk, Kim 2000. 'Biotourism, *Fantastic Voyage*, and Sublime Inner Space', in Janine Marchessault and Kim Sawchuk, eds, *Wild Science: Reading Feminism, Medicine and the Media*. London: Routledge. 9–23.

Schivelbusch, Wolfgang 1979. *The Railway Journey: Trains and Travel in the 19th Century*, trans. Anselm Hollo. New York: Urizen.

Schwenger, Peter 1992. *Letter Bomb: Nuclear Holocaust and the Exploding Word*. Baltimore, MD: The Johns Hopkins University Press.

Seabrook, Jeremy 1996. *In the Cities of the South: Scenes from a Developing World*. London: Verso.

Sedgwick, Eve Kosofsky 2003. *Touching Feeling: Affect, Pedagogy, Performativity*. Durham, NC: Duke University Press.

Shapin, Steven 1999 [1988]. 'The House of Experiment in Seventeenth-Century England', in Mario Biagioli, ed., *The Science Studies Reader*. London: Routledge. 479–504.

Shaviro, Steven 2010a. *Post-Cinematic Affect*. Winchester: Zero Books.

——2010b. '*Splice*', http://www.shaviro.com/Blog/?category_name=film (accessed on 15 February 2012).

Shaw, Philip 2006. *The Sublime*. London: Routledge.

Shohat, Ella and Robert Stam 1994. *Unthinking Eurocentrism: Multiculturalism and the Media*. London: Routledge.

Smelik, Anneke 2008. 'Tunnel Vision: Inner, Outer, and Virtual Space in Science Fiction Films and Medical Documentaries', in Anneke Smelik and Nina Lykke, eds, *Bits of Life: Feminism at the Intersections of Media, Bioscience, and Technology*. Seattle: University of Washington Press. 129–46.

Sobchack, Vivian 1991. *Screening Space: The American Science Fiction Film*. New York: Ungar.

Sontag, Susan 1994a [1965]. 'The Imagination of Disaster', *Against Interpretation*. London: Vintage. 209–25.

——1994b [1964]. 'Notes on "Camp"', *Against Interpretation*. London: Vintage. 275–92.

——1994c [1965]. 'On Style', *Against Interpretation*. London: Vintage. 15–36.

Sothcott, Jonathan 2001. 'Robert Fuest Bio', DVD extra on *The Final Programme*. Anchor Bay/Studio Canal.

Stacey, Jackie 1997. *Teratologies: A Cultural Study of Cancer*. London: Routledge.

——2010. *The Cinematic Life of the Gene*. Durham, NC: Duke University Press.

Stewart, Garrett 1985 'The "Videology" of Science Fiction', in George E. Slusser and Eric S. Rabkin, eds, *Shadows of the Magic Lamp: Fantasy and Science Fiction in Film*. Carbondale: Southern Illinois University Press. 159–207.

Suvin, Darko 1979. *Metamorphoses of Science Fiction: On the Poetics and History of a Literary Genre*. New Haven, CT: Yale University Press.

Tal, Kalil 2002. '"That Just Kills Me": Black Militant Near-Future Fiction', *Social Text* 20.2: 65–91.

Thomas, Troy S. 2002. 'Slumlords: Aerospace Power in Urban Fights', *Aerospace Power Journal* (Spring): 1–15, http://www.airpower.au.af.mil/airchronicles/ apj/apj02/spr02/thomas.html (accessed on 15 February 2012).

Tinkcom, Matthew 2002. *Working Like a Homosexual: Camp, Capital, Cinema*. Durham, NC: Duke University Press.

Traweek, Sharon 1988. *Beamtimes and Lifetimes: The World of High Energy Physics*. Cambridge, MA: Harvard University Press.

Trilling, Lionel 1951 [1945]. 'Art and Neurosis', *The Liberal Imagination: Essays on Literature and Society*. London: Secker and Warburg. 160–80.

Tuck, Greg 2008. 'When More is Less: CGI, Spectacle and the Capitalist Sublime', *Science Fiction Film and Television* 1.2: 249–73.

Tudor, Andrew 1989. *Monsters and Mad Scientists: A Cultural History of the Horror Movie*. Oxford: Basil Blackwell.

Vaughan, Dai 1990. 'Let There Be Lumière', in Thomas Elsaesser with Adam Barker, eds, *Early Cinema: Space, Frame, Narrative*. London: BFI. 63–67.

Vint, Sherryl 2009. 'Science Studies', in Mark Bould, Andrew M. Butler, Adam Roberts and Sherryl Vint, eds, *The Routledge Companion to Science Fiction*. London: Routledge. 413–22.

Vint, Sherryl and Mark Bould 2009. 'There is No Such Thing as Science Fiction', in James Gunn, Marleen S. Barr and Matthew Candelaria, eds, *Reading Science Fiction*. Basingstoke: Palgrave Macmillan. 43–51.

Wallerstein, Immanuel 2004. *World-Systems Analysis: An Introduction*. Durham, NC: Duke University Press.

Weiskel, Thomas 1976. *The Romantic Sublime: Studies in the Structure and Psychology of Transcendence*. Baltimore, MD: Johns Hopkins University Press.

Wells, H.G. 1980 [1933]. 'Preface to *The Scientific Romances*', in Patrick Parrinder and Robert Philmus, eds, *H.G. Wells's Literary Criticism*. Sussex: Harvester. 240–45.

Wells, H.G. 2004 [1927]. 'Mr. Wells Reviews a Current Film', in Greg Rickman, ed., *The Science Fiction Film Reader*. New York: Limelight. 5–12.

Westfahl, Gary 1998. *The Mechanics of Wonder: The Creation of the Idea of Science Fiction*. Liverpool: Liverpool University Press.

——1999. 'Scuse Me While I Kiss the Sky: An Open Letter to a Young Science Fiction Scholar', *Interzone* 147: 53–54.

——2000. 'From the Back of the Head to Beyond the Moon: The Novel and Film *This Island Earth*', *Science Fiction, Children's Literature, and Popular Culture: Coming of Age in Fantasyland*. Westport, CT: Greenwood. 49–68

——2007. *Hugo Gernsback and the Century of Science Fiction*. Jefferson, NC: McFarland.

Williams, Evan Calder 2011. *Combined and Uneven Apocalypse*. Winchester: Zero.

Williams, Linda 1990. *Hardcore: Power, Pleasure, and the 'Frenzy of the Visible'*. London: Pandora.

Willis, Martin 2006. *Mesmerists, Monsters and Machines: Science Fiction and the Cultures of Science in the Nineteenth Century*. Kent, OH: Kent State University Press.

Wood, Robin 1986. 'The American Nightmare: Horror in the 1970s', *Hollywood from Vietnam to Reagan*. New York: Columbia University Press. 70–94.

Wyatt, Justin 1998. *Poison*. Trowbridge: Flicks Books.

Žižek, Slavoj 1997. 'Multiculturalism, Or, the Cultural Logic of Multinational Capitalism', *New Left Review* 225: 25–81.

——2003. 'Not a Desire to Have Him, But to Be Like Him', *London Review of Books*, 25.16: 13–14.

INDEX